BARBARA BENNETT WOODHOUSE

HIDDEN *in*
PLAIN SIGHT

THE TRAGEDY OF
CHILDREN'S RIGHTS FROM
BEN FRANKLIN TO LIONEL TATE

PRINCETON UNIVERSITY PRESS   PRINCETON AND OXFORD

Requests for permission to reproduce material from this work
should be sent to Permissions, Princeton University Press

Published by Princeton University Press, 41 William Street,
Princeton, New Jersey 08540
In the United Kingdom: Princeton University Press, 3 Market Place,
Woodstock, Oxfordshire OX20 1SY
All Rights Reserved

British Library Cataloging-in-Publication Data is available

Library of Congress Cataloging-in-Publication Data

Woodhouse, Barbara Bennett, 1945–
Hidden in plain sight : the tragedy of children's rights from
Ben Franklin to Lionel Tate / Barbara Bennett Woodhouse.
        p.   cm.   —(The Public Square Book Series)
Includes bibliographical references and index.
ISBN 978-0-691-12690-6 (hardcover : alk. paper)
1. Children's rights—United States—History.   2. Children—Legal status, laws, etc.—
United States.   3. African American children—Civil rights—History.   4. Convention
on the Rights of the Child (1989)   I. Title.
KF479.W66 2008
342.7308'772—dc22   2007026840

This book has been composed in Sabon with Trajan Displays

Printed on acid-free paper. ∞

press.princeton.edu

Printed in the United States of America

1   3   5   7   9   10   8   6   4   2

TO MY FAMILY

CONTENTS

LIST OF ILLUSTRATIONS

Ruth O'Brien

W e've all met children who push their parents' limits. These children challenge their rules, criticize their decisions, and complain about their incompetence. Visiting a household with children behaving like this, we might well find them annoying. But, guess what? Cultural anthropologists, most notably Annette Lareau, argue that this so-called argumentative child now found in middle-class and upper-middle-class homes is not a "problem child." Quite the contrary, they are on the road to having a happy, productive life. It is precisely the pushing, tugging, and pulling at their parents that gives children voice and agency, teaching them how to effectively manage their own time, make big life decisions, and engage in healthy and productive relationships with their peers. According to Lareau, the disadvantaged child is the one raised the old-fashioned way—with parents who discourage their children from questioning authority or trying to negotiate the rules, instead demanding their honor, respect, and obedience.

In this elegantly written and well-argued book Barbara Woodhouse extends this notion of voice and agency to children's rights. She uses narratives to show how children throughout American history have exhibited great courage by raising their voices, taking agency, and trying to forge their own human rights. While Woodhouse sheds new light on familiar historical figures like Benjamin Franklin and Louisa May Alcott, she also brings to life the stories of children who struggled during key moments in history but remained nameless. The book examines children's rights not vis-à-vis the parents, but rather the state. She tells stories about how the state failed to safeguard the children who were sold into slavery; denied education; abused physically, sexually, and emotionally; persecuted for religious practices or their sexuality; exploited by masters and employers; as well as those excluded from court and separated from their families without so much as due process of law.

To Woodhouse, children's rights stem from children's needs and their natural capacity for growth. We shouldn't study children from an "adult perspective," she writes, but rather "each child can tell us something about other children." "Just as human rights are derived from an idea of what it means to be human, *children's* rights are derived from an idea of what it means to be a *young* human" who has different needs for dignity, survival, voice, and agency at different stages in their lives during different moments in history.

Woodhouse traces the resistance children's rights activists and the children themselves face. In particular, she focuses on why the United States refused to sign the United Nations Convention on the Rights of the Child, one of the most successful of all human rights charters. Blocked by the religious right, on top of the United States' longstanding suspicion of international law, this treaty lacked an American signature because of a debate falsely staged between liberals and conservatives about whether existing laws give children too many rights and/or could endanger a family's autonomy and right to privacy. She purports that the principles underlying this treaty well represent American law, policies, and values and therefore should have been signed.

What makes *Hidden in Plain Sight* powerful is that Woodhouse constructs neither a legal nor a social science argument to make these points. Rather, she relies on the narrative. Whether it is Frederick Douglass or the unknown children who marched in the civil rights movement, Woodhouse recounts their stories, making it possible for a reader to watch a child's development unfold. Illustrating their real lives, not idealizing them, her narratives focus less on society's reaction to children and more on the children themselves.

She captures the interplay of a child's developmental stage in conjunction with specific events and places.

What is more, by telling stories Woodhouse gives power to children—children of color who were enslaved and then later faced racism; children with disabilities; girls facing sexism and sexual exploitation; and boys and girls who were as children sexually, emotionally, and physically abused. She places these marginal groups at the center of the discourse about children's rights. But none of her stories are tearjerkers. Nor are they based on romantic stereotypes. Woodhouse writes with hope and dignity about how the American state should offer children both hope and dignity by extending them human rights. And because these stories are so effective, she helps move the cause of children's rights forward by breaking open the debate. Whether or not readers agree with her about children's rights, she puts to rest the idea that these rights undermine parental rights or violate the autonomy of the family. In challenging the very terms of the debate, *Hidden in Plain Sight* helps us raise or build the Public Square.

PREFACE

When the editors of Princeton's new series, The Public Square, presented me with a chance to speak on a topic that too often has been overlooked, I jumped at it. Children, their rights, and their role in the American experience have much to teach us. To the extent that young people and their voices are excluded from our histories and our debates, we walk blind and deaf into our future.

This book, my first, is a very different project from the thousands of pages of articles and book chapters I have written during twenty years as a scholar. It is different from the dozens of legal briefs I have authored and the mountains of memoranda I produced as a law clerk to Justice Sandra Day O'Connor. In this book, I tell a story about children's rights, trying to make it as free of legal and academic jargon as I can, so it may be accessible to all. After two chapters devoted to theory, the book is a series of essays blended with narrative and tied together by law and history. Academic debate and endnotes play a supporting, not a starring, role.

In this book, I draw upon a lifetime of research and experience as an academic but also as a child and daughter, nursery school teacher, parent and foster parent, and a grandparent. My professional involvement as a law professor and an advocate for children has spanned more than two decades. Along the way, I have invariably learned more from my colleagues, friends, family, students, and clients than I could ever have imagined or repay.

For this reason, it would be impossible to thank by name all the individuals who contributed to this book. I thank my teachers at Columbia Law School, Jane Spinak and Andy Schepard, for providing me with my first role models of multidisciplinary and child-centered practice. I thank all those with whom I worked as a codirector of the Field Center for Children's Policy, Practice, and Research at the University of Pennsylvania, especially Annie Steinberg, Alyssa Burrell Cowan, Sacha Coupet, Carol Wilson Spigner, Richard Gelles, and Ira Schwartz, and my former colleagues at the University of Pennsylvania Law School, especially Lani Guinier, Howard Lesnick, and Susan Sturm.

At the University of Florida, where I joined the faculty in 2001 to found the Center on Children and Families, I have been blessed with a new group of wonderful colleagues, and I am grateful to all, especially Iris Burke, Chris Slobogin, Kenneth Nunn, Sharon Rush, Katheryn Russell-Brown, Alyson Flournoy, John Cech, Berta Hernandez, Bill Page, Monique Haughton Worrell, Claudia Wright, and Danaya Wright. Without the encouragement and insights of my codirector Nancy Dowd this book would never have been possible. Deans Jon Mills and Robert Jerry and funding from Levin College of Law supported my research and gave me the space to write. The David H. and Fredric G. Levin families, through their financial support of the David H. Levin Chair in Family Law and the Center on Children and Families, contributed enormously to this project.

I owe a great debt to the students, too numerous to list, who worked on research that found its way into this book. Beginning in 1989, with my first research assistants Randi Stock and Cathy Miller, and stretching to the present, well over seventy-five young law students have contributed in one way or another to this project. Many of them were student fellows at the Center on Children and Families, at the University of Florida Levin College of Law. Among them, Libby Maxwell and Grace Casas deserve special thanks. Debbie Kelley Willis, the Center's program coordinator, has been an invaluable part of this project and is the heart of our Center.

I am grateful also to the many family and child law scholars and attorneys who welcomed me into the fold, including Martha Fineman, John Eekelaar, Peg Brinig, Sanford Katz, Carl Schneider, Marsha Garrison, Dorothy Roberts, Marty Guggenheim, and all my colleagues at the International Society of Family Law, as well as the late dean of family law scholars, Lee Teitelbaum. I am grateful to leaders from the public interest arena, including Howard Davidson of the ABA Center on Children and the Law, Bob Schwartz of the Juvenile Law Center, Marvin Ventrell of the National Association of Counsel for Children, and Frank Cervone of the Support Center for Child Advocates, as well as the "wise owls" Jane Spinak, Lewis Pitts, and Bob Fellmeth.

I owe a large debt of gratitude to Frank Furstenberg Jr., for his early encouragement, and Ruth O'Brien, the series editor for Public Square, for believing in my book. I owe more than I can say to my wonderful editor at Princeton University Press, Brigitta van Rheinberg, who gave generously of her wisdom and insights.

I am especially thankful for my friends. Betty, Dale, Kate, Michiko, Molly, and especially Sally, provided lifelong role models of girl solidarity. Sandra began as my mentor, became my friend, and remains my inspiration. My former co-clerks, Kent, Scott, and Gail, have been like siblings and their children like nephews and nieces.

Last but not least, I thank my family. The amazing family into which I was born has evolved over sixty odd years, through marriages, births, adoptions, deaths, and reunions, into a different and even better family, and I, to my surprise, am now the matriarch and not the child. My parents, Anne and Boyd, are gone but still in my heart. My brothers Charlie and John Tony and their families are a great source of joy. My children Jessica and Kenneth, son-in-law Mitchel, and grandson Sacha give me tremendous pride, and they have all contributed to my understanding of what it means to be part of a family. Most of all, I am grateful to Charles Woodhouse, my best friend and my spouse of forty years. His love and support gave me the confidence to set forth on the journey of challenge and discovery that gave life and breath to this book. Any errors or shortcomings in this book are, of course, my own.

HIDDEN IN PLAIN SIGHT

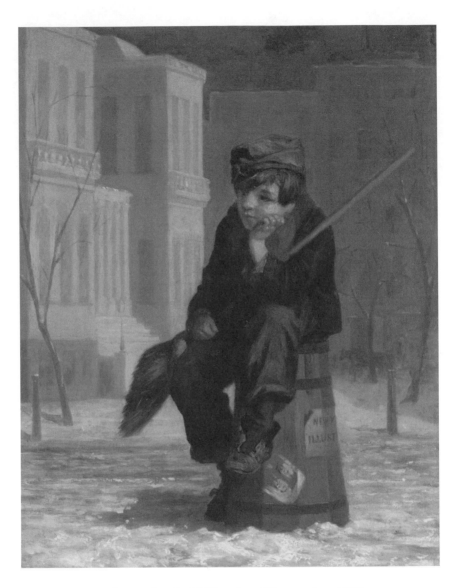

Frontis. *New York Newsboy* by William Penn Warren, circa 1870.
Courtesy of the author.

AIN'T I A PERSON?

Ain't I a person? Ain't I got rights?
> —Questions posed by a thirteen-year-old foster child

The great strength of history in a free society is its capacity for self-correction. This is the endless excitement of historical writing—the search to reconstruct what went before, a quest illuminated by those ever changing prisms that continually place old questions in a new light.
> —Historian Arthur M. Schlesinger Jr.[1]

The boy I shall call Tony was not very tall or strong for his age, but he was intense, intelligent, and articulate. Tony had been removed from his mentally ill mother's care at age four because of medical neglect. He and his younger half sister had spent the previous nine years in various foster homes. He saw his mother often but she remained unable to care for him. When Tony was thirteen, the attorney for the state had decided to file a motion, known as a TPR, to terminate the parental rights of Tony's mother. A TPR is the ultimate sanction—the "death penalty" of family law. The judge had asked an interdisciplinary team, composed of a lawyer, a psychiatrist, and a social worker, to evaluate mother and children. I was not Tony's lawyer. My job was to advise the child psychiatrist and the social worker on the relevant law. But

Tony knew I was a lawyer, and he had a lot of questions about his rights.

Everywhere but the United States, the answers would have been readily available in "child friendly" language, in booklets describing the United Nations Convention on the Rights of the Child, popularly known as the Children's Rights Convention or CRC. The United States is alone in refusing to ratify the CRC, the most rapidly and universally accepted of all human rights charters.[2] Although the CRC was widely supported by mainstream organizations from the American Bar Association to the PTA, ratification in the United States had been blocked by opposition from the religious right because of concerns about undermining the traditional family and because of a pervasive American distrust of international law. Many Americans assumed our laws already gave children all the rights they could need or handle. Others feared that giving rights to children would threaten the autonomy of American families and open the privacy of the home to state intervention.

Meanwhile, Tony and hundreds of thousands of other American children were growing up in the custody of the state—essentially being raised by the government—with few rights and precious little family. For Tony, state intervention in his home life was a given. He lived each day with the state looking over his shoulder, deciding where he would live and what he would be allowed to do. In the words of another foster child, Malcolm X, he was stigmatized before his peers as a "state child" with no real home of his own.[3] Whatever family ties Tony had were at the mercy of the state. A child in state custody, as Tony's story graphically illustrates, even more than an adult in custody, needs legal assistance to navigate the system and correct its mistakes and failures. The U.S. Constitution requires that the states provide lawyers to adults when they are placed in state custody—in prisons or psychiatric institutions, for example. However, abused and neglected children in the United States have no constitutional right to a lawyer and are lucky in some states to have a civilian representative to speak for them. Tony happened to live in a forward-looking state that had passed laws providing lawyers to children in foster care. But with a caseload of several hundred child clients, Tony's lawyer was not returning his phone calls. Tony had been saving up some tough questions and now here was a lawyer—myself—to answer them. I was stuck with the job of explaining to him that, under the law of his state, he did not have "standing"—the right to file papers on his own behalf—to oppose the TPR that would forever sever any legal relationship with his mother and remaining family members.

His disbelief and outrage were palpable. "She's my mother, ain't she? Ain't I got rights?" he demanded. "Look here," he said, pointing to the text of a pocket size U.S. Constitution I had given him. "It says here 'all persons born in the United States are citizens.' And it says 'nor shall any State deprive any person of life, liberty or property.' Ain't I a person? Ain't this my life? Ain't I got rights?" Tony had never read the 1851 speech delivered by the African American abolitionist Sojourner Truth marked with the refrain, "Ain't I a Woman?"[4] His cry, like hers, arose from the heart of his own experience of frustration and injustice in a system that treated him not as a person who could feel pain and loss and desperation, but as an object.

The TPR that brought our team into this case seemed to have had a vicious domino effect on Tony's life. The TPR was a knee-jerk reaction to a new law, the Adoption and Safe Families Act, but it bore no rational relation to Tony's developmental needs. Tony was an articulate thirteen year old, and he made a persuasive case that a TPR at this late date simply made no sense. He said, "I don't need an adoptive mother. I got a mother—the one sitting right here," and he pointed to his mother sitting next to him. He admitted his mother was not capable of caring for him and his sister, but he had a plan and it made sense to him. "In four more years," he told us, "I'll be going to college. I'll get me an apartment and my Mom and my little sister can come live with me." Perhaps his plan was unrealistic, but he had given it a lot of thought. He didn't want to be adopted by some stranger. He wanted to get an education and a job and make a home where they could be together as a family.

Tony's longtime foster mother understood and had supported Tony in his efforts to resist the TPR. A few weeks after our meeting, the state agency suddenly decided that her home was "out of compliance" with its regulations. Tony's social worker called him one morning and instructed him to put his and his sister's belongings in a bag and bring them to school. She explained that he was being moved to a "respite shelter" and she wanted to avoid a scene with his foster mother. Tony refused. He knew enough about bureaucratic double talk to suspect that respite was a synonym for limbo and that the caseworker was up to no good. Like any sane person would, he demanded to know where he was being sent, and why. He demanded a chance to state his objections to the move and told the caseworker that, if she wanted him, she would have to come and get him.

Tony was courting disaster. Technically, by refusing to follow orders, he could be designated as "ungovernable," and subject to detention in a locked facility. If he resisted physically he could be charged with assault of a government official—a felony. For a child in state custody, being sent from the "dependency" system into the "delinquency" system signals the end of childhood. While adults cannot be evicted for failure to pay rent without being given a court hearing, in many states a child can be sent away from a foster home without a hearing, for any reason or no reason at all.

Tony's complaints about the foster care system had begun long before the state's filing of the TPR. Why, he asked me, had the state not made any attempt to locate his father during the nine long years that he had been in foster care? A few years before we spoke, on his own initiative, Tony had found out who his father was and where he was living. He had telephoned him in another state, and they had talked. Before they could meet, however, his father passed away. Tony had another question. As his father's sole survivor, he was entitled to Social Security survivors' benefits. He wanted to save for college, he told me, but the checks were being taken by the state. How could the state just take his money, he asked? And how come the state said he could not visit his paternal grandfather who had invited him to spend some time down south with his cousins?

His grandfather had sent him a ticket. Shouldn't Tony have a right to visit his own grandfather?

Dr. Annie, the child psychiatrist leading our team, asked him gently, "Why is it so important to you to know your grandfather, or your father, for that matter? Why does it matter so much to you?" He looked at her as if she had lost her mind. But he tried to answer her strange question.

"You know, a person wants to know where he comes from. He wants to know his roots. Sometimes, when I was a young 'un, I used to cry and say, 'Where's my Daddy? Where's my Daddy?' It tore me up inside. I want to see my Granddaddy so he can tell me about him—what my Daddy was like as a boy; how it was when he was coming up." He paused and looked down at his hands. "Sometimes, I just feel . . . kinda' . . . mad . . ."

Tony's face crumpled and he broke down in bitter tears as he tried to explain how much this lost relationship meant to him. Of course he was angry. Anyone would be angry after what had happened to him. Nine years when maybe he could have lived with his own father, instead of in foster care, were gone forever. He was being kept from knowing his only living male relative and now he was about to lose his mother. No wonder he asked, "Ain't I a person? Ain't I got rights?"

There are too many Tonys. At any given time, there are over half a million children in foster care in the United States and half of these are twelve or older. Most Americans are vaguely aware of the existence of this system. They read about it in the newspaper or see stories on TV of kids killed, lost, starved, or abused, and they are shocked. They imagine that shows like *Judging Amy*, where foster children are listened to and treated with respect, reflect real life.[5] Most would be astonished to learn that abused and neglected children in state custody have fewer rights than accused criminals. While a long line of Supreme Court cases has addressed the rights of adults to counsel when taken into state custody, to protection of their property from unjust takings, and to protection of their familial ties, the Supreme Court has never held that a foster child has a right to legal representation, a right to speak in his own court case, a right not to be deprived of property without due process, or a right to contact with his family. The situation of children in foster care is but one example of our failure to recognize and protect the human rights of American children. One questioner at a recent lecture responded to Tony's story by saying, "This is a horrible, tragic story. But isn't the answer to fire all the people who messed up and hire people who will do a good job?" This answer is too simple—it has been tried, over and over, and has failed. Despite the systemic flaws in the child welfare system that are so evident in Tony's story, I believe the system is filled with hard-working and dedicated people. They carry heavy caseloads, lack adequate funding, and get little pay and no respect for doing one of the most difficult jobs ever invented. How can we expect them to succeed at protecting our children when we, as a people, devalue children and deny recognition of their basic rights?

We like to think of ourselves as a young and forward-looking nation. As Americans, we are proud of our nation's role in extending rights beyond the narrow circle of landed gentry to working people, people of color, women, and ethnic and religious minorities. American children and youth have played an important role in the struggle for a more perfect union, from revolutionary and civil wars, to the antislavery and women's suffrage movements to the civil rights, disability rights, and labor movements. Yet they are still waiting for rights of their own. Formalization of children's rights in the United States has been stalled for decades in superficial debates that pit conservatives against liberals and parent advocates against advocates for children. The purpose of this book is to spark public debate about the meaning of rights for children and to force a closer examination of our national resistance to children's rights. I use dramatic narratives about children, drawn from both historical and contemporary sources, to give meaning to the abstraction of rights for children and show how American children have earned their claim to rights.

The story of children's rights has been "hidden in plain sight." History has been purged of stories about children's agency and voice that make adults uncomfortable. Adults do not like to advertise the pivotal role played in American history and culture by acts of youthful defiance. We are more comfortable with George Washington's confession ("I did it with my little hatchet") than with Ben Franklin's precocious political activism. At sixteen Ben was publishing satires that infuriated the Boston censors and at seventeen he was a fugitive from justice, breaking the terms of his apprenticeship and lying his way into a job in Philadelphia.

History has also been purged of stories about children's suffering and exploitation that adults find too disturbing. Like stories about slavery, stories about children's real lives are prettified to make them more palatable. But the fact remains that this nation was built with the sweat of children, many of them enslaved or serving long terms of indenture. Children fought in our wars, toiled in our factories, marched on picket lines, and went to jail for civil rights.

Some of the child protagonists profiled in this book grew up to become famous men and women. Others lived and died in anonymity. By weaving together in each chapter the stories of famous and unknown children, the book presents children, both as individuals and as a group, as leaders in the American struggle for justice. These stories lay the foundation for a new conversation about the meaning and purpose of children's rights. A deeper understanding of children's rights can open a deeper discussion in America about human rights, by expanding the notion of rights to encompass dependency and difference as well as liberty and equality.

It is an American tragedy that Ben Franklin's homeland is now the only civilized nation where a twelve-year-old like Lionel Tate could be sentenced to life in prison without parole. While children's rights have gained universal acceptance around the world, the American debate about rights for children is polarized and mired in simplistic imagery. One reason is simply a failure of imagination. Rather than envisioning children marching against racial discrimination or unsafe working conditions, the typical American tends to think of children's rights in very personal terms, as involving children seeking liberation from parental authority. Adults laugh uneasily and joke about children refusing to take out the garbage or even hiring lawyers to "divorce" their parents. Concerns about the balance of legal rights within the family, and in contexts such as divorce or custody where family members ask courts to resolve their disputes, while difficult and important, are the topic for a different book.

Children's rights, and this book, are about something far more serious than children hiring lawyers to sue their parents or refusing their parents' reasonable commands. This book is about children's human rights in relation to the power of the state. While the children in this book may sometimes be at odds with their parents, the primary focus of these stories is the systematic denial of children's basic human rights. The children profiled in this book have been indentured and sold into slavery, denied equal education, persecuted for religious and gender differences, physically and sexually abused, exploited by employers, excluded from court proceedings, and separated from their homes and families without due process of law. These children, side by side with their elders, have been leaders in the struggle against oppression and injustice, playing important roles in American movements for fair labor practices, women's equality, and civil rights.

Many contemporary Americans seem to see children's rights as a threat to family integrity and parental authority. This concern about children's rights as a wedge to open the doors to state intervention in the family cuts across categories of liberal and conservative, uniting critics from both ends of the spectrum.[6] On the left, critics voice concern that child rights will be misused as a weapon against the poorest and most vulnerable families to justify intrusive state intervention. On the right, critics fear that emphasizing children's rights will imperil adult authority within the traditional family. I will argue that a fuller and more nuanced description of children's rights, encompassing not only rights of protection but also of family privacy, and acknowledging needs-based as well as capacity-based rights, will address the fears voiced by critics on each end of the political spectrum.

Americans' cautiousness in embracing rights for children also reflects a fear we have seen before that new rights (such as those of women and people of color) would result in erosion of established rights. But human rights need not be a zero sum game, especially when it comes to children and families. Adults' rights and children's rights can be complementary as opposed to mutually exclusive. Recognizing that children have rights need not subtract from the rights of parents. Instead, recognizing rights for the child adds to the armory of the parent who is defending a child from harm or seeking assistance in meeting the child's needs.

Defining children's rights as complementary to parents' rights and as a part of the universal quest for human rights may calm the concerns of some Americans, but it stirs up a different set of concerns in others. A widespread disaffection with international rights agencies makes many Americans wary of international authority. A look at Web sites discussing children's rights illustrates the radical disconnect between those who see the international movement for children's rights as a beacon to follow and those who reject it as an invasion of American parental autonomy and national sovereignty. The specter of blue-helmeted United Nations storm troops invading the American home and internationalizing American family values is clearly alarmist, but the desire to protect American political, cultural, and religious autonomy strikes a chord with large numbers of citizens. In addition, many conservatives reject the very notion of expanding recognition of rights beyond those specifically enumerated in the U.S. Constitution, believing it should be up to the democratic majority to distinguish between just and unjust laws. Yet the concept of rights more fundamental than either the will of the majority or the fiat of the king is deeply embedded in American constitutional democracy. The Declaration of Independence begins with the proposition that certain truths are "self-evident" and certain rights "unalienable."

Even Americans who generally favor the extension of human rights at home and around the world may hesitate at the idea of rights for children. What good are rights to persons who lack the maturity to understand them or the autonomy to assert them in a court of law? Who speaks for children too young to express their views—and how authentic can any adult be in claiming to speak for children? By claiming autonomy rights for children, do we sacrifice their needs for special protection? At what point do children's rights to protection from harm give way to rights to self-determination? And how shall we define children and childhood? Childhood means different things in different times and places. Given the chasms that divide children not only by age and cognitive ability but also by race, class, gender, ethnicity, and historical moment, how can we draw upon any shared concept of "childhood" to construct a coherent theory of children's rights?

To complicate matters further, the United States is not only a highly religious but also a religiously and culturally diverse society. Americans harbor conflicting images of children's proper place. Should children honor and obey, should they be seen and not heard? Or is their place on the front lines of the revolution, whether it is a political revolution, or a revolution in technology, popular culture, or human sexuality? Do we need to protect children from themselves or worry more about protecting ourselves from them? As the narratives in this volume suggest, children's proper place defies easy definition. Obedience and defiance, courage and recklessness, the need to make choices and the need for protection from bad choices, are all essential elements of children's developmental journey to adulthood.

Despite conceptual challenges and political, religious, and cultural tensions, it is time for Americans to grapple seriously with children's rights. Our ambivalence toward rights for children has isolated the United States from the world community. Isolationism has its defenders, but the reasons behind our hostility toward children's rights deserve more systematic analysis. Outside the United States, the CRC is universally recognized as the framework for analyzing laws that affect children. It provides the basic metric for measuring a nation's progress in meeting its obligations to respect and protect its children. Inside the United States, the CRC is virtually unknown. When the CRC was cited by the U.S. Supreme Court, in a recent decision striking down the death penalty for juveniles as unconstitutional, the Court's reference to the CRC was attacked as pandering to international opinion and ignoring American democratic values.

The CRC, however, has provided citizens around the world with a comprehensive language for talking about rights for children that is sorely needed in America. The basic human rights principles of the CRC are already deeply embedded in American history and tradition. By fully exploring the concept of rights from a child-centered perspective, I will show that rights for children are the natural outgrowth of American constitutional, democratic, and moral values.

But why, one might ask, build a book around stories about children if the purpose is to explore the theoretical and legal issues discussed above? Why not simply describe the CRC and our current constitutional laws and the theoretical issues they pose? Narrative enables the reader to revisit familiar territory with a fresh perspective. It brings the marginalized voice into the center of the conversation. Feminists used oppositional narrative to expose the ways in which women's stories and concerns had been made invisible by their lack of power within a patriarchal society. Telling the story of rights from the children's perspective fosters a critical analysis of unexamined truths. Of course, no adult, including the author of this book, can craft a story of children or childhood that is fully authentic, since we must either imagine or remember what it means to be a child and since childhood itself is a contested idea, defined as much by culture as by nature. Such obstacles should inform but not deter children's advocates from helping children, past and present, to begin to tell their own stories. A core principle of children's rights is the obligation of government to foster the direct participation of children in civil life, but Americans must first accept that children have something important to say.

Narrative allows for complexity and ambiguity. Stories about children's lives offer a more contextually rich terrain for exploration of children's rights than philosophical reasoning or legal doctrine standing alone. Children's situation, like that of adults, is rarely unambiguous. Elements of dependence and independence, victimization and heroism, authenticity and group identity coexist and can never be fully resolved. In the context of narratives, children's rights may be more clearly seen as involving negotiation and compromise between competing values and interests rather than as absolute demands.

Narrative humanizes. It challenges at a very personal level the stereotypes we use to make those whom we marginalize seem less than fully human. The stories in this volume invoke the respect and admiration Americans share for people who see and challenge injustice, who refuse to become jaded or accept defeat, who pull themselves up by their bootstraps. By using quintessentially American stories, I expose the fundamental connections between children's rights and American values.

Readers who have walked with children like Sheyann Webb in the civil rights movement or stood beside children like Lionel Tate in a criminal court will better understand the importance to children of equal protection and due process of law. Readers who have heard Helen Keller speak and visited with severely and profoundly retarded children like Mara in their schools will better understand why children like Helen and Mara need the right to an education. Readers who have walked with children of color in the civil rights movement and stood beside them in the modern juvenile courts will better understand the importance to children of equal protection and due process of law. This book aims to *show* rather than merely tell why rights matter to children and should matter to adult citizens.

I use historical materials in this book but I also use stories drawn from today's headlines and from my own work with children. Before I became an academic I was a lawyer, and before that a preschool teacher and a biological, adoptive, and kinship foster mother. Children in each of these settings have taught me much of what I know. In narratives involving children with whom I have worked or talked, I will sometimes use pseudonyms and change dates and personal details, to protect the children's privacy, or combine several cases into one to enhance anonymity and efficiency. Some of my quotations are verbatim where I was able to draw upon a written or recorded transcript, but others are paraphrases of remembered conversations. However, all the children in this book are real children, and I try to reflect each child's unique voice and to be faithful to each child's story.

But before turning to the stories of individual children, in chapters 1 and 2 I will lay out a framework for thinking about rights for children. The framework for thinking about children's rights that I have developed and will apply throughout this book is not meant to compete with or displace the CRC. Rather, it is intended to clarify and explain to Americans what an American scheme of rights for children might look like. I start by visualizing rights as generated by certain universal human rights values and then apply the lens of developmental theory to understand what these values mean in relation to children. Far from calling for a simplified or dumbed-down version of rights for adults, the project of defining rights for children poses especially complex and difficult challenges. It challenges us to rethink the very meaning of human rights through a less individualistic and more ecologically and developmentally sensitive lens. Many would agree with me that having and raising children is what turns adults into grown-ups. Thinking seriously about justice for children can have the same maturing effect on our capacity to understand the fundamental meaning of human rights.

You may be wondering what happened to Tony. I introduced him to you, but left you in suspense after he defied the state and refused to pack his things and move to "respite care." He could have run away, as many children do, from foster care. He could have been sent to a secure institution for refusing to cooperate with adult authority. He could have been browbeaten into accepting a TPR that made no sense to him. The experience was a watershed for Tony, but not in the ways one might have feared. Instead of cowing him, it convinced him that he would rather be adopted than remain in foster care, always at the mercy of the arbitrary decisions of the system. But he insisted he would not be adopted by strangers. He made a list of adults he would like to adopt him. One of these adults, a woman I will call Ms. Barnette, had befriended Tony at the church he attended with his foster family. She was active in her community, lived in a tidy two bedroom apartment, had a good job "with benefits," and her children were all grown. She enjoyed Tony's lively company and would invite him for milk and cookies after church. One time, she gave him a paper with her phone number and said, "If you ever need me, you just call me." So he did. He asked her if she would adopt him and his little sister. Ms. Barnette agreed on the spot. Amazingly, the plan encountered resistance from the agency—perhaps the workers resented how Tony had taken charge of his own case, or perhaps they were just too surprised to respond flexibly. Instead of telling her she might be eligible for adoption subsidies and for Medicaid for the children, they tried to discourage her by warning her that Tony's and his sister's medical care could be a big burden, and they cited rules such as the one that boys and girls cannot share a room. Ms. Barnette was not deterred. Her insurance would cover the children once they were adopted. As for the requirement that Tony and his sister each have a separate room, that was easy. Tony could have the spare room, his sister could have Ms. Barnette's room, and Ms. Barnette would sleep on the Barcalounger in the living room. So the children made their transition to their preadoptive home and were settling in nicely the next time we saw Tony.

Ms. Barnette came to the session with Tony and his little sister, since our role had now shifted to evaluating the adoptive placement. She was a large woman with a big bosom and motherly body language, and you could see both kids sinking comfortably into her embrace. Ms. Barnette understood how they felt about losing their mother and, like many African Americans, she saw no sense in an adoption cutting off a child's family ties. "She will always be your mother," she assured them. "She will always be welcome in our home." She would also be sure that the children had plenty of chances to visit with extended family and that Tony could visit his paternal grandfather on summer vacations. And once Tony was adopted, he would get his Social Security survivors' benefits and together they would save for his future education. So Tony's story had a happy ending, and it was an ending that he wrote himself. In common with many children you will meet in these pages, Tony exemplifies not only children's needs for stability, protection, and nurture, but also children's voice and agency—their understanding of their own needs and their capacity to mold and shape their own lives.

CHAPTER 1

HOW TO THINK ABOUT CHILDHOOD

Look at them, looking, their eyes meeting the world.
— William Carlos Williams, poet and pediatrician,
as he watched children drawing pictures[1]

Childhood has many meanings.[2] To physicians and psychologists it is a stage of human development to be studied and analyzed. To historians it is a term whose meaning varies from epoch to epoch and according to race, class, and region. To anthropologists it is a social phenomenon to be observed in cultural context. To lawyers it is a time for invoking age-based legal protections and imposing age-based legal disabilities.

A relatively new academic field, "childhood studies," has emerged committed to studying the meaning of childhood from all of these perspectives. As an advocate for children, I had always been convinced of the critical importance of interdisciplinary practice and research. How could a lawyer represent "the best interest" of a child without drawing upon developmental psychology, social work, and health sciences? How could a lawyer listen to and understand a child client without understanding children's gradual development of language and cognitive skills? How could a lawyer understand justice for children without knowledge of history? Several years ago I was invited to join a group of academics gathered at the Kahn Institute at Smith College to consider how we might use our knowledge from different disciplines to understand children better and make better policies for children. We were anthropologists, psychologists, educators, theologians, philosophers, and legal scholars, trained in a variety of research methods. After several days of discussion, a consensus emerged that the time had come for a broad "rethinking" of childhood. This was not an original idea. Each generation, to some extent, rethinks the meaning of childhood. For our generation of twenty-first-century Americans, it seemed clear the process must involve integrating our growing understanding of child development with our growing awareness of how environmental and cultural influences define children's worlds. It would also require integrating what we have learned about children's agency and voice—their active engagement in shaping their own lives. As Peter Pufall and Richard Unsworth explain in their Introduction to the book *Rethinking Childhood,* which emerged from our discussions:

> Rethinking childhood makes sense only when it is not driven either by our fear or by our idealizing visions. It is not a call to a romantic view of children that equates respect and active listening with handing over the keys to the kingdom. Rethinking requires a thorough examination of this apparent ambivalence in society's estimation of its children—patronizing on the one hand and idealizing on the other. It is a challenge to understand children as they are and where they are by listening to them and understanding the ways in which they act to create their own futures.[3]

We know a tremendous amount about *how* children grow. We also are learning that *where* and *when* they grow—the families and communities, cultural settings and historical moments in which a child's development takes place—are crucial elements. Not only history and geography but also race, class, and gender determine the meaning of childhood in a given time and place. For example, compared to their nineteenth-century counterparts, twenty-first-century middle-class American children go through a prolonged period of maturation, remaining dependent into their middle or late twenties even after they have finished their educations and found employment.[4] In many developing countries, as in America's urban ghettos and rural pockets of poverty, school leaving, premature parenthood, or incarceration spell an early end to childhood. If childhood has so many meanings, how is it possible to separate out children as a special group with special rights? While childhood may be a cultural construct that differs from place to place, the study of child development exposes commonalities between children from every culture and historical period. *All children change as they grow*. These changes are both physical and mental. While debate continues about the relative roles of nature and nurture, hard wiring and environment, certain developmental tasks seem to be shared by children the world over.[5] Childhood studies attempts to integrate the biological and behavioral models of child development with the work of historians, anthropologists. and sociologists studying childhood in historic and cultural context.

In his newest book, *Huck's Raft: A History of American Childhood*, historian Steven Mintz identifies a number of themes that run through the American experience of childhood.[6] First, he shows how the definition and experience of childhood have changed over the course of American history. Second, he shows that childhood has never been an uncontested concept, and people in each historical era have argued about its meaning. Third, he highlights how American childhood is marked by diversity—age, sex, class, and race differences make one child's experiences very different from another's. Fourth, he shows that power relationships between adults and children have never been stable and have shifted over time. Fifth, he reminds us that every generation has experienced its own "moral panic" over the demise of childhood and the state of "today's" children. And finally, he asserts that children have agency—even in times past, children played a large role in shaping their own lives. Mintz reminds us that the meaning of childhood is contextual and historically contingent. As I explore our knowledge of child development in this chapter, it is important to remember how much of what we know is guided by the questions and concerns of our times.

In modern-day America, parents who once turned to Dr. Spock now turn to Dr. T. Berry Brazelton and other doctors for practical advice. Brazelton and Stanley Greenspan have identified six irreducible needs of children: (1) the need for ongoing nurturing relationships; (2) the need for physical protection, safety, and regulation; (3) the need for experiences tailored to individual differences; (4) the need for developmentally appropriate experiences; (5) the need for limit setting, structure, and expectations; and (6) the need for stable, supportive communities and cultural continuity. A seventh need, which they call protection of the future, is the need for a safe and sustainable global environment.[7]

Brazelton and Greenspan have not drawn these ideas out of thin air. They base their recommendations on evidence-based studies of child development and on their many years of practice with children. In the following pages I will sketch with broad strokes some basic approaches to thinking about the process of child development that have influenced experts' thinking. The theories set forth here are not the only theories nor are they the newest theories. But they are among the most influential theories and provide the foundation for training of most professionals working with children. No one theory fully describes children's development; instead, each theory provides a lens or perspective for viewing how children grow.

A Developmental Perspective on Childhood

Scientists studying human and child development have proposed various theories to explain the commonalities as well as the differences in children's development from one setting to another.[8] Some examine emotional development, some look at cognitive development and the growth of logical thinking, some at moral or spatial thinking. Most have pictured childhood as a series of stages of development.

Swiss psychologist Jean Piaget, born in 1896, was perhaps the most influential thinker about child development in modern times. Piaget challenged the notion that young children were simply less intelligent. He discovered that younger children were not "dumber" than older children but seemed to think in a different way. Piaget arrived at his insights by suspending his adult preconceptions. He learned by observing and listening to children. Piaget's model identifies four general periods of development.[9] In the first period (birth to one), children develop *sensorimotor intelligence*, sucking, grasping, and dealing with the immediate environment. In the second period (two to seven), children develop *preoperational thought*, and learn to think and use symbols and images, but in a way very different from adults, less logical and organized. In the third period (seven to eleven) of *concrete operations*, children develop the capacity to think systematically but only when they can refer to concrete objects and activities. During the fourth period (eleven to adulthood), children develop the capacity to reason on an abstract level using hypothetical thinking. While Piaget observed that different children progress at different rates, he believed all children move through the stages of cognitive development in the same sequence. He also believed, observing infants teaching themselves, that the capacity to learn and develop was inherent. Current theories of child development may build upon, modify, or reject Piaget's model, but all are influenced by his work.

Another influential thinker was Erik H. Erikson. Born in 1902 in Germany, he moved to America in 1933, fleeing Nazi persecution. While Piaget's model focused on how children learn and think, Erikson explored relationships between the child and his social world. He saw child development as a series of stages in which children tackle a series of "crises," or critical tasks. Successful completion of each stage adds a new "ego strength" as the child progresses toward maturity. In stage one, the focus is on *Trust versus Mistrust*. Even if children encounter frustrations and hurts, as long as the caregiver is dependable and meets their essential needs, they are able to develop a basic sense of trust, or "hope," that enables them to move forward with optimism to take up new developmental challenges.

In the second stage, the focus becomes *Autonomy versus Shame and Doubt*. Erikson viewed the drive to autonomy as inherent. Biological maturation entails doing things on one's own—standing, walking, using hands and fingers, controlling the sphincter muscles, feeding oneself. As children struggle to control their bodies and dominate their surroundings they meet resistance from rules ("don't hit") and social expectations ("don't soil your pants") that introduce shame and doubt. A child who emerges from this stage with a healthy balance between autonomy and shame/doubt, acquires what Erikson called rudimentary "will"—defined as "the unbroken determination to exercise free choice as well as restraint."[10]

In stage three, the primary task is balancing *Initiative versus Guilt*. The child becomes more goal-directed, competitive, and capable of planning and imagining the future. At the same time, children must internalize taboos and social prohibitions that limit their goals and actions. The child's natural exuberance and daring are now offset by self-control and self-punishment. Ideally, the child emerges from this stage with a healthy sense of guilt but also a strong sense of "purpose," defined as "the courage to envisage and pursue valued goals."[11]

Stage four, according to Erikson's model, is characterized by *Industry versus Inferiority*. During this period, children focus on learning and mastering skills—in a simple society they may learn hunting and weaving by working next to their parents, while middle-class children in twenty-first-century North America usually go outside the home to learn reading, writing, computation, and to hone their skills in sports, creative activities, and peer relations. Ridicule and bullying, so common during this stage, can cause children to develop a sense of inferiority. Parents and teachers, influenced by race, class, and gender stereotypes, can discourage some children from trying and can undervalue their achievements when they do try. Ideally, however, children emerge from this stage with "competence," defined as "the free exercise of intelligence and skill in the completion of tasks, unimpaired by excessive feelings of inferiority."[12]

The fifth stage is one of *Identity versus Role Confusion*. The task of identity-formation reaches a crisis as adolescents go through rapid physical and hormonal changes while simultaneously trying to forge for themselves a sense of individual and group identity. Biological changes, such as puberty, are not set in stone—the onset of puberty has accelerated due to changes in nutrition and the environment.[13] But the combination of social and physical change involved in puberty and adolescence presents a significant challenge to child development. Successfully emerging from this stage allows the individual, now a young adult, to "form and sustain freely pledged loyalties"—an ego strength Erikson called "fidelity."[14]

Erikson saw childhood and adolescence as part of a continuum of growth, and he believed the individual continued to develop through stages of *young adulthood,* where the primary challenge is intimacy, through *adulthood*, where the primary task was developing a sense of "generativity," a commitment to caring for others as opposed to self-absorption and stagnation, into *old age*, where the struggle is between ego integrity and despair. Erikson's model shows how physical, intellectual, and moral development are intertwined in the individual's passage through the stages of human experience.

Theories like those of Piaget and Erikson are only a few among a number of influential theories that are being tested and revised as researchers develop more sophisticated methods and tools to study children's development. With the invention of MRI and other new technologies, scientists have developed ways to measure brain functioning under different stimuli and at different stages of maturation, and we can expect an explosion of research in precisely how the child's brain develops. Modern geneticists looking at DNA have provided fresh insights into connections between inherited traits and social and environmental influences. Although their methods and conclusions may differ, most modern theorists start from the premise that each child is an individual, born with certain genetic traits, and with a capacity to develop spatial, relational, cognitive, and moral thinking in interaction with his environment.[15]

An Ecological Perspective on Childhood

Piaget's and Erikson's models focus primarily on the child and her immediate surroundings, but other scientists attempt to place the developing child in a larger context. Urie Bronfenbrenner's ecological model invites us to visualize children as part of a larger universe of relationships and forces that affect both individuals and society. Bronfenbrenner saw persons, including children, as active, growing, complex organisms possessing evolving, interrelated, dynamic capacities for thought, feeling, and action. He also brought into focus the dynamic relationship between the child and the immediate settings in which he lives, the relations between these settings, and the larger contexts in which the child and these settings are embedded.[16] The ecological model of childhood is often represented as a series of concentric, often overlapping circles with the child at its center. We place the child at the center not merely because the child is the subject of our inquiry but in recognition of the child's own active and dynamic capacities.[17]

Very young children inhabit a small zone, where interactions with caregivers define their worlds. As children develop, their lives expand beyond family and home into many other zones that ecological theorists call *microsystems*. Microsystems are those settings in which the child actually lives, works, and plays—day care or school, neighborhood or village, faith community, extended family, peer group. In times past, the workplace, whether factory, mill, or farm, figured prominently in an average American child's universe. Today, middleclass North American children are more likely to be found at the mall or on the Internet than in the factory.[18]

Areas where these microsystems overlap are called *mesosystems*. When mesosystems are in harmony, life is simple. When they are sites of conflict, children can suffer (but also grow) because of the tensions between them. The values and expectations of parents may conflict with those of teachers and schoolmates. The peer group may make demands on the child that violate those of the faith community.

The ecological model does not stop with the child and her immediate surroundings. Outside the circles of microsystems, imagine a series of concentric circles that represent places and forces external to the child's world that nevertheless affect the child in profound ways. Developmental scholars call these *exosystems*. A child may never have visited his parent's workplace yet he feels the impact of its policies. A parent's job can provide flex time and health benefits or it can impose mandatory overtime and pay less than a living wage. The market economy is another exosystem that affects children, even in developed countries where child labor laws prevent direct exploitation of children. As unemployment rises, so do domestic violence, substance abuse, and divorce.[19] Commercial enterprises market food, entertainment, and clothing to children, cultivating the next generation of consumers and changing the environments of their physical and mental maturation.[20] Just as the ecology of childhood is different from place to place and from time to time, it also changes as the child ages.

All of the systems identified above—micro, meso, and exo—are embedded in a cultural *macrosystem*. A cultural macrosystem is the patterning by history, power, and ideas of the broader society in which the child lives. It includes prejudices, politics, ideologies, religions, moral values, and even the very concept of childhood itself.[21] The concept of the macrosystem allows those studying children to place children in the context of the intimate systems that affect them and also to examine the pervasive influences of surrounding political, religious, and economic systems in children's lives.

The work of Glen H. Elder Jr., at University of North Carolina, attempts to bring together stage theories, such as those of Piaget and Erikson, and ecological theories, such as those of Bronfenbrenner, with a historical perspective on childhood. He theorizes that each child is born into a time and place within a society that moves through phases of stability or change. The influence of these events depends on the stage of development of the person experiencing them.[22] His theories highlight the complicated interplay of internal stages of growth, external events, and societal forces in defining and shaping a particular experience of childhood.

Recognizing Children's Agency, Voice, and Action

While biology and environment each play a critical role, the child, as a unique individual, is the final critical variable in children's development. A fundamental lesson learned by scientists observing children's development is that children are neither passive objects nor empty vessels. From infancy, when a baby cries for a mother's breast or mirrors a father's smile, children are actively engaged in making and defining their own worlds. Modern scholars of childhood have adopted the terms "voice" and "agency" to describe this dynamic engagement of children with their surroundings and their own development.[23] *Voice* is that "cluster of intentions, hopes, grievances, and expectations that children guard as their own" and that is often overlooked by adults who do not listen to what children have to say. *Agency* recognizes the fact of children's self-determination, as they grapple with new developmental challenges and strive to "make sense of their world and construct a good fit within it." "Voice is an expression of agency. It puts the focus on children's commitment to make known their ability to act on their own behalf, whether to ensure their own interest or to modify the world around them."[24]

No parent or teacher has to be convinced of the importance of agency and voice. Just as we need no experts to tell us about developmental stages, we need no experts to tell us that children have minds of their own. We create folklore about "the terrible twos" and "impossible teens." But we also know that each child approaches and experiences these stages in a unique way and that children make distinctive choices and express distinctive viewpoints in spite of parental and societal efforts at management and control. When my son was two, his agency had grown faster than his voice, or at least his command of syntax. "*I* cut it, meat!" or "*I* tie it, shoe!" he would announce firmly. Another favorite was "*I* am the boss of my food." It is remarkable that stereotypes of children as passive and malleable have survived so long in the face of such cogent evidence of children's agency. In part, these stereotypes have been convenient mechanisms for avoiding the inconvenience and conflict that comes with listening to dissenting voices. Families are not pure democracies, one person one vote. For children's sake, adults must be in control. It is easier for adults to maintain control and justify dominion over children if children are seen as lacking in insight and capacity for action. But acknowledging children's agency and voice should not mean that adults abdicate responsibility for decision-making and control.

Across the many fields of childhood studies, all disciplines are increasingly emphasizing the role of children's agency. Historian Steven Mintz, examining children in slavery, observes they "were not simply slavery's victims; they were also active agents, who managed to resist slavery's dehumanizing pressures." Mintz shows how enslaved children invented games, like "hide the switch" and "auction," to cope with slavery's stresses and gain a sense of control and self-worth. "Play helped forge a sense of solidarity among enslaved children and allowed them to create a semiautonomous realm, beyond the direct control of their masters."[25]

Harvard psychiatrist Robert Coles was a pioneer in listening to children.[26] Working with children in a variety of settings, from polio wards in hospitals, to the civil rights movement, to the slums of Brazil, he developed a methodology for listening to children as they grappled with difficult moral and spiritual challenges, paying careful attention not only to their words but also to their drawings. Coles goes beyond providing a set of data points for mapping children's development. He treats children themselves as moral agents and spiritual thinkers. While there have been criticisms of Coles's work and methodology, it has had a huge impact in many fields beyond psychiatry.

Following in Erikson's, Bronfenbrenner's, and Coles's footsteps, sociologist James Garbarino integrates theory and practice in his influential volume *What Children Can Tell Us*. His goal was to improve the validity and ethical soundness of adults' efforts to communicate with children. He has applied ecological theory to study many aspects of childhood in social context, insisting on the importance of children's own experiences. Many other researchers have begun to allow children's interests and activities to define the research agenda. For example, Allison James studies the way children construct their own social order on the playground and in the marketplace for children's food. She insists that we get beyond deterministic age-based models of the child and look at the actual child before us. In her view, the greatest challenge for the future of childhood studies will be "exploring and understanding how *this child*—the one who stands in front of us—helps to shape our expectations of childhood and what children can and cannot do. . . . [T]his child can tell us something about all children and may, through his or her actions, lead us to shift our thinking about who children are and what childhood is like."[27]

When Does a Child Become an Adult?

When does childhood end? From a developmental perspective, there is no one answer to this question. This is why Allison James calls age-based developmental models "deterministic." Adulthood, if defined as the taking on of adult roles and responsibilities, can come very early in some societies and for some children, and very late for others in different settings. The timing of transition from childhood to adulthood is strongly influenced by issues of class and culture as well as by issues of race and gender.

This indeterminacy in measuring when childhood ends is evident in the laws that set certain ages as benchmarks for young people to take responsibility for their actions and to make decisions without supervision or veto by adults.[28] These benchmarks seem arbitrary and inconsistent. Why should a boy too young to drive or marry be subject to trial and sentencing as an adult? Why should a minor girl be able to obtain an abortion but not a tattoo without parental consent? Many of the age-based rules have little to do with child development and much to do with our ambivalence about children and our struggle to resolve the tensions between images of children as incompetent innocents and dangerous predators.

In one area of the law, however, the science of child development has had a significant impact. In legal terminology, we call a person's ability to reason and understand his "capacity" or "competence." Traditionally, minor children were deemed to lack capacity and could not testify in courts of law. Research has shown that "capacity" does not appear suddenly when one turns eighteen, but evolves through stages of development. Three-year-olds do not reason in the same way as ten-year-olds, but each child has something to tell us as long as we use what we know about child development in asking and in listening.[29] Modern rules of evidence now allow children's testimony without demanding proof that the child is competent in the sense of having the ability to reason like an adult and to understand the meaning of the oath "to tell the whole truth so help me God." Instead, juries are allowed to consider the child's testimony and give it the weight they believe is appropriate based on the particular child's abilities to observe, report, and reason.[30]

Child development has also had a major role in thinking about children as victims or perpetrators of crime. The criminal law looks at the ability to distinguish right from wrong, to understand cause and effect, to observe and report, and to act independently of external influences. In March of 2005, the U.S. Supreme Court used data about adolescent brain functioning to reject application of the death penalty to crimes committed by persons under age eighteen, concluding that they lack full capacity to understand the gravity of their conduct or to control their impulses.[31] The Supreme Court has also looked at children's cognitive and emotional development in cases involving child witnesses' capacity to testify and in allowing children to testify via television or videotape.[32] Because of differences between children and adults, these procedures are necessary to protect the child from trauma and to assure that the information obtained is as accurate as possible.

The developmentally based concept of "capacity," as we shall see in the next chapter, also plays a critical role in international thinking about children and the law. The CRC, while it describes children as holders of rights, makes parents the guardians of these rights. Parents are to provide "appropriate direction and guidance" consistent with the "evolving capacities of the child."[33] This developmental approach makes sense to parents. Most American parents and grandparents know from experience what to expect from toddlers and teens, and how much autonomy they can be allowed given their developmental stage and cognitive and moral capacities.

are constantly learning about the stages and the ecology of child development and about the role of the child's own actions in creating his or her world. Rather than studying children from an adult perspective, a child-centered perspective looks closely at what children do and say, as individuals and as a group. Each child can tell us something about other children and about childhood in general.

Knowing about children's development, however, is not enough. Totalitarian regimes have used knowledge of child development to subvert and manipulate children rather than to protect them or advance their interests. Any theory of rights must be built upon a system of values. I have borrowed a term from Erik Erikson for the overarching value that ought to inform America's public policies regarding children—"generativity." Erikson uses this term to describe that quality of commitment to the flourishing of the next generation that exemplifies human maturity.

I have called this philosophy *ecogenerism*, to remind us to look at children in a developmental context, as growing organisms. As earlier children's rights advocates understood, children's rights are natural rights. This is how Raymond Fuller described the origin of rights for children in an essay on *Child Labor and Child Nature*, published in 1922 during the campaign to enact national child labor laws. "Out of the nature of children arise their needs; and out of children's needs, children's rights."[3] Children's rights were not the product of some lawmaking body but inherent in the human condition. Just as "the wing of the bird indicates its right to fly," so children's natural dependency and capacity for growth established their right to be nurtured on the path to adulthood.[4] Adults, recognizing this moral claim, were obligated to take action to protect children from harm and exploitation.

The core insight of early child advocates, that children have special needs and that those needs should be recognized as human rights, remains vital today. Just as rights are derived from an idea of what it means to be human, *children*'s rights are derived from an idea of what it means to be a *young* human.[5] Since those early days of the children's rights movement, there have been many movements advocating "rights" for children. In the beginning, the focus was on children's needs for nurture, protection, and education. Child-savers removed children from poor families, rescued them from exploitation as workers, and mandated that they attend school. In the 1970s, a children's liberation movement emerged that shifted the focus from adults' protection of children to children's own claims to autonomy. Children's liberationists urged that children be released from schools and adult-imposed rules that imprisoned and oppressed them.[6] Modern theorists like myself use developmental theory to integrate these values of dependency and autonomy.

As humans, children are covered by the broad set of human rights principles that apply to all humans. But certain rights are unique to children and other human rights values must be tailored to meet children's needs. Human rights should not be confused with other forms of legal entitlement. Most Americans, when they hear the term "rights," think immediately of the U.S. Constitution and its Bill of Rights. Or they may think of rights defined in legislation such as the Civil Rights Acts. They assume rights lead inexorably to lawsuits. These assumptions are not necessarily accurate when it comes to human rights. In order to understand children's rights, it is important to see the place and function of human rights in legal context.

Human Rights: The Ozone Layer of Law

One way to visualize human rights in relation to other forms of law is to imagine a series of concentric spheres, like zones in the atmosphere, surrounding children and parents.[7] The innermost zone, in which children and their families operate on a daily basis, is the sphere of *common law*. These are customary rules so deeply rooted in tradition and instinct that we do not think of them as laws at all, even though they channel our conduct. When a child cries, her caregivers feed and comfort her, without thinking whether they have a common law duty to feed and comfort her or whether she has a right to be fed and comforted. Next is the zone of *statutory rights* created by laws enacted by federal or state legislatures or other state and local lawmaking institutions. An example would be the right of a child like Tony to receive Social Security survivors' benefits when his parent dies. Congress created this "right" and Congress can modify it or take it away. Another example would be children's rights, under a state's divorce laws, to receive child support. The basic right to a father's support existed under English common law, but it has been codified in legislation in every state and has been extended to both parents.

The next layer is where we find *constitutional rights*. The United States and each of the fifty states all have written constitutions, and certain rights are expressly or implicitly protected by these constitutions. Although children are never mentioned in the U.S. Constitution, courts have held that various rights apply to children as well as adults. Usually, the rights are modified to meet the special situation of children. Examples of constitutional rights that apply to children as well as adults are the right to a fair trial, the right to be free from race and gender discrimination, and the right to religious and intellectual freedom. State constitutions often include an explicit *state constitutional right* to education.

Finally, international human rights charters like the CRC articulate *human rights*. They form the outer zone, the ozone layer, so to speak, of the legal environment. The CRC is the most recent and comprehensive charter of children's rights, but not the first. In 1924, the League of Nations proclaimed a Declaration of the Rights of the Child, and the United Nations issued a Declaration of the Rights of the Child in 1959.[8] In contrast to these brief declarations, the CRC provides a detailed scheme of children's rights. It has become the most universally applied model for describing the human rights of children. Other charters of rights for children include the 1990 African Charter on the Rights and Welfare of the Child and the European Convention on the Exercise of Children's Rights.[9] These charters create an atmosphere of protection and respect for children and promote development of specific rights at the constitutional and statutory levels. Lack of a robust theory of rights for children, like holes in the ozone layer, changes the environment at the macrosystemic level, making it less friendly to children's healthy growth.

Many Americans assume that a convention such as the CRC would become law enforceable in our courts immediately upon being ratified by the United States. It is true that the Constitution establishes that treaties, like federal law, are the supreme law of the land. But the United States would undoubtedly designate the CRC as a "non-self-executing" treaty.[10] This means that its provisions would only become enforceable in American courts as laws were enacted at the federal, state, or local level to make the CRC principles operational. This process places the design and implementation of human rights with local lawmakers and allows universal human rights principles to be adapted and molded to fit the contexts of nations with diverse legal, political, and social cultures.

Regardless of whether ratified by the United States, the CRC will affect U.S. law. The history of the U.S. Constitution has been expansion of rights to formerly excluded groups. As the ideal of children's human rights becomes more firmly entrenched around the world, U.S. courts can be expected to extend current constitutional doctrines to cover this new generation of rights-holders. I call this process, already underway, the "constitutionalization" of children's rights.[11] By this process, general principles of human rights are accepted, adopted, and adapted to local and national settings and traditions. Americans must also understand that, like the ozone layer, human rights do not respect national borders. At the 2002 U.N. Special Session, the Bush administration insisted on deleting all references to children's rights and substituting the term "children's interests," before it would support the Session Documents. But the United States, standing alone against the world, cannot prevent children's rights from becoming enforceable in U.S. courts as customary international law, or *jus cogens*—universal norms of international law that demand respect.[12] Ratification of the CRC is a practical necessity if we wish to retain any influence over the evolution of children's rights around the world and at home.

Five Basic Human Rights Principles Examined through the Lens of Children's Needs-Based and Capacity-Based Rights

Certain fundamental human rights values are both universal and deeply rooted in American history and tradition. Tailoring rights to fit the American child involves re-visioning these values in the context of the American *child*'s experience. Building on the work of Harvard professor Martha Minow, I have identified five basic human rights values reflected in contemporary understandings of human rights and embedded in American values.[13] Like American childhood, American values can mean many things to many people. But the core values I identify are present in the Declaration of Independence and the Constitution and appear in crucial historical moments in the American experience such as the Civil War, the women's suffrage movement, and the civil rights movement of the 1960s. These basic values are: (1) the privacy principle, (2) the agency principle, (3) the equality principle, (4) the dignity principle and (5) the protection principle. These values do not and cannot mean the same thing to children as they do to adults. In order to understand their specific application to children, we must look at them from a child-centered perspective. Because children's natural state is one of growth, children's rights must rest on strong developmental foundations.

Legal scholars, looking at rights from an adult's perspective, generally divide the world of rights into *negative* and *positive* rights. Negative rights are rights to be let alone, free from government interference or abuse, while positive rights are rights to claim a positive good or benefit from government. Americans are quite familiar with negative rights, since most of the rights guaranteed by our Constitution are rights to be free from government intervention and to fair treatment at the hands of government. Another common way to divide or classify rights is between *civil* and *political* rights, which entitle the rights holder to participate in public life; *economic* or *welfare* rights, which entitle the rights holder to economic justice and to basic necessities such as food, shelter, and health care; and *social* or *cultural* rights, which protect personal and community values.[14]

These ways of thinking about rights have generally presumed that the rights-holder is an autonomous person making mature choices about whether or when to exercise his rights. Children are not born autonomous. From an infant's perspective, a right to be left alone without any corresponding right to care would amount to a sentence of death. Children's special situation exposes the emptiness for children of any theory of rights that ignores the interdependency of individuals, families, and communities. But to presume that all children are helpless and naive because it is true of some children ignores the child's individuality and capacity for growth to autonomy.

I have proposed a new language for talking about children's rights that recognizes their dignity as humans and integrates their essential dependency with their capacity for growth.[15] Instead of classifying children's rights as negative or positive, I would divide them into needs-based rights and capacity-based rights. Let me illustrate this language using the dignity principle. All children, no matter how young, have a right to human dignity—the right to be recognized as fully human individuals despite their differences from adults and from one another. While a child's ability to reason and decide evolves over time, the child's dignity rights are fully present at birth. Recognition of human dignity calls on us to acknowledge that the child, despite his or her lack of present autonomy, does have rights based on present humanity as well as the potential for autonomy. In making these rights operational, the law must reflect children's dependency but also honor their emerging capacity for participation and, ultimately, control. Both needs- and capacity-based rights are critical to this task. Needs-based rights include the positive rights to nurture, education, food, medical care, shelter, and other goods without which children cannot survive, let alone develop into autonomous adults and productive citizens. Children's needs-based rights would also reflect children's needs to test the wings of their increasing autonomy. Capacity-based rights reflect and respond to the child's development and recognize children's agency and voice even before children reach the state of maturity that allows them to make decisions without adult assistance and guidance.

It is not the capacity to exercise one's rights that creates the right. Individuals who lack the capacity to act autonomously—for example, mentally retarded persons, patients in a coma, mentally ill persons—nevertheless have rights to be treated with dignity, rights to protection and to be free of invidious discrimination. While many Americans might argue that decisions about life and death should be made in the privacy of the family, and many others believe that human dignity requires the state to preserve life at all costs, few believe the nonsentient person, even someone in a vegetative state, is simply a lump of flesh that the state can dispose of at will. Each of my principles incorporates both needs and capacity analysis, and it is to each of the principles that I now turn.

The Privacy Principle

The privacy principle, while not enumerated in the Bill of Rights, is inherent in the very notion of a right to the "pursuit of happiness" noted in the Declaration of Independence. Respect for intimate family relations are at the core of this human rights value. The Civil War, in large part, was a reaction to the horrors of slavery. Abolitionists found the laws of slavery profoundly inhumane and unjust above all because they ignored or destroyed intimate family relationships. As Peggy Cooper Davis has shown, family privacy and respect for family relationships was a core value that surfaced again and again in the congressional debates about the Fourteenth Amendment.[16] Family privacy is as firmly entrenched a part of constitutional values as free speech and freedom of religions, values that are explicitly enumerated. The term "liberty" as used in the Fourteenth Amendment has been interpreted to include the rights to form intimate relationships, to marry, to beget and bear children, and to live one's personal life free of legalized oppression.[17]

But privacy as a form of liberty is a strange concept when applied to very young children. Children are not free to choose their parents or siblings. Their daily care involves routine intrusions on bodily privacy—diapering, washing, dressing, feeding—that would be unacceptable to all but the most disabled or aged adults. The key to understanding young children's privacy rights lies in their developmental needs. We know that children must be able to forge attachments to their caregivers in order to survive, let alone develop the cognitive capacities and ego strengths described by Piaget and Erikson that are needed to function in the wider ecological environments described by Bronfenbrenner. For young children, the basic unit of privacy is not the individual but the relationship between child and caregiver. As children mature, their needs for privacy develop in different ways. As they grow, relations with peers and adults outside the family circle become more important. In adolescence, as children's bodies mature and develop sexually, the need for bodily privacy increases. The capacity to make choices about intimate relations also increases.

The children's stories in this book will explore children's privacy rights in both these dimensions, as a capacity-based right to define one's self, and as a relational right to family integrity. In the Introduction you have already heard the privacy principle powerfully expressed by Tony, a foster child who claimed the right to be raised by his own family and not the state.

The Agency Principle

A basic tenet of American values is the right of the individual to a voice and to play an active role in shaping his or her own destiny. I will adopt the term "agency" for this value, because it links so directly with research and theories about human development. The agency principle is reflected in the democratic constitutions that established our political structures at both state and federal levels. Citizens speak through their elected representatives and have the right to speak directly to government themselves. Only aliens, felons, and persons below age eighteen are now precluded from voting. Voting is not the only form of agency and voice of the individual in society.

The rights to be heard in courts of law and in public debate are important components of the agency principle that do not depend on citizenship, but extend to all.

The old saying, "Children are to be seen and not heard," illustrates how adults once drew the lines that excluded children from participation in civic and social life. Increasingly, children are being heard in family discussions, in courts, and in public discourse. The Internet has accelerated this process by giving young people ready access to the public square. Looking at children's agency through the lens of needs-based and capacity-based rights, children should be able to exercise their capacities to speak and act within a framework that acknowledges their stage on the road to adulthood. They need practice in learning to exercise independent judgment and voice informed opinions. As citizens in training, they should always have a voice in matters that affect them even though, in many situations, they are not ready to take responsibility for the ultimate choice. Child custody decisions provide an example of children's right to a voice even when they are too young to be burdened with making the ultimate choice. Judges in most jurisdictions are required to consider the child's preferences, giving due weight to the maturity of the child. But the judge is the decision-maker, and it should be made clear to children that the choice is the judge's, and not the child's, to make.[18]

Many of the stories in this book show children's agency and voice in action. Children's words and actions have played a far greater role in shaping the American experience than most people realize. From eighteenth-century revolutionary times to nineteenth-century labor movements to twentieth-century civil rights movements, American children have been seen *and* heard. Their voices and actions have often made a critical difference in the unfolding of American history.

The Equality Principle

The words "All men are created equal" in the Declaration of Independence established an idea that may have been revolutionary in

1776 but has become universally accepted as a bedrock principle of human rights. The original U.S. Constitution failed to deliver on this promise of equality—it tolerated slavery and voting rights extended only to white men with property, a small segment of the population. It took the Civil War and passage of the Fourteenth Amendment to make the equality principle explicit in the Constitution. The Fourteenth Amendment's guarantee that "no state shall deny to any person the equal protection of the laws" has been the primary means for extending constitutional rights to previously excluded groups. The equality principle appears in countless other forms, including laws that prohibit discrimination against disabled or elderly citizens. At the core of the equality principle is the conviction that it is wrong to treat people differently because of irrelevant traits such as their race or their gender. Classifications based on race are generally unconstitutional and classifications based on gender or sex must be supported by objectively real and important differences, not stereotypes or myths.[19]

But very young children *are* different from adults, and age is not an entirely spurious measure of their right to equal treatment. A rule of absolute equality among all humans would leave children to fend for themselves, unprotected by the special laws that recognize and protect their vulnerability. The tension between children's claims to "equal justice under law" and the fact of children's essential dependency forces us to find more nuanced ways of thinking about equality in relation to children. Equality for children must mean both more and less than formal rules that treat all persons exactly the same. Equality has many possible meanings—equal treatment, equal resources, equal impact, to name a few. One facet of equality is the idea of equality of opportunity. This principle seems especially important in the lives of children, who inherit at birth the inequalities that shaped their parents' lives. Applying the twin measures of children's needs and their capacities for autonomy to equality rights for children would refocus our sights on creating an environment for children that supports their capacities for growth and achievement of their natural potential. In North American social and political culture, parents have primary responsibility for meeting children's needs for nurture. But communities and nations also have responsibility for children. A society that possesses sufficient resources for all children and allows some of its children to go without necessary health care, food, and education is failing in its moral duty. As children mature and their dependency diminishes, equality of opportunity together with the notion of capacity-based rights suggests we should give children the space to try their wings and take more responsibility for shaping their own opportunities.

The stories I will tell include many examples of children fighting racial and gender barriers to equal access to schools and professions. But no scheme of rights for children can ignore the fact that children do not begin life on an even playing field. A society committed to the values of equality will strive to give all children a fair start on their developmental journey and a fair chance at arriving safely at their destination.

The Dignity Principle

An indispensable part of human rights values is the principle that every human has a right to be respected as an individual. The Declaration of Independence envisions all men not only as created equal but also as endowed with "unalienable rights" to "life, liberty, and the pursuit of happiness," a phrase that captures the notion of inherent human dignity. While this phrase is not part of the Constitution, many of the details of the constitutional scheme are designed to recognize the worth of the individual and to protect against assaults on human dignity. The Bill of Rights includes rights to due process of law, against self-incrimination, and against cruel or unusual punishment, all examples of rights based in respect for the dignity of the individual.[20] The Court has also given a broad reading to the word "liberty" in the Fourteenth Amendment, as protecting not only freedom from bodily harm and restraint but also those personal freedoms "essential to the orderly pursuit of happiness by free men. In a Constitution for a free people, there is no doubt that the meaning of 'liberty' must be broad indeed."[21]

Recognition of the individual dignity principle has been a long time coming for children. Law has treated children almost as if they were the property of adults. Early child custody laws gave absolute parental authority to fathers and did not consider the child's attachments or the child's welfare in deciding child custody. Poor children whose parents could not support them could be taken from their parents and put to work in pubic workhouses. In the mid-nineteenth century, courts began to look at children's needs in custody cases. At first, looking through a Victorian lens, judges presumed that a young child needed his mother. By the twentieth century, the "best interest of the child" had become the dominant rule in child custody.[22] Laws that penalized innocent children for the sins of their parents began to look inhumane. Children born out of wedlock were no longer punished for their illegitimate status.[23] We have come to accept that children, unlike chattels, have rights as individuals, even if law assigns authority to assert those rights to elders.

Looking at the individual dignity principle through the lens of children's needs-based and capacity-based rights suggests that children's dignity must be honored within the context of their dependency and not just in the context of their capacity for autonomy. Dignity exists even in the absence of autonomy. Treating children as individuals means we should focus on the child, and assess the individual child's needs even if he is too young or disabled to assert his own views. It also suggests we ought to listen with great care even to very young children so we can give weight to their perspectives and experiences in assessing their needs and interests. The dignity principle asks that we respect children's intrinsic value and capacity for growth.

The Protection Principle

The protection principle is perhaps the most basic principle of law. Civilized societies cannot exist where the law of the jungle prevails and the strong are free to harm the weak in order to get their way.

The protection principle applies with even greater force when an entire class of persons is in a weaker and more vulnerable position. The law has long recognized that parents have the obligation to protect their children. When children had no parents or their parents failed to protect and support them, the state took the parents' place under a doctrine called *parens patriae* that empowered government to protect those who could not protect themselves.[24]

Parents, however, were given great latitude in the use of force to discipline their children. Only in the early 1970s did physicians begin to understand the severe risks to children posed by excessive use of force on growing bodies. We also discovered that the incidence of sexual abuse of children was far greater than previously believed. During the last decades of the twentieth century, we have developed elaborate child welfare systems for protecting children from abuse and neglect.[25] Striking the proper balance between family privacy and child protection remains an elusive goal. Advocates for children split over whether the focus should be on protecting children by assisting their families to care for them, or whether the focus should be on removing children who were abused or neglected from their homes to places of refuge.[26] Inevitably, the realities have required a blend of both approaches. Where risks to children arise from poverty and lack of skills, provision of resources and services to ensure family preservation is the ideal, but where risks arise from severe pathologies that cannot be changed, child protection becomes the primary goal.

A separate but related form of child protection is the notion that adults have an obligation to protect children from themselves. We tend to think that adults will ask for protection when they want it and otherwise should be left alone, free to make foolish, even fatal, mistakes. A child-centered developmentally informed view of protection, however, recognizes that children have the drive and motor skills to act long before they acquire the capacity to understand the risks and consequences of their actions. Both the family and society play important roles in this "paternalistic" form of protection. Parents protect the toddler who reaches for the electric socket from the consequences of his curiosity. Adolescents too young to fully comprehend or internalize the health risks and hazards of drinking, smoking, and speeding in cars must be protected by society from their own impulses to look and feel more mature. Persons too young to have consensual sex or to marry wisely are protected from their own immaturity by laws that prohibit statutory rape and underage marriage.

A key event in the American experience was the creation of special courts for juveniles. These courts recognized that children who committed crimes were too immature to understand their acts and could be rehabilitated.[27] We have seen a shift toward more punitive approaches that treat children as adults when they commit criminal acts even though they are not considered mature enough to make simple personal decisions without adult assistance. In the stories that follow, we will see many examples of the tensions between values of child protection and children's desire to assert competing rights, including individual dignity, equality, agency, and privacy rights.

Autonomy and Dependency: Two Sides of the Same Coin

Children's rights are not different in quality from those of adults but flow from the same set of basic values: dignity, agency, equality, privacy, and protection. Children are constantly in transition, developing before our very eyes, and their lives involve a complex dialogue between dependence and independence. Studies of child development tell us, however, that autonomy and dependency are two sides of the same coin. From the first eye contact with a caregiver, the first game of peek-a-boo, the first step, children are engaged in testing the boundaries of self and other. Their survival, flourishing, and growth depend on our success and theirs as we try to balance their need to operate independently and their need for support, direction, and protection. I believe this duality to be true of humans generally, but it is unmistakably true of children.

Thinking of needs-based and autonomy-based rights as intertwined highlights the creative tension between autonomy and dependence. These terms recognize that the balance between children's needs for care and for independence changes as they travel the road from birth to adulthood. Children possess rights from birth, but the power to exercise those rights lies first with the child's parents who guide him according to his "evolving capacities."[28] As children mature, they become increasingly able to express and assert their rights, first under the guidance of parents and other adults and eventually as fully mature rights-bearing citizens. Sometimes more than one of these basic human rights principles is reflected in a specific right of the child. For example, a child's right to education is both a "needs-based right" and a "capacity-based right." Children need to be provided with access to education in order to function in a competitive world, but the process of education not only shapes but also is shaped by their capacity. Education meets survival needs but also promotes autonomy, dignity, and equality. Sometimes two principles or rights may come into conflict. For example, the agency principle often conflicts with the protection principle. No matter how strongly felt and authentic the two-year-old's drive to cut his own meat, when he seizes a razor-sharp steak knife, the values of autonomy have to give way to the values of protection. Or one child's right to education may come into conflict with another child's right to free expression. Every day in every classroom, teachers are balancing children's rights to free expression and their rights to learn, searching for the compromise that promotes an optimal learning environment. Just how that compromise is struck differs from culture to culture and from era to era. It even differs from family to family, and child to child, as parents learn when they find that one child thrives in a structured environment while his brother does much better in a relaxed environment.

I have been using the terms child, children, and childhood almost as if they were interchangeable. Actually, the meanings of these terms are highly dependent on whom you ask and why you ask. A child psychologist, a pediatrician, and a lawyer might define the terms quite differently. For purposes of international human rights law, the United Nations Convention on the Rights of the Child answers this question in Article 1. Childhood, for purposes of the CRC and other human rights documents, is the period before legal emancipation. The CRC applies to all persons below age eighteen unless the law of the child's country grants majority status at an earlier age.[29] In many countries, age eighteen is a major benchmark. In others it is relatively insignificant, dwarfed by benchmarks such as leaving home for marriage or work. Generally, age eighteen is the age of majority in the United States; under the Twenty-Sixth Amendment, at eighteen we are allowed to vote. Eighteen provides a convenient bright line between adults and children. But no one believes that a child is transformed instantly into an adult on his or her eighteenth birthday. Instead, we recognize childhood as a period of transition and growth. Laws that set different age limits in different contexts illustrate that childhood is a moving target. In my state, Florida, a child cannot drive a car until age sixteen or get a tattoo until age eighteen, but the same child can be sentenced to life in prison without parole or bypass parental consent to obtain an abortion at age twelve. At common law, a child under the age of seven was believed too young to charge with a crime. In Florida, there is no minimum age for criminal responsibility.

One thing is clear when we examine the role of chronological age in American law. Americans have an ambivalent attitude toward children. We patronize children when they are young, underestimating their capabilities. At the same time, we idealize children as the embodiments of innocence and romanticize childhood as a time of carefree play. As they grow in autonomy and begin to challenge adult control, our tendency to patronize turns to anxiety and mistrust. An understanding both of children's development and of the impact of the natural and social environment on their growth is essential to thinking about children's rights. As our knowledge of child development increases and as the environments of childhood in America change, we must revisit and examine stereotypes and preconceptions about children and test them against children's real experiences.

But theories, in the abstract, lack the persuasive power of history and experience. This is why I have built this book around children's stories, reaching back into the past as well as looking at present-day children. The American experience and American history play a large role in the constitutionalization of children's rights and their adaptation to fit the American context. While I am looking at American children's stories as a means of understanding children's rights, rather than as a means of describing America's past, history, law, and the emergence of rights are inextricably intertwined. Each emerging right looks backward as well as forward. For this reason alone, the history of children and youth in America would be important to thinking about our children's rights.

The U.S. Supreme Court has developed a set of tests for deciding whether a claimed right that is not specifically mentioned in the Constitution is truly fundamental. The justices look at whether the value at stake is so deeply rooted in tradition and so basic to the notion of justice that it is implicit in the concept of ordered liberty.[30] Different justices take varying views on how specific the historic tradition must be. A minority would look to the most specific level of historical fact at the time the drafters wrote the constitutional text. Under this view, capital punishment of juveniles must be constitutional today because it was practiced and accepted at the time the Bill of Rights, prohibiting cruel or unusual punishment, was written. Most justices have taken a more general approach. They believe that practices such as executing juveniles, discriminating against illegitimates, and prohibiting interracial marriage that were once accepted or tolerated can become offensive to the values embodied in our Constitution as American values and perspectives on human rights evolve over time.

In Their Own Voices: American Children's Stories

If called upon to draft a brief for the Supreme Court of the United States in support of children's rights, I would use American history and tradition as important arrows in my quiver of arguments. The stories of children are important as narratives but also as historical evidence that justice for children is integral to America's fundamental values. The stories also provide proof that American children, through their own agency and voice, have earned their right to claim rights.

In the stories that follow, I invite you to consider how human rights evolve into legally enforceable rights in American law. Consider, as well, how theories about children's development and about children's rights are reflected in the real lives of children. Think about the concepts of agency and voice, as demonstrated in these stories. Consider the developmental crises that challenged these children to grow and the particular cognitive tools these children brought to their interactions with and understanding of their worlds. And consider the interplay between the child's developmental stage and the historic times, places, and communities in which the child lives, from the intimate settings of microsystems and mesosystems, to the culturally and historically diverse settings of exosystems and macrosystems. All of these tools and concepts are important to thinking about children's rights in the context of American values.

PART I

THE PRIVACY PRINCIPLE: STORIES OF BONDAGE AND BELONGING

CHAPTER 3

BOYS IN SLAVERY AND SERVITUDE

Frederick Douglass

I am but a boy, and all boys are bound to someone.
 —Frederick Douglass, age sixteen[1]

As a boy growing up in slavery, the great orator and abolitionist Frederick Douglass acknowledged and reflected on his common bond with children everywhere. In his bleakest moments, during a time when his master was trying to break his will at hard labor, he took comfort from the fact that his bondage did not set him so far apart from his peers. "I am but a boy," he reflected, "and all boys are bound to someone." Looking around him, as an American child in the early 1800s, Douglass could see that no child was really free. All were subordinated to some adult's control. The young Douglass articulated one of the central puzzles of children's rights. How can we assert as a foundational principle that liberty is the birthright of all Americans and yet accept that American children are not free? How can we honor children as persons and yet make them subordinate by their very status as children? We know in our hearts that Frederick Douglass's status as a slave was different from the bondage of free children. Yet the historic similarities between the powers of masters and the powers of parents are striking. Historically, parents and guardians had legal authority to use the same techniques as overseers—whippings, deprivation of food, solitary confinement, silence, and forced labor—as forms of control in the home. American childhood is rooted in seemingly conflicting images of personal liberty and of youthful obedience to adult authority.

We are all familiar with the tragic history of slavery, a shameful heritage that Americans have rejected. Yet between the lines of the story of children in slavery is an overlapping and related history—the story of children's status as property. All slaves were defined by law as "chattel," articles of living property. In the case of children born into slavery, however, their status as children and as slaves—the double disabilities of age and race—combined to further justify their status as a saleable commodity. This double disability made the deprivation of their liberty as *children* seem normal and natural and their treatment as *things* rather than as persons relatively unremarkable. In the early years of the Republic, children, as a class, suffered from a complex system of interlocking legal discriminations based not only on race or ethnicity but also on poverty, illegitimacy, and youth. In this chapter and the next, I will ask you to envision childhood through the eyes of boys and girls who endured and also, as agents of their own emancipation, resisted and escaped the bonds of slavery.

The stories of children growing up in slavery and servitude illustrate how legal subordination to another's will has always been a feature of American childhood. But these stories also push us to articulate why, having rejected the laws that bound children in slavery, we honor as a fundamental right the bonds arising out of the parent/child relationship. I will argue that the child's right to family privacy—the developmentally based right to intimate nurturing relationships—is what makes us reject one hierarchy as slavery and protect the other as essential to freedom.

The child who would one day become Frederick Douglass was given the name Fred Bailey at birth (Fig. 1). He was born in February of

1818 to a slave named Harriet Bailey, who belonged to Captain Anthony, a landholder in his own right and the overseer at Wye Plantation. Fred's first memories were of Betsy Bailey, his grandmother. He knew that she was not his mother—his mother was her daughter, Harriet—but Betsy raised him from infancy and he loved her dearly. As Fred soon realized, the laws of slavery controlled him from birth. His grandmother lived in her own cabin near the Tuckahoe River, as the "wife" of Isaac Bailey, a free black woodcutter, but Betsy Bailey was a slave and could never be legally married. Most children's status was defined by the status of their father, but a different rule applied to children of enslaved women. A child born to a black woman inherited the status of his mother. Since Betsy was a slave, Fred's mother Harriet was a slave, and so Fred was born a slave.

Fred heard whispers that Captain Anthony, his mother's owner, was his father. But he was never allowed to learn the truth of his parentage. Legally, he was not the child of his father but the chattel of his mother's owner. Separated from his mother in infancy, so she could return to her toil as a field hand, Fred could not recapture a memory of his mother from his first six years. He grew up playing in the woods and streams, sharing the hard but independent life of the Baileys. At six, this brief childhood was over and Fred was turned over to his owner. He recalled walking down a dusty road holding his grandmother's hand on the way to a strange brick house. He would go to sleep and wake up to find his grandmother gone.

The overseer's home stood within sight of elegant Wye House, where one of the Eastern Shore's "oldest" families lived a life of ease. For the first time in his memory, Fred was aware of knowing his own mother, who came often to see him and battled to ensure he received adequate food. He observed the cruelty and attempts at kindness of those around him, and felt the vivid contrast between his life and the life of the young master of Wye House, to whom Fred became both playmate and servant. But when Fred was eight, once again his life changed abruptly. He was put aboard a ship sailing to Baltimore, on the western shore of Chesapeake Bay. Captain

Engraved by J.C. Buttre.

Frederick Douglass.

Fig. 1. Frederick Douglass as a young man (with permission of The Granger Collection).

Anthony no longer had use for him, and he had loaned him to Baltimore relations in need of a child servant. Fred's new master and mistress, Hugh and Sophia Auld, lived in the Fells Point section of the crowded city. In the 1820s and 30s, Fells Point was a crossroads of commerce and shipping with a large population of free blacks, many of whom had purchased their freedom with wages earned from skilled labor.[2]

In Baltimore, a new world opened to this bright and curious child. Like many other youths before and after, Fred found a city space where he could experience relative freedom, away from the strict divisions between white and black that characterized plantation economy and rural society. At first, eight-year-old Fred was set to work looking after two-year-old Thomas Auld. There was nothing odd about this arrangement, since assigning older children to run after toddlers was commonplace in families of all kinds. Soon, Fred was helping with household tasks and running errands that took him into the busy streets of Fells Point, gateway to the larger world of boys. In many ways, his life was no different from that of the ragtag band of boys who were his Baltimore playmates in the alleys around Durgin and Bailey's shipyard. All worked as well as played, and many of them were indentured servants or apprentices, living in the homes of their masters and separated from their families of origin. Unlike these white children, however, Fred was forbidden to attend school. Yet he learned to read and write, becoming a skilled orator and famous author.

The story of how Fred came to read was the single most important episode in his journey from bondage to freedom. He first learned his letters from Sophia Auld's Bible, but these lessons ended abruptly, with an angry lecture from Master Hugh on the importance of keeping slaves in ignorance. The lecture made an indelible impression on Fred. " 'A nigger should know nothing but to obey his master, to do what he is told to do. Learning would *spoil* the best nigger in the world. Now,' said he, 'if you teach that nigger (speaking of myself) to read, there would be no keeping of him. It would forever unfit him to be a slave.' " This furious outburst, which "sank deep into [Fred's] heart, . . . explained dark and mysterious things" that had puzzled this highly intelligent child. Finally, "the white man's power to enslave the black man" had been revealed to him, and he suddenly "understood the pathway from slavery to freedom."[3]

Fred carefully kept his new knowledge a secret from the adults, but he seized every chance to learn to read and write. He recalls, "I was much better off than the poor white children in our neighborhood," as bread was in plentiful supply at the Auld house. He gave his friends bread and they gave him lessons from their copybooks— the bread of knowledge. Years later, when all were grown men and Fred was safely in the North, he concealed the little boys' names "out of gratitude and affection," and concern that they would be punished for the "almost unpardonable offense" of teaching a slave to read.[4]

Fred's first debates about slavery were with other children. "I used to talk this matter of slavery over with them. I would sometimes say to them, I wished I could be as free as they would be when they got to be men. 'You will be free, as soon as you are twenty-one, *but I am a slave for life!* Have not I as good a right to be free as you have?'"[5] There were no dissenters among his audience. "I do not remember ever having met with a *boy*, while I was in slavery, who defended the slave system."[6] Adults, especially white adults, however kind, were not to be trusted. One day, passing some free hours on the dock, Fred pitched in to help some Irish sailors unload stones from a scow. When the task was finished, one of them came to Fred and asked if he was a slave. Fred answered that he was. The Irishman pressed him further: " 'Are ye a slave for life?' I told him that I was. The good Irishman seemed to be deeply affected by the statement. He said to the other that it was a pity so fine a little fellow as myself should be a slave for life."[7] These men told him he could be free if he ran away to a free state in the North, but Fred pretended not to be interested and acted as if he did not understand them. However, from that time he resolved to run away.

By now Fred was about twelve, and had taught himself to read. As Hugh Auld had predicted, "there would be no keeping of him." Fred learned from cast-off newspapers the real meaning of mysterious words like *abolition*, overheard in adult conversation but never explained and too dangerous to ask about. He soon got his hands on "The Columbian Orator," a primer filled with patriotic speeches containing "bold denunciations of slavery" and vindications of human rights. In its pages, he would have discovered Abbé Fauchet's eulogy to Benjamin Franklin, praising the autobiography of the famous man's youth as the "foundation of American morality," planting the seed for Douglass's chronicle of his own coming of age.[8] Fred grew increasingly bold, and began to read openly, infuriating his mistress who seemed to turn against him as his intellect and body grew.

By the time he turned fifteen, he was no longer a precocious little boy but a physically and mentally powerful youth. Once again, Fred's owner ordered him shipped across the Chesapeake Bay, this time to Thomas and Lucretia Auld, Hugh Auld's brother and sister-in-law, who had inherited Fred as a chattel at Captain Anthony's death. Perhaps the white adults who owned him feared he would escape, or perhaps he was simply the victim of grown-ups' family squabbles over their human property. Letters between Thomas and Hugh Auld indicate that Thomas's wife Lucretia was angry at being saddled with Fred's crippled cousin Henny, while her brother-in-law had the use of a strong and healthy boy. She demanded that Hugh either take the useless Henny off her hands, or send Fred back.[9]

Thomas Auld was a tradesman in St. Michaels, a busy port on Maryland's Eastern Shore, and he found the defiant teenager Fred impossible to handle. When whippings failed to subdue his spirit, he was hired out to a local wheat farmer with a reputation as a "nigger breaker."[10] The farmer worked Fred mercilessly, determined to teach this uppity boy his place. Years later, Fred recalled how he would lie exhausted on a hillside overlooking the Chesapeake Bay and dream of following the white sails of the vessels northward to freedom. It was then that he comforted himself with the knowledge that all boys were bound to someone. But he was determined not to be "a slave for life."

When Frederick was eighteen, the Aulds discovered that he had plotted and almost succeeded in carrying out a plan of escape. It was clear that he could not be dominated by force, and Thomas

Auld decided he would be worth more as a trained artisan than as a surly field worker, with little to live for and nothing to lose by fleeing North. Fred was sent back to Hugh Auld's home in Fells Point, and in 1836 he was hired out to a master shipbuilder to learn the skilled trade of ship caulking, at the time a common trade among Baltimore's free blacks. The prospect of earning his freedom was dangled before him, as an incentive to win his compliance. Hugh Auld made vague promises of manumission—implying that if Fred learned well and worked hard, and turned every penny of his wages over each week, perhaps he would be manumitted from slavery when he reached age twenty-five.

Fred's first apprenticeship was both frustrating and dangerous. He was severely beaten by a gang of white apprentices from the shipyard, angry and fearful at competition from a black. For once, Hugh Auld came to Fred's defense, and marched the bleeding boy down to the magistrate, demanding damages for the injury to his property. The boy shared his owner's outrage when the magistrate told them that Fred's testimony was useless, and a cause of action could only be lodged if a competent white witness to the assault would come forward.

Hugh Auld decided to take charge of Fred's training in the shipyard where Auld himself worked. Fred learned the craft of caulking and was soon earning six dollars a week. His wages, however, were not his own and he deeply resented the weekly ritual in which he handed his earnings to a scowling Master Hugh. Schooled in rhetoric from the pages of the "Columbia Orator," Fred later deployed the language of property rights, and their antithesis—seizure by arbitrary power—to explain his outrage. "I contracted for it; I earned it; it was paid to me; it was rightfully my own; yet upon each returning Saturday night, I was compelled to deliver every cent of that money to Master Hugh. And why? Not because he earned it,—not because he had any hand in earning it,—not because I owed it to him,—nor because he possessed the slightest shadow of a right to it; but solely because he had the power to compel me to give it up. The right of the grim-visaged pirate on the high seas is exactly the same."[11]

But Fred instinctively understood that his own ability to earn a skilled wage gave him some measure of power over the man who claimed to own him. The difference between the market value of enforced slave labor and the wages the same slave could earn as a skilled craftsman provided Fred with the currency to buy back a small slice of his freedom. He negotiated an agreement with Hugh Auld, allowing him to live on his own, pay his own upkeep, bargain with employers for his work, collect his own wages and, in exchange, he would pay three dollars a week to his master, rain or shine, whether he had found work or not. As Fred later observed, "This arrangement it will be perceived, was decidedly in my master's favor. It relieved him of all need of looking after me. His money was sure. He received all the benefits of slave holding without its evils; while I endured all the evils of a slave, and suffered all the cares and anxieties of a freeman."[12] Added to his master's side of the ledger was the fact that Fred, as a slave and a minor, had no legal standing to enforce such an agreement, if his master were to breach it.

This compromise might have lasted indefinitely, but one Saturday in summer of 1838 Fred failed to pay his three dollars on time and Auld flew into a fury. Auld did not use physical violence, but throughout his life the adult Douglass recalled Auld's threats and curses in humiliating detail. Fred's first response was to go on strike, refusing to look for work so that he would earn nothing and have no wages to turn over on Saturday. Having made his point, he shifted to feigning cooperation, in order to avert suspicion from his plot to escape. Fred had met the girl he would later marry, Anna Murray, a free woman born to manumitted slaves who had migrated from the Eastern Shore to Baltimore.[13] Fred went back to work, meekly paying every cent he earned to his master, and borrowed from Anna the money he needed to escape. On September 3, 1838, still six months shy of twenty-one, Fred's plans were complete—he slipped out of Baltimore on his way to New York, and "left [his] chains" forever.[14]

In the *Narrative of the Life of Frederick Douglass, an American Slave Written by Himself*, we see slavery through the eyes of a little

boy as he grows into a powerful young man. His psychological
struggle against enslavement was shared by countless other children
growing up in slavery. As Walter Johnson has remarked, "From
an early age, enslaved children learned to view their own bodies
through two different lenses, one belonging to their masters and the
other belonging to themselves."[15] Many enslaved children shared
similar recollections of a childhood that ended abruptly, of grief at
the loss of a mother, of a father whom they never knew, of play and
work, hunger and beatings, and of sudden and arbitrary separations
from all people and things familiar. His story is both uniquely a
story of slavery and universal to every child of his time who was
burdened by poverty, dependency, and illegitimacy.

In fact, Frederick Douglass never completely left behind the
chains of slavery. He returned again and again in his adult life to
examine the details of his early years, searching for an understanding of his identity as an adult through the perceptions and experiences of the child he had once been. In 1845, when he committed
to paper his recollections of a childhood in bondage, he was about
to emerge on the national scene as a powerful spokesman against
the evils of chattel slavery. His story draws its power not only from
the injustice of slavery but also from the powerlessness of a child,
growing to adulthood, under a legal regime that allowed the adults
around him to exploit his value as a chattel while denigrating his
value as a sentient human being. His narrative of a childhood in
slavery, and his insights into the condition of children generally,
show us that injustice toward children is deeply rooted in our history. The modern movement for children's rights is only the latest
stage in the battle for human rights—a continuing struggle for justice that reaches back to the earliest days of this nation.

The seeds of American children's rights were planted in the Declaration of Independence. Of course, neither Thomas Jefferson nor
his compatriots intended to foment a children's rights revolution.
When they declared it self-evident that all men were created equal,
they certainly did not mean to emancipate their slaves, their women,
or their children. They had much to lose from challenging a status
quo that made women's and children's liberties depend entirely on

the will of their husbands and fathers. The protection of liberty and property in the minds of many was intimately tied to protecting vested rights, including a man's right to the obedience and labor of his household members—slaves, indentured servants, women, and children. However, the intellectual seeds sown by the American, and later the French, revolutions showed a stubborn tendency to spread like weeds beyond their original boundaries. The authors of the Declaration articulated the notion that in order to be just, a grant of power to one human being over another could not be hereditary, but must be grounded on some form of consent and predicated on inherent equality. The same principles that justified a revolution against the British monarchy would eventually challenge the domestic monarchy reflected in the notion that "a man's home is his castle" and his wife and children vassals within the domestic realm. First, however, America had to deal with the greater evil of slavery.

Slavery was a uniquely horrible injustice, but the principle that one person could hold complete and arbitrary power over another spilled over into other legal relationships as well. Although only children held as slaves were ever actually designated by law as "chattels personal," in many ways, the laws applying to children as a group had much in common with the laws of property. Rhetoric about children, as well as the actual treatment of children, remained deeply analogous to assumptions made in the prevalent thinking about property.[16] Comparing children's status with that of slaves should not be taken as a trivialization of slavery or as a claim that the evils of children's subordination were equivalent to the evils of slavery. Children, unlike enslaved African Americans or women who have fought for "equal" rights, are not equal with adults and do need adult protection. Most observers, today as well as in the early years of the Republic, would agree that children cannot become free adult citizens without someone to provide love, authority, and care as they grow. The strength of children's deep attachments to those who nurture them is nature's proof of this vast difference between family bonds and the bonds of slavery. Nevertheless, the fact remains that the status of children owes much to theories of ownership, as well as to theories of human relationships. This historic connection, invisible to adults, was clear to the young Frederick Douglass.

The concept of human property, of which slavery was the most notorious vestige, had ancient roots. The notion of children as their father's property flowed naturally from the story of procreation as told by a patrilineal society—according to the ancients, it was the father's "seed" that, once planted in the mother's womb, grew into his likeness within the woman's body. Flesh of their father's flesh, children rightly belonged to the patriarch, to be worked, traded, and given in marriage in exchange for money. Had you tried to engage Aristotle in debate over the question of parental powers versus justice for children, the debate might have ended almost before it began. He would have contended: "There cannot be injustice towards that which is one's own; and a chattel, or a child, until it is of a certain age and has attained independence, is as it were a part of oneself; and nobody chooses to injure himself (hence there can be no injustice towards oneself) and so neither can there be any conduct towards them that is politically just or unjust."[17]

Subsequent Western European political theorists such as Thomas Hobbes and John Locke attempted to map out other arguments justifying adult power over children. Hobbes argued that parental power was based on an implicit contract—the infant "agrees" to obey the parent in exchange for the parent's forbearance from allowing the helpless infant to perish. Locke contended that God was the true owner of children. God created children and gave them into their parents' care, therefore parental powers were a form of trusteeship of the Creator's property. This conception of parental right as a reflection of parental responsibilities appeared in the writings of American scholars like William Blackstone.[18]

Under Roman law, fathers possessed the power of life or death over their children. Even in the American Colonies, laws in many places provided capital punishment for a child who struck or cursed his parent—although no record exists of such sentences being carried out. As late as 1920, a parent who killed a child in the course of punishment could claim a legal excuse for homicide in no fewer than nine states.[19] Well into the nineteenth century, a father could enroll his male children in the army and collect the enrollment bounty, betroth his minor female children to persons of his choice, and put his children to work as day laborers on farms or factories and collect their wage packets. Like Frederick's owners and masters, a father had the power to decide where and with whom his child would reside, and to transfer his children in his will, by testamentary disposition, often to someone other than the mother.[20]

As Fred Bailey realized, long before he became Frederick Douglass, the lines between freedom and bondage, between persons and property, were patrolled and reinforced by concepts of minority and dependency, as well as by concepts of race and color. It was simply a fact of economic and social life that all children were "bound" to somebody. The United States was settled, in large part, by working indentured children—many of whom were bound out for long terms of service and separated by an ocean from their parents. Over half the people who settled the Colonies south of New England came to America under contracts of indenture, binding them in many cases past the age of majority. Many were poor children taken from the streets of English cities, often without their consent. The average age of an indentured servant was fourteen to sixteen and the youngest was six.[21] The Constitution itself protected adults' vested rights to the involuntary servitude of persons who had been bound out as children. Article IV, Section 3, clause 3, which formed the basis for the Fugitive Slave Acts, covered "all persons held in Service or Labour" and obligated neighboring states to return them if they escaped across state lines.[22]

In Frederick's retelling of the story, it did not appear to surprise the Irish sailor that Fred was in bondage—it was the notion of slavery *for life* that so horrified the Irishman and caused Fred such anguish. In Douglass's day it was ordinary to exploit a child as an economic commodity. Free children belonged to their fathers, who had a right to their labor, in exchange for education and sustenance. Except for those few children born into wealthy families, children typically spent much of their youth working for others, whether "rented out" by their fathers in exchange for wages, bound out to employers in long-term indentures, or apprenticed to a master to learn a trade.

Almost as draconian as racialized status were the consequences for children of illegitimacy. In combination, race, poverty, illegitimacy, and minority were used to deprive parents of their children and to deprive children of many valuable rights. Again, Douglass's story is illustrative. If it was true, as Frederick Douglass believed, that Captain Anthony was his father, he should by birth have been among the lucky few children who might live a life of leisure and learning. However, under the one drop rule, a child with a drop of African blood was deemed black, deprived of his father's wealth, and because his father did not and could not marry his mother, he was illegitimate—all of which were interlocking and mutually reinforcing disabilities. Black children in antebellum America, in an exception designed to perpetuate and reinforce racialized slavery and to guarantee a renewable source of human capital, did not belong to their fathers. In every slave state, as in Maryland, their status was defined by that of their mother. White men who fathered children with black women were able to "own" their own children, without having to share their wealth or their status with them.[23] Another large class of children, children born out of wedlock, was stigmatized as bastards. Considered *filius nulius*, or children of no one, regardless of their color or class status, they had no right to claim their fathers' or mothers' names or inheritance.[24] Since legal marriage was denied to slaves, and interracial marriage was a crime, children like Fred could rarely escape becoming "chattels personal" of their mother's owners. Frederick Douglass's childhood illustrates the uncertain existence of a "chattel"—a form of moveable personal possession with attributes both of thing and of human being, to be used to satisfy the needs of his owners.[25] The implications for Fred's cousin Henny were especially stark, since her master's frustration at being saddled with a child who was an economic liability seems to have escalated into a pattern of vicious physical abuse.[26]

Children of unmarried mothers, whatever their color, were extremely vulnerable to being treated like chattel, transferred to the most economical use, and separated from their kin. Even after un-married mothers were given rights of custody to bastard children, Poor Laws, patterned on those of England, continued to authorize local authorities to remove any child lacking support, and to offer the child for indenture as a servant or laborer until the age of ma-jority. Although single mothers were more likely to be destitute, the laws applied to all families unable to care for their young, and many children with two living married parents found themselves involuntarily indentured. Mulatto children born to white mothers received still harsher treatment, which was intended to discourage miscegenation. They were indentured at birth until they reached age thirty-one. Indenture provided a process of redistributing labor and also a method of controlling unmarried and interracial sexual activity and of privatizing responsibility for the poor, who would otherwise be a drain on the community's resources.[27]

As Fred's experience in Fells Point illustrates, the boundaries among the labor of free, indentured, and slave children often blurred in practice. During the first half of the nineteenth century, many blacks migrated to urban centers, either in the custody of masters or after securing their freedom. In commercial economies like that of Baltimore, slave children were put to work by their masters in business, commerce, and craft settings, and worked side by side with free black children and with whites who had been bound out by their parents or the Poor Law authorities. All such children were at risk, although black children far more than their white counterparts, of being abruptly sent away from their homes and families. Children in slavery or indenture also were constantly at risk of being demoted from training in service or skilled crafts, which at least gave some promise of security even to those who were "slaves for life," and being assigned menial labor and field hand's work.[28]

In the hierarchy of servitude, apprentices stood at the top. In the-ory, the child's consent was required, and he was entitled to training as part of the bargain. Under some apprenticeship agreements, the father of a child might turn to the courts to enforce a master's bro-ken promise to train and educate him, or might petition to revoke an illegal assignment of the child to another master. The typical indenture gave more latitude for assignments and fewer assurances of useful education and training. Racism in both North and South created an overlay of legal and economic disabilities, placing additional burdens on free black children in apprenticeships and indentures, withdrawing many of the protections afforded white apprentices, and further blurring the lines between free and bond labor.[29] A slave child like Fred Bailey was at the very bottom of the ladder of power. His owner owed no duty of education or training to him and was legally as well as practically free to use, sell, or abuse the child as he wished, limited primarily by public opinion, which (according to Douglass) might approve of whipping a child but would censure starving her.[30]

As the episode of Fred's assignment to the "nigger breaker" plantation owner illustrates, the ability to transfer a minor child's custody and control from one user to another provided not only economic benefits but also a means of maintaining control. Rebellious youths could be removed from bad company or temptation and sent to more restrictive surroundings, where these bad habits might be broken. We know that slave youths were at the mercy of their owners. Nonslave children also could be sent away by their parents, and they could be seized by persons charged with maintaining public order and protecting the young.[31] During the nineteenth century, charities formed to rescue children from the deviance of poor families. Charitable and religious organizations founded Houses of Refuge, Asylums, and Reform Schools, committed to controlling as well as teaching the young. The boundaries between education, protection, and incarceration were extremely vague. A child could be detained in these asylums until age twenty-one, against his will and without due process of law or any charge of criminal behavior. Courts rebuffed challenges to children's seizure and incarceration by pointing to the educational mission of these institutions. Parents were warned that if they failed to control their children, to feed and clothe them, or to teach them appropriate morals, the state would take over the parental role. Those readers familiar with Oliver Twist's life in the Poor

House would recognize the following description of a New York asylum: "In summer, they are about fourteen hours under orders daily. On parade, at table, at their work, and in school, they are not allowed to converse. . . . For every trifling commission or omission, they are "cut" with rattan. . . . The endurance of the whip, or the loss of a meal—deprivation of play or the solitary cell. On every hand their walk is bounded; while Restriction and Constraint are their most intimate companions."[32]

Thus, limitations of slavery, involuntary servitude, and incarceration overlapped in powerfully symbolic ways with the limitations on the freedom of children as a class. Since all children must be subject to the custody and control of some responsible adult, laws prohibited the manumission of slaves (even if their master consented) until they reached age twenty-one.[33] What distinguished free children—white or black—from slave children, as twelve-year-old Douglass knew, was the free child's coming of age, which arrived for boys at twenty-one and for girls at eighteen or at marriage. Yet, for mulatto children and even for white children in long-term indentures, as we have seen, age twenty-one was not a magic number signaling the end of servitude, because apprenticeships and indentures lasting past majority were commonplace.

Blacks and children both were burdened as well with the stereotype of "childlike" irrationality, deceitfulness, and helplessness.[34] These adjectives describe many individuals, of all ages and colors, but they presumptively described all blacks and all minors, regardless of their individual traits. This categorical stereotyping justified the imposition of numerous civil and legal "disabilities" that prevented both classes of persons from participating in civil life. Because of his race, young Frederick Douglass lacked "legal capacity" to testify against his assailants—regardless of his obvious capacity as an intelligent individual to observe, report, and analyze. The same rule applied to all minors. With few exceptions, minors could not bring a legal action except through a parent or legal guardian, lacked the legal "capacity" to take the oath needed to swear out a complaint or testify in court, and could not enter into contracts or dispose of property. If a child of any color or condition of servitude ran away, whether from his parent or his master, he could be chased and forcibly returned to their custody. A father whose son was whipped, or whose daughter was raped, could recover damages from the assailant, but the child could not. Rape and assault were treated as a diminution of the father's property rights rather than as violations of the child's dignity rights.

Within the private sphere of parental powers, fathers' and mothers' unequal rights attracted some criticism, but the notion of sweeping parental authority was hardly questioned. In the public sphere of the marketplace, however, children's employment provoked increasing concern as the critique of slavery sharpened. The rejection of slavery was part of a larger revulsion toward the entire concept of coerced labor, and this concern spilled over into a growing uneasiness with child labor and especially with indenture of children. Historian Marilyn Irvin Holt reports a telling incident that occurred in 1858, the same year in which the Supreme Court handed down its decision in the case of *Dred Scott*, which I discuss in chapter 4. Orphans, street children, and unemployed youths had become a growing problem in urban centers like New York City, and charities had begun experimenting with the practice of sending poor children to live and work with rural families in the prairie states, where labor was in short supply. There was nothing new about this concept, other than its interstate element, since Poor Laws had for centuries authorized the indenture of children of the poor to relieve the public of the costs of their care. But when a representative from the Five Points Mission in New York's slums arrived in Springfield, Illinois, with a train car of forty children from the poorest and most crowded tenements, and began offering them for indenture, a local Springfield newspaper editor gave the project a scathing reception.

"There are a great many good Christian families about Springfield," he wrote, "that are wealthy and do not wish their sons and daughters to do manual labor—are not partial to colored servants—are very religious: could not bear the thought of slavery." He predicted that the city children would be put to work in what amounted to chattel slavery, and "not half beloved and respected as the black man and his children." He concluded: "If some Missionary Agent had taken that many little negroes from the plantations of Louisiana to Springfield . . . our good abolitionist friends . . . would all have fainted at the horrid thought."[35] The comparison between chattel slavery and child indenture provided an opening to charge Northern abolitionists with self-serving hypocrisy and also an opening wedge to re-visualizing the historic treatment of children as property.

At this pivotal moment in American history, as slavery was abolished by the Civil War and the Thirteenth Amendment, the Fourteenth Amendment was also added to the Constitution, providing that no state should deprive any person of the "equal protection" of the law or of "life, liberty, or property" without due process of law. Some modern jurists have claimed that the Fourteenth Amendment was only about slavery and has nothing to do with family privacy or integrity. As Peggy Cooper Davis has shown in her book *Neglected Stories: The Constitution and Family Values*, one cannot interpret the meaning of these words without placing them in historical context. Discussions of family values and family governance played a central role, and family rights formed a core part of the abolitionist critique. Over and over again, enslaved African Americans and their advocates described the dehumanizing effects of a legal system that refused to acknowledge their family ties. Davis gathers these neglected stories of slavery to illustrate that the concepts of "liberty" and "equality" referred to in the Fourteenth Amendment were inextricably linked to issues of family—especially marriage, child custody, and procreation.

Antebellum images of family, however, often relied on concepts of hierarchy and innate inferiority, and were invoked by slavery's supporters as well as by its opponents, the former using them to justify slavery, and the latter to define freedom. Paternalistic images were a staple of romantic defenses of slavery in the antebellum South. Apologists depicted blacks as simple and primitive people belonging by nature under the dominion of whites. They likened plantation life to family life and blacks to children who needed guidance, structure, and protection—and against whom society needed protection as well. These images made slavery seem as natural as male domination of women, and adult domination of children, neither of which appeared wrong or immoral to the typical American, whether he lived above or below the Mason-Dixon line.

Ironically, opponents of slavery often described the enslaved man's claims to freedom and equality in terms that linked a man's liberty to his ownership of others. In claiming the status of a free man, the former slave quite naturally sought equal access to the powers and privileges that white men enjoyed—including the right to control their children. Davis persuasively shows that the denial to slaves of family rights was a recurrent theme in the attacks on slavery and that, in the post–Civil War Reconstruction era, many former slaves protested the deprivation of their rights as parents. She explains,

> [i]n the common understandings of the day, rights of contract, of property, and of the equal benefit of the law encompassed rights of marriage and family integrity, for the right to marry was understood as a right of contract; rights of family integrity were understood as male rights to possession or ownership of wives and children; and the provision of rights equal to those of white citizens was understood to guarantee former slaves the traditional and common law rights of marriage and parental custody and control.[36]

Abolitionist Theodore Weld offered a normative description of the opposite of slavery in terms that would have struck a familiar chord with Tony as well as with the young Frederick Douglass: all persons must have

> ownership of their own bodies, of the use of their own limbs and muscles, of all their time, liberty, and earnings, of the free exercise of choice, of the rights of marriage and parental authority, of legal protection of the right to be, to do, to go, to stay, to think, to feel, to work to rest, to eat, to sleep, to learn, to teach, to earn money, and to expend it, to visit, and to be visited, to speak, to be silent, to worship according to conscience, in fine, their right to be protected by just and equal laws, and to be amenable to such only.[37]

It is striking to see that Weld's litany of inalienable freedoms included the right of parental authority—to control the bodily and mental freedom of children.

Senator Jacob Howard, defending the power of Congress to enforce general citizenship rights through the Civil Rights Act in 1866, defined freedom thus: "Is a free man to be deprived of the right of having a family, a wife, children, home? What definition will you attach to the word "freeman" that does not include these ideas! . . . [i]n all common sense is he not entitled to those rights which we concede to a man who is free?"[38] Among these rights was the right to use physical violence with impunity. In a vignette that takes on a different coloration when viewed from a child's perspective, historian Eric Foner reports that "Georgia freedman James Jeter was beaten for claiming the right of whipping his own child instead of allowing his employer and former master to do so."[39] The notion of the child as property not only survived abolition but also hitched a ride on the freedom train disguised as an essential element of the liberties of "free men."

The Emancipation Proclamation did not end the servitude of children, black or white, but servitude fell especially heavily on newly emancipated children. Within a month of the end of the Civil War, with the complicity of the Reconstruction government, in Maryland alone, 2,500 African American children were apprenticed to former slave owners. All over the South, formerly enslaved children were removed wholesale from their parents, without their or their parents' consent, and bound out to white masters until age twenty-one and beyond.[40]

During the same period, however, we see a gradual shift in the way parental authority over children is conceptualized. In early child protection cases like *Mercein v. People*, parents no longer "own" their children, but are entrusted by law with their nurture. Children are not possessions acquired by procreation but rather future citizens of the Republic. In the realm of custody law, we see protection of parental ownership giving way to protection of the child's interests. This shift reflected the maturing of American democratic values about the moral conditions for one person to assert authority over another. But, to this day, notions of the child as property still infect our treatment of children.

I opened this chapter with the story of the child Fred Bailey, who later became the famous writer and orator Frederick Douglass. Slavery was the dominant injustice of Fred's status, but it was one of several interlocking injustices that prevented Fred from being free and equal. The abolition of slavery would not have provided the thirteen-year-old Fred Bailey with the right to an education, nor the fifteen-year-old Fred Bailey with the right to choose his own trade or profession, nor the seventeen-year-old Fred Bailey with the right to keep and spend his own wages. Under antebellum laws, emancipation from slavery would not have saved this child from being treated like chattel, or have prevented the child's arbitrary relocation and exploitation, the denial of his identity, the constant uncertainty that marked his early years.

Looking at Fred's story through a developmental lens, we can see the collision between his growing sense of agency and his growing awareness of his status as a slave. Both his needs and his perceptions changed as he grew from a small child into a powerful young man. We can also see how the ecology of his childhood was shaped by the specific settings and historical times in which he lived. We can identify the full range of common experiences and themes that linked him to other children in his times and remain universal themes in children's lives today. Many of Fred's experiences are quintessentially modern, not relics of some ancient history. Each of the basic human rights principles that I have articulated as core to children's rights is present in his story. The agency principle becomes less abstract as we see Fred struggling to teach himself to read and, later, bargaining for his own freedom. The equality principle could not be clearer than when we hear Fred compare his own future as a "slave for life" to that of his white playmates. The privacy principle is conspicuous in its absence from Fred's life. Denied as a child any right to legal protection of his intimate relationships, Fred had to escape in order to claim the basic privacy rights of family relationship, marriage, and procreation. Whenever Fred was beaten or starved, the protection principle was made starkly real. The dignity principle, the right to be treated as a human being and not an article of property, was what motivated Fred to resist the dehumanizing forces of slavery and, ultimately, to escape it.

His story makes very real the unjust oppression of children as children, because of their age as well as their race or gender. It illustrates how unjust laws can empower the strong to oppress rather than to protect the weak, and shows the interplay of dependency and autonomy in every child's growth to maturity. The challenges Fred faced remain alive in the stories of all the children who have been treated like possessions by adults battling over their custody, who have been unjustly deprived of parental relationships, or arbitrarily removed from homes and caregivers they loved, who have been exploited for others' gain, abused out of anger and frustration, or gone hungry when those around them had plenty.

Fred's story also illustrates children's resilience and capacity for growth. Fred's striving for autonomy—his drive to learn, to understand, to act—was nurtured in small ways, even as his rights were being systematically violated. The grandmother who gave him a secure early childhood, the mistress who first taught him to read, the master who, in spite of himself, had to give Fred some freedom or risk losing him entirely, all contributed to the story of his growth to manhood. His experiences have been shared by generations of resourceful children who have struggled to overcome obstacles to education and individual achievement, child witnesses who have felt faceless and voiceless in courts of law, and youths who have persisted in understanding their own place in life and in seeking to identify their own roots in the face of adult conspiracies of silence. Like Fred Bailey, children deserve our respect for their ability to absorb and rebound. Many other children who might have been crushed by childhood oppression have managed to draw upon their own powers of agency and action to make their bold escape and complete the dangerous passage to adulthood with their spirits intact.

Most importantly, Fred's story illustrates how we can reject slavery as evil and yet accept the subordination of children. Fred's experiences of separation, hunger, hard labor, and youthful rebellion were not unusual for his time and place. But his status as a chattel struck at the child's core sense of self. Preventing him from knowing his father, removing him at a young age from his family, denying him education, confining him to menial work were all designed to make him a slave for life. I thought of Fred when I read about an enslaved child whose mistress used to tell the children she was feeding them so they would " 'grow likely for the market.' Having staked a right to her slaves that stretched into the very fibers of their form, she would turn them out to run laps around a tree in the yard, lashing them to make them 'nimbler,' forcibly animating their bodies with the spirit she imagined buyers would desire."[41] This story embodies the crucial difference, from a child's perspective, between slavery and belonging to a nurturing parent.

As family law matured, American law increasingly characterized parents as the guardians not the owners of their children.[42] Parental rights were regrounded in a presumption that parents are motivated by love for their children, share a deep commitment to their children's future, and will act in their children's best interests. Adult authority in general—the authority of teachers, for example—is justified by its function in protecting and guiding children in their journey to adulthood. Laws that treat children as a form of property rather than persons with rights of their own, laws that deny children basic human dignity lack the central developmental justification that distinguishes the free child's journey from dependency to autonomy from Fred's oppression as a chattel and a slave for life.

CHAPTER 4

GIRLS AT THE INTERSECTION OF AGE, RACE, AND GENDER

Dred Scott's Daughters

> They were virtually free before, having achieved their freedom by their heels, what the more conscientious Dred could not secure by ten years of litigation.
>
> —St. Louis *Daily Evening News*, reporting on Dred Scott's runaway daughters, 1857

Frederick Douglass's story illustrates how history has been blinded to the implications of his status as a minor by the spotlight it has shown on his status as a slave. What about the enslaved children whose stories were even more marginalized because they were not only young and black, but also female? While we are used to thinking of history in terms of the lives of famous white men, modern scholars, seeking to explore the interlocking roles of seemingly separate aspects of identity and status, are rapidly building a more complex and nuanced history. Old studies are being reexamined to expose hidden stories that were omitted, misunderstood, or willfully distorted in earlier tellings. Often invisible to history and therefore missing from our collective memory, these shadowy supporting players can be made visible by a careful retelling of a familiar story from their unique perspective. Consider the case of Eliza and Lizzie Scott.

In the autumn of 1838, about the same time as Douglass was escaping north into Pennsylvania, Eliza Scott came into the world on a Mississippi River steamer heading south from free territory toward Missouri. Her mother, Harriet, had grown up in Pennsylvania, and had been brought to Indian Territory by her master Major Taliaferro, stationed at Fort Snelling, a rough frontier garrison with a few Dakota villages scattered around it, located at the confluence of the Mississippi and Minnesota Rivers. As uncivilized as it may have seemed to the teenaged Harriet, it had the advantage of being in free territory. Twenty years earlier, the admission of Missouri to the Union had kindled a heated debate between North and South over slavery's extension to newly acquired territories and new states. The result was the Missouri Compromise of 1820. While Missouri would enter the Union as a slave state, slavery henceforth was prohibited in all the territories and newly admitted states north of the line at 36 degrees and 30 minutes that marked Missouri's northern boundary.[1]

While at Fort Snelling, seventeen-year-old Harriet had met and married Dred Scott, a manservant of about forty whose master, Dr. Emerson, was a medical doctor. Harriet's master, Major Taliaferro, was a justice of the peace. He performed the civil ceremony and recorded it in the Fort Snelling logbooks. Shortly before their first child was due, her husband's master, who had traveled to Louisiana Territory, called Dred to rejoin him, and Harriet went with Dred. Logbooks from the journey show that Harriet gave birth to baby Eliza on the steamer *Gypsy*, while it was still north of the line between slave and free territory. Before the year was out, baby Eliza and her parents had returned to Fort Snelling. When Eliza was about two, the family left Fort Snelling for good, and moved to St. Louis, Missouri.

Sometimes the Scott family worked for Dr. Emerson and his wife, but from the time Eliza was about three or four, her parents were hired out for wages. We know very few details of Eliza's early childhood, but the economics of slavery in St. Louis made field-work unprofitable compared to services, trades, and commerce. We can assume that, as soon as she was old enough to work on her own, she would have been hired out as a day worker.[2] When Eliza was about eight, the familiar world of work and play suddenly took a strange turn. Her parents' master died and his widow inherited the family. The Scotts began to fear that the family might be split apart and sold downriver. A new baby, Lizzie, had just arrived. It must have been scary to Eliza, in all this confusion, to see the comings and goings of the white men who were her parents' lawyers. Strange new words like "cause of action" and "pleading" and "deposition" would have entered her vocabulary.

If her parents explained what was happening, they might well have said it was nothing very unusual. Freedom suits were commonplace in Missouri in the 1840s.[3] A line of cases established that, once a slave had lived in a free state or territory, he or she became a free person. All the Scotts had to prove was that they had lived in free territory with their master's consent and now were being held as slaves—falsely imprisoned and deprived of their liberty.

All of this may have seemed far away and abstract to Eliza. But one day when Eliza was about fifteen and Lizzie about seven, they were dragged kicking and screaming into the very center of their parents' struggle for freedom. Dr. Emerson had died and, as mentioned, his widow had inherited his worldly goods, including the Scott family. Now Mrs. Emerson's brother had come to town to beat some sense into his sister's errant slaves. White men they had never seen before grabbed Eliza and Lizzie and dragged them into a barn. The girls were taken before their mother and father, who had both been whipped and locked up in the barn as punishment for their insolence in daring to file a lawsuit. As the parents watched, unable to intervene or protect them, the men pulled up Eliza's skirts and whipped her on the buttocks, and then did the same to her sister.[4] The message to their father was unmistakable: you and your womenfolk have received our first lesson in obedience, and next time you can expect something far worse. But the Scotts were more outraged than intimidated. Dred Scott filed another lawsuit, this time in a federal court, charging the assailants with false imprisonment and an unlawful battery upon himself, his wife, and his children. The next time the men came looking for Eliza and her littler sister, they were nowhere to be found. It seems the two girls had taken to their heels and had no intention of coming home until the court battle was over.

Lea VanderVelde and Sandhya Subramanian, feminist historians exploring the intersections between race and gender, have opened a fascinating window into the neglected story of Harriet Robinson Scott. Although this woman's name is virtually unknown, she is instantly recognizable when identified as "Mrs. Dred Scott." These historians skillfully uncover, hidden between the lines of the famous case of *Dred Scott v. Sandford*, the story of a woman's struggle to control her own life and the lives of her two daughters.[5] Harriet's case, they argue, was even stronger than Dred's for showing that the Scott family members had been emancipated by operation of law. Had Harriet remained in Pennsylvania, the state of her birth, she would have been manumitted by law at age twenty-seven. Harriet's master had been the commanding officer at a garrison in free territory when he performed her marriage ceremony. Since slaves were prohibited from marrying, the officer's act in performing and making a written record of her civil marriage ceremony was tantamount to freeing her, in which case her children were also free.

Nevertheless, the lawyers representing the Scotts in their federal case decided Harriet's claim need not be argued separately. So her claim was dropped. In historical context the lawyers' decision is not at all surprising. The prevailing doctrine applying to "free" married women—the law of *couverture*—placed married women's property and persons under the power of the husband. To cast the Scotts' claim in terms of Harriet's legal rights, rather than Dred's, would have required a re-visioning not only of race but also of gender. Such a shift in consciousness would have been a major feat even for Harriet's abolitionist attorneys, not to mention the

Supreme Court justices of 1857, six of whom were slaveholders and none of whom was female. Many abolitionist sympathizers who thought Harriet Scott was entitled to be treated as a citizen would have balked at the notion that their own wives, let alone a black female like Harriet, should be entitled to vote, bring a legal action on her own, sit on a jury, or hold property in her own right. Even many ardent abolitionists defended hierarchy within the sphere of the family as not only natural and normal, but divinely ordained. Thus, Harriet's subordinate status as a person of African descent was compounded and complicated by her status as a woman.

The strategic decisions of Dred Scott's attorneys provide a striking example of the complex interactions of racism and patriarchy. The laws that applied to Harriet as a slave reduced her to property but recognized her productivity—both as a worker and as a child bearer. Albeit for all the wrong reasons, the antebellum legal system attributed to Harriet the slave a high economic value and provided that her children would inherit their status, as free or slave, from their mother. Ironically, Harriet's claims to freedom were made invisible because her lawyers treated her as Dred Scott's wife—defining her not as a free woman, but as the consort of a man claiming his freedom. Viewed by the laws of slavery as chattel, she belonged to her owner, and so did her children. Viewed by the laws of free men as a woman, she belonged to her husband, and so did her children. Because her attorneys saw her in the culturally and legally ascribed role of dependent, which described the norm for all "free" women, they assumed Harriet's case depended on Dred's, and that the key to her freedom lay in proving that Dred was a free man. In fact, the key to Dred Scott's case lay in Harriet's story. If Harriet was free, her children were free. Moreover, if Harriet was free, then Dred himself must be free, since no man could be both a slave and a "free" woman's husband.[6]

Hidden between the lines of Mrs. Dred Scott's story is the unexplored story of Eliza and Lizzie. This is not newly discovered evidence, but information that was known all along. The archival records and the Supreme Court and lower court documents include many references to the girls, and newspapers of the time printed a drawing of the two girls, arm in arm in their Sunday dresses. They were even the topic of a presidential debate.[7] But when I presented a talk on this case at a 1999 conference at the University of Buffalo on Urban Girls, I was mobbed by young black girls at the end of the session. "I didn't know that Dred Scott had daughters," they exclaimed. "Why didn't we know that? Why didn't they tell us that in school?"

The same intersection of race and gender that made Harriet Scott invisible to history, obscured the crucial role played by her daughters. Just as Mrs. Dred Scott was deemed to be "one" with her husband, the Scott girls' rights were subsumed in those of their father. This concentration of power over both women and children in the head of household is illustrated by the theory behind the claim that Dred Scott's lawyers used to gain access to the federal courts. Federal courts were open to citizens of two different states to provide a neutral forum for deciding their cases. Dred Scott, in his bid to be recognized as a "citizen" of Missouri, for purposes of federal diversity jurisdiction, filed a claim stating that a citizen of New York had assaulted himself, his wife, and his two children, and "for that collective indignity Dred Scott does ask nine thousand dollars in damages." The claim grew out of the whipping incident described earlier. Dred Scott's claim was as the patriarch for damages to his family members. The jury, however, accepted the defense of Sanford, one of the men doing the whipping—that the blows had been inflicted in the course of "instruction" in obedience, a perfectly legal act when performed by a master or master's surrogate on a slave. No slave or indeed black person of any age, man, woman, or child, was safe from such beneficial "instruction."

The historians who have refocused the spotlight on Mrs. Dred Scott treat her two daughters primarily as beneficiaries of and motivations for her strategy to keep the family together. But because of their status as children, they are deprived of agency even in the skillful retelling of Mrs. Dred Scott's story. Yet what little is known about them suggests that they were key players in the famous case. Helen Catterall, the early twentieth-century scholar of slave law, believed we had Eliza to thank for forcing the Supreme Court to rule on the constitutionality of the Missouri Compromise. If the Missouri Compromise was constitutional, Catterall writes, "Eliza, though born of a slave mother, was free. Consequently the constitutionality of the Missouri Compromise act had to be decided in order to reach a determination of her case."[8] The Supreme Court was forced to reach deep into the heart of the controversy and hold that Americans of African descent, whether free or enslaved, were simply not citizens.

Looking at Eliza and Lizzie's experience through a developmental lens, we can see how their world was affected by the confluence of history and their own stages of development. Contemporary sources establish that Eliza was born in autumn of 1838, north of the Missouri state line.[9] Although the records of the second daughter's age are more confused, it seems most likely that Lizzie was about eight years younger than her sister.[10] Using these dates as a template, we can imagine eight-year-old Eliza's feelings when Dred Scott and Harriet Robinson Scott filed their first state court case in 1846, just as a new baby arrived in the household. Eliza was about sixteen at the time of the federal case filing in 1853, and Lizzie would have been about eight. Eliza was a young woman of nineteen when the Supreme Court handed down its opinion deciding the case in 1857, and Lizzie would have been about eleven. Undoubtedly, this case must have dominated their childhoods, framing their understanding of their own status and prospects in life much as Master Hugh's diatribe on the evils of teaching slaves to read had framed the issue of "slavery for life" for eight-year-old Fred Bailey. To imagine the impact of this case on Eliza and Lizzie, one must try to imagine being young, black, and female in St. Louis, Missouri, not today—a time when childhood for black girls in St. Louis is tough enough—but between 1846 and 1857. Simply because they were female, their experience of St. Louis was hardly likely to have been the liberating experience Frederick Douglass found in Baltimore. As females, their life prospects were far different from Fred's. A boy (even a slave) might be apprenticed to learn a trade. A girl was destined to do laundry and cleaning and cooking, then as now menial tasks. Physical abuse was a constant for girls as well as boys. When Fred was fifteen, he was sent to a plantation to be taught his place with the lash. Eliza was fifteen when Sanford seized her father and mother and whipped them. The coup de grâce, however, was Sanford's "spanking" of Dred's daughters, a "collective indignity" designed to show their father his subservient place. The spanking of seven-year-old Lizzie might be thought appropriate, but the disrobing and spanking of a fifteen-year-old girl would be an especially offensive assault.[11]

This incident illustrates an especially cruel aspect of patriarchy, especially when compounded by racial or ethnic hatred—the notion that a man can be humiliated by abusing his human possessions, his wife and children, especially his "innocent" daughters. In slavery, as in war, girls such as Eliza could expect to be used as object lessons for males, and their subservience enforced not only by physical assault but also by sexual assault. Had Eliza been sold downriver, her sexuality would have been included in her economic value, which treated every form of the female slave's labor, including childbirth, as an asset of the master. Subject to being abused by white men, and "bred" to black men not of their own choosing, unable to nurse or keep the babies to whom they had given birth, and conscripted to nurse and tend the master's legitimate offspring, females in slavery experienced a different and even more profound form of sexual oppression than males.[12]

Historians have questioned why the Scotts did not flee north when they were in free territory, or conversely, why they did not bring their suit earlier. Again, the girls may have played a pivotal role. Flight was an especially risky option for a family. Traveling in a band including women and children often ended in tragedy.[13] The timing of the suit may also have been influenced by fear of family separation. Dr. Emerson's widow would likely want to sell her human chattels, as she had sold other portions of her husband's estate. Slave sales of girls peaked between thirteen and twenty. Sold at auction, a healthy adolescent girl would command over three hundred dollars.[14] An estate sale raised dramatically the likelihood that the Scott family members would be separated and sold to different owners. Even worse than being sold to different Missouri owners was the specter of being sold to a trader traveling to the cotton and sugar plantations of Mississippi and Louisiana, where conditions were far worse. From a mother's perspective, there was much to fear.

How much of this context did Eliza and Lizzie understand, and how did it shape their childhood and girlhood? They had lived a relatively secure life in St. Louis, but surely, especially as they grew older and more skilled in reading between the lines of adults' conversations, they began to understand the ominous uncertainty of their futures.[15] Where Fred Bailey saw ships sailing north up the coast toward New England, Eliza saw Mississippi side-wheelers carrying slave traders' coffles downriver into the Deep South. Gender made a large difference in the prospects for and paths to freedom. Fred Bailey, being a male, was able to negotiate a de facto emancipation from his master. He became an independent young man living on his own, by agreeing to support himself and pay a bounty to Hugh Auld as the price of his own freedom. "Free" white boys apparently made similar bargains with their fathers. One boy of seventeen was allowed to leave farming for school mastering, but only if he hired a substitute out of his wages to take his place on his father's farm until he turned twenty-one.[16] For girls, such de facto emancipation was seldom an option, given the pervasive restrictions on female autonomy.

For girls like Eliza and Lizzie, the distance to freedom in East St. Louis, Illinois, visible just across the Mississippi, must have seemed tantalizingly close yet unbridgeable. But the cases on fugitive slaves show that riverboats were a prime means of escape for boys. A slave boy named Louis, worth nine hundred dollars, was hired out by his owners to work on a riverboat as a fireman. He escaped when the boat docked at Cincinnati, Ohio. The owner sued the steamboat captain but lost. The court remarked, "it is not the custom for boats hiring slaves on board to iron them or confine them when entering a free port. . . . where a slave is hired as a boat hand, we must presume the owner is fully aware, that every facility for escape is afforded by the very nature of the service."[17] While the economic value of boys was exploited by giving them greater liberty, that of girls was exploited by keeping them close to home as house workers and breeders. Many reported cases show how girls were promised freedom, but only after they had passed their childbearing years or produced a certain number of offspring. Catherine Bodine's will set her slave Jenny free "whenever she should cease child-bearing," and Kitty's master Mr. Winston promised her freedom in twelve years, but meanwhile sold her for $150 to a Mr. Chambers, "to have and to hold said girl Kitty for the term aforesaid, and her increase during said term absolutely and forever."[18]

In narratives of slavery, the notion that a girl needs a male protector forms a recurrent theme, sometimes appearing as a restraint on her ability to flee and sometimes as a threat to coerce her into sexual compliance. In a telling passage of *Incidents in the Life of a Slave Girl*, Harriet Jacobs describes a period in her adolescence when she was tormented by the unwanted sexual attentions of her master.[19] She recalls planning with her younger brother William how they would someday escape north. One major impediment was the opposition of her grandmother, a woman who, like Fred's grandmother, had a home of her own—and nursed the hope of earning enough money through baking cakes to buy her grandchildren. Here is how Harriet describes the tension between her own youthful passion for freedom and her grandmother's mature fears. "As for Grandmother, she was strongly opposed to her children undertaking any such project. . . . To me, nothing seemed more dreadful than my present life. I said to myself, 'William must be free. He shall go to the north, and I will follow him.' Many a slave sister has formed the same plans."[20] The modern reader is struck by the contrast between the girl's spirited resolve and her assumption that the road to freedom was for men to travel. She could not think of her own escape until a fourteen-year-old boy, two years her junior, had gone ahead.

While some narratives of girls in slavery reflect vulnerability and dependency, the narratives of figures like Sojourner Truth and Harriet Tubman run counter to such "feminine" images. These females were often depicted, even by their friends within the abolition movement, as oddities—noble savages or exotic Amazons. By their enemies, they were depicted as de-sexed Aunt Jemimas or oversexed Jezebels.[21] All girls, but especially girls of color, were disabled by the myths that defined the sexes in dichotomous stereotypes: strong or helpless, powerful or fragile, chaste or promiscuous. As female children and adolescent girls, Eliza and Lizzie were situated at a very complex time and place, made extraordinarily dangerous by the confluence of their race, gender, and status as minors.

What were their beliefs and behaviors, confronted with the facts of slavery and emancipation? How did they act to "make their own world?" There are hints in the meager historical record that Eliza and Lizzie may have shown more independence and power than conventional images of girlhood would have allowed them. Contemporary reports noted that the girls had "run away" while the case was pending.[22] We do not know for certain whether they planned their escape with or without the blessing of their parents. Young people, to the dismay of parents, do not always place family unity ahead of personal freedom. The narratives of slavery show that children began to understand that they were slaves around the age of six or seven, that slavery was a topic of intense discussion with other children during preadolescent years, and by early adolescence, many were already plotting their escapes.[23] Many a slave, male and female, ran away while still legally a child, leaving a father, mother, or grandmother behind who could not or would not leave.[24] We have learned to recognize Harriet Scott as an individual with agency and must do the same for her teenaged daughters.

The Scott girls did not return to their parents' home until they were no longer slaves. The Supreme Court announced the *Dred Scott* decision in March of 1857, holding that persons of color were not citizens under the Constitution. Neither changes in popular sentiment nor Congress itself could alter the fact that the Constitution originally envisioned blacks as by nature subordinate to whites and had protected their owners' property rights in the document. Among those who protested this reading was Frederick Douglass, now the editor of an abolitionist publication called *The Frederick*

Douglass Papers. He pointed to clear evidence in the same constitutional texts, including limitations on the perpetuation of the slave trade, that the framers believed slavery was contrary to fundamental human rights principles on which the new Republic had been founded. Looking at the document as a whole, and in its parts, he showed how slavery violated its basic premises.

> Take, for example, the prohibition of a bill of attainder. That is a law entailing on the child the misfortunes of the parent. This principle would destroy slavery in every State of the Union. The law of slavery is a law of attainder. The child is property because its parent was property, and suffers as a slave because its parent suffered as a slave. Thus the very essence of the whole slave code is in open violation of a fundamental provision of the Constitution, and is in open and flagrant violation of all the objects set forth in the Constitution.[25]

Abraham Lincoln, debating a different Mr. Douglas on the subject of the *Dred Scott* decision, spoke with particular frankness about Dred Scott's daughters and the hypocrisy of those who argued that abolition would lead to mixing of the white and black races.

> Dred Scott, his wife and two daughters were all involved in the suit. . . . Could we have had our way, the chances of these black girls, ever mixing their blood with that of white people, would have been diminished at least to the extent that it could not have been without their consent. But Judge Douglas is delighted to have them decided to be slaves, and not human enough to have a hearing, even if they were free, and thus left subject to the forced concubinage of their masters, and liable to become the mothers of mulattoes in spite of themselves—the very state of case that produces nine tenths of all the mulattoes—all the mixing of blood in the nation.[26]

In May of 1857, two months after the Supreme Court decision was announced, in a move that surprised many observers, a new owner manumitted Dred Scott and his family. Newspapers covering this development reported that Dred's daughters "were, virtually, free before, having achieved their freedom by their heels what the more conscientious Dred could not secure by ten years of litigation. Their whereabouts have been kept a secret." The reporter speculated, perhaps reflecting stereotypes about paternal omnipotence, "Their father knew where they were, and could bring them back at any moment. He will doubtless recall them now."[27] Indeed, the girls had returned to their parents' home by late June, when reporters from *Frank Leslie's Illustrated Newspaper*, the most popular periodical of its day, featured portraits of Dred and Harriet and of Eliza and Lizzie, in their prettiest dresses, hand in hand (Fig. 2).[28] The girls look calm and poised. The family's reunification lasted for less than a year. Dred Scott died in 1858, followed by Eliza in 1863 and Harriet in 1870. Their deaths were most likely caused by tuberculosis, the great equalizer that had also claimed their master, Dr. Emerson. Lizzie married, had a family, and lived until 1884.[29] Unlike Frederick Douglass, neither of the Scott sisters left us a published narrative of her childhood. We do know, however, from the narratives of girls like Harriet Jacobs that slavery held uniquely different terrors for girls than for boys, and we know that their gender circumscribed their avenues of escape. As Henry Louis Gates Jr. says of *Incidents in the Life of a Slave Girl*, "Jacobs . . . charts vivid detail by vivid detail precisely how the shape of her life and the choices she makes are defined by her reduction as a sexual object, an object to be raped, bred, or abused."[30] We also know that many slave girls, in spite of or because of this specter, did "take to their heels" at great peril to themselves and against the wishes of parents who feared losing their child to the unknown more than they feared the known evils of slavery.

The stories of these girls illustrate the mutually reinforcing qualities of race, sex, and minority. These qualities generate cultural stereotypes, which in turn generate laws based on these disabling stereotypes. We can see these elements combine and recombine in complex formulas that unjustly empower or disempower classes of persons, without regard to individual qualities and merits. Such stereotypes seem to have a symbiotic relationship, each feeding on

Fig. 2. Lizzie and Eliza Scott with Dred and Harriet Scott (courtesy of the Library of Congress).

and nourishing the others. As scholar Dorothy Roberts has observed, "Racism makes the experience of sexism different for Black women and white women. But it is not enough to note that Black women suffer from both racism and sexism, although this is true. Racism is patriarchal. Patriarchy is racist. We will not destroy one institution without destroying the other."[31] The same can be said of the interlocking disabilities experienced by girls like Eliza. The cultural and legal images of women, children, and people of color as naturally subordinate beings lacking in rational capacity were rooted in the same fertile soil of inequality. Discrimination against children seemed to thrive in symbiotic relationship with discrimination against blacks, the poor, and females. A challenge to injustice toward any of these groups tends to expose the interconnections among them.

The insecurity and perils of female lives in slavery provide a motivating plot that shaped the story of the *Dred Scott* case. Like Frederick Douglass, Eliza and Lizzie's lives were marked by slavery. But they were more fortunate than Fred in one respect. They were raised by their own father and mother. The greatest indignity Fred suffered was being deprived of both the status and the reality of growing up as the child of his own parents. For Eliza and Lizzie, the indignity of their status as slaves was buffered by the dignity of their status as precious and irreplaceable children. The dominion that Dred and Harriet exercised over their daughters may have resembled bondage or property rights in its form, but it was qualitatively different. In a democracy, a parent's goal is not to produce good slaves—to make them "nimble" or "grow them likely for the market"—but to raise a new generation of human beings and citizens.[32] Setting of boundaries, imposition of adult authority, are essential developmentally to a child's safe passage to adulthood. These forms of authority meet children's needs-based rights.

Historians like Steven Mintz and Peggy Cooper Davis have pointed to the loss of family as among the most severe hardships inflicted on enslaved children. Separation from family was almost a universal experience. Children showed their agency by bonding with fictive kin whom they called Auntie or Sister or Brother. But these adults were unable to provide nurture when slaveholders strictly controlled food and time. Poor children of all colors suffered from hunger and went without clothing or care. Enslaved children, in contrast to free poor children, died of neglect and malnutrition in households and plantations where white brothers and sisters were well fed and thriving. In the same households where white children ate decent meals from bowls with forks and spoons, enslaved children were fed at communal troughs using oyster shells to scoop up meager rations of cornmeal mush. In a reversal of the natural order, where hungry young receive priority, enslaved children were starved throughout childhood but found their rations doubled when they were old enough to work.[33]

These are stark examples of child abuse, drawn from our most shameful historical heritage, that would now be criminalized as child abuse. The abuses were made possible by a system that treated humans as property. But the lines between adult authority as a form of abusive bondage and adult authority as a bridge to freedom are not always easy to draw. Parents who abuse their authority by inflicting gratuitous harm cross that line. In such situations, the privacy right of children and parents gives way to values of protection. In addition, as children develop and mature, the privacy principle gradually takes on a different meaning. Children's developmental tasks shift to understanding who they are, separate and distinct from those who nurtured them. As they approach adulthood, they gain the capacity to make important decisions and to forge independent relationships—even becoming parents in their own right. While personal privacy may mean little to an infant, it looms large to a teenager. As children near adulthood and adult responsibilities, privacy takes on a more individualistic cast as an aspect of defining one's own identity. In this stage of a child's life, good parenting involves allowing a child to test his capacities but knowing how much freedom he can handle. Americans place a high value on privacy, defined as the right to be left alone in a zone where government does not intrude. In most cases and contexts involving children, that circle of privacy is drawn around the family as an interdependent unit. In rare cases, for example, a mature minor's choice to bear or not bear a child, it is drawn around the minor as an autonomous unit. Both concepts honor aspects of privacy that are developmentally important to children and both must acknowledge children's agency. Young children separated from biological parents, in adoption for example, will naturally bond with loving caregivers, creating new families of their own. As we see in the stories of enslaved boys and girls, young people who feel or fear being unjustly confined, exploited, and robbed of agency will "take to their heels"—in a word play based in democratic ideals, we call this "voting with your feet." In Fred's case, he ran away from slavery so he could have a home and family of his own. In Eliza and Lizzie's case, they ran away from home because of laws that threatened to separate them from their family.

In browsing amazon.com recently, I came upon a children's book that filled me with delight. Authored by Gwyneth Swain, it is titled *Dred and Harriet Scott: A Family's Struggle for Freedom*. Published in 2004, it is aimed at readers as young as age nine. Although it is extremely well researched and replete with detailed bibliographical materials, it is classified as "juvenile literature" and thus unlikely to come to the "serious" scholar's attention. Swain interweaves the children's story with that of their parents. Rather than peripheral characters, the girls are central to her plot. In framing her narrative, Swain does not describe it as a story about a man or a woman, but as a story about children.

> Historians say the Court's decision was all about states' rights, citizenship rights, and a host of other big and important ideas. But to Dred Scott and Harriet Robinson Scott, it was simple. It was about children. It was about how precious their daughters were to them. It was about a dream Dred and Harriet had. They dreamed that their children—the daughters of slaves—would be free.[34]

Swain's research adds a poignant epilogue to my own—apparently Lizzie did tell, if not write, about her experiences. As a grown woman, she shared memories of being hidden away and feeling forgotten while the *Dred Scott* case swirled around her. She also remembered the harshness, uncertainty, and fear of slavery, and the goodness of being free. I am glad that future generations of girls, especially black girls like those who attended the Urban Girls Conference, will know the names of Eliza and Lizzie and appreciate the role they played in shaping American history.

CHAPTER 5

GROWING UP IN STATE CUSTODY

"Tony" and "John G."

If you are going to take children in, treat them as your own, not just a castaway. Don't make them feel like you were the only one that would give them the time of day and whatever you give them is sufficient, even if you treat them like trash.

  —Advice of teenager in foster care[1]

As a society, we were, by force of law, the parents of these young people while they were in foster care. We need to see the job through. We would do no less for our own children.

  —Gary Stangler, director of the Jim Casey Youth Opportunities Initiative[2]

In chapter 3, we saw that emancipation did not free black children. Thousands of children who had been enslaved were taken from their parents by the state and placed in involuntary apprenticeships or indentures. In those days, an era when most children worked, these children were put out to work as servants and field hands, often with their original masters, and effectively reenslaved. I thought of these children when I learned of three young children in a rural county who had been forced to work in the tobacco fields by their foster family. This enslavement occurred in 2006 and involved children who had been removed from their family by Florida's Department of Children and Families. While it is no longer legal to put neglected or abused children to work to earn their keep, the fact remains that over half a million American children are growing up in foster care, as wards of the state. Children of the poor and children of color are at far greater risk of growing up in state custody, deprived of many of the freedoms enjoyed by other children including the basic privacy right of being raised by families of their own. Separated from their families of origin, these children are too often treated as burdens or objects rather than valued as young human beings.

Modern children growing up in state custody suffer double disabilities, from their status as minors and their status as objects of state control. As minors, they have diminished expectations of privacy and are presumed to be in need of adult control. There are many wonderful foster parents who provide the kind of parenting that we would wish for our own children, often paying out of their own pockets to meet their foster children's needs. But, as wards of the state, foster children have no assurance that their daily needs for nurture, structure, and love will be met at all, much less with the deep-seated commitment and spirit of love and sacrifice most children can expect from their parents. When child protection and juvenile justice systems are working as they should—to prevent abuse, to heal children who have been hurt, and to prepare them for adulthood—children's dignity and privacy rights are preserved. Too often, however, the key ingredient that provides a moral justification for children's subordination to adults is missing. We trust parents to make decisions grounded in their love and concern for their children. We cannot make the same presumptions about the state in its relationship to children. When the state steps in as *parens patriae*, children are deprived of the care of parents and must deal instead with an often neglectful and sometimes abusive system. Laws and policies may entitle them to medical care, education, and protection of their persons and property, but who will fight to secure these benefits if the state fails in its responsibilities?[3] Children in state custody, even more than incarcerated or institutionalized adults, need a powerful voice, not only to hold the state to a standard of care to serve their needs but also to get our attention when the state fails to treat them as valuable young human beings.

Who are the guardians of these children? In a democracy, the state is not some alien "other"—it is "us." These children are literally "our" children. You and I, as American citizens, have taken them under our collective care. Do we treat them as we would our own children, or are they treated as second-class citizens? Does invidious racial discrimination still burden these children, as it did during slavery? Northwestern University professor Dorothy Roberts has argued that the current systems for protecting children from abuse are destroying minority families and communities much as they did in the aftermath of the Civil War. While her claim seems stark, history and the modern data support her concerns.

Consider the story of thirteen-year-old Tony, whom I introduced in my Introduction. Tony was an African American child growing up in foster care. After nine years in the same foster home, he was suddenly told the state would terminate his relationship with his mother so strangers could adopt him. No one wanted to hear his objections. Tony's question, "Ain't I a person?" speaks eloquently to the sense of powerlessness and lack of dignity he felt as a child in state custody.

The removal of children from their families strikes a painful chord in African American history. It strikes a painful chord as well for unmarried mothers who, despite laws to the contrary, still lose their children because they cannot afford to feed and house them or because they are victims of domestic violence. Poverty, race, and gender of their parents often determine whether children will live at home or become wards of the state.[4] While children of color make up only 42 percent of our child population, they make up 58 percent of the children in out-of-home care. African American children are four times more likely to enter out-of-home care than white children, and once in care, they stay significantly longer before exiting. Poor children and children of color face a greater risk of growing up in state care because they are more likely to be reported abused or neglected. This is not simply because the incidence of abuse is higher among poor families and families of color. As Jane Waldfogel shows, by defining neglect broadly to reach situations where neglect is due to parents' poverty, and by making access to government resources contingent on a finding of neglect, America has converted the child protection system into a service delivery system. Ironically, it is failing miserably in that role, since only a fraction of the reported cases result in services.[5] Other factors besides poverty, including lack of community and private resources, greater opportunities for state intrusion, the stresses of life at the edge, and unconscious bias by decision-makers, combine to make poor children and especially poor children of color overrepresented in the child welfare system. And race itself plays a role we are only beginning to understand, affecting informal decisions about which cases to prosecute and which to refer for voluntary services.[6]

Historically, Americans have paid little attention to the foster care system until some horror story hits the headlines. Responding to individual tales of child abuse or neglect, we indulge in both over- and underintervention, and lose sight of the larger picture of children's welfare *while* in care. It is becoming increasingly inexcusable for the public, as guardians of these half million children, to evade responsibility for monitoring their welfare. The Internet provides us with much of the information we need to judge the effectiveness of our child welfare systems. The Child Welfare League of America has created a database that allows visitors to obtain customized reports on the demographics of child abuse. You can find out how your state is doing across many different measures by visiting this site.[7] Here is a thumbnail sketch of the national picture. Nationally, more females are reported victimized than males (405,056 girls to 378,037 boys in 2003) and children of color are disproportionately likely to be reported abused or neglected (about 419,375, or twelve per thousand, white children in 2003 compared to 219,000, or twenty per thousand, African American and Hispanic children). African American children, Pacific Islander children, and American Indian or Alaska Native children had the highest rates of victimization at 19.9, 17.6, and 15.5 per thousand children of the same race or ethnicity, respectively. While about 148,877 of these reports involved physical abuse, a stunning 78,188 were reports of sexual abuse. Girls of all ages are more likely to be sexually abused than boys, and high school girls are twice as likely as boys to report being sexually assaulted (11.9 percent of girls and 6.1 percent of boys). African American girls are almost twice as likely as white girls to be sexually assaulted. As of 2004, the Centers for Disease Control stated that 12.3 percent of black students, 10.4 percent of Hispanic students, and 7.3 percent of white students reported that they had been forced to have sexual intercourse.[8]

For some of these children, foster care is a necessity. They are truly at risk of serious harm if left in their own homes.[9] While the risks to maltreated children may diminish after placement, they do not end. In recent years, approximately six out of a thousand children are maltreated each year while in foster care, while victimization rates in the general population averaged about twelve children per thousand.[10] While removal is sometimes necessary to save the life of a child, being separated from their families of origin has profound effects on their future development as well as on their communities. In some inner city neighborhoods and Native American communities, 10 percent of the children are in foster care.[11] For families in some African American inner city neighborhoods, the fear of losing one's children to "the system" is as ever-present and ominous as the fear felt by parents in slavery times.

And some children do actually get lost in the system. Four-year-old Rilya Wilson made national headlines in 2002 when Florida's Department of Children and Families discovered that she was missing from foster care and had been missing for sixteen months. Rilya was never found, and suspicions remain that her foster parents killed her. But her story brought national attention to the problem of children missing from foster care, especially Florida's more than five hundred missing children. Florida authorities were further embarrassed when reporters from the *Orlando Sun Sentinel* were able to find children the department had been missing for years.[12] Within a few months of this news story breaking, Florida had found most of the children then missing from care. But this improvement was short-lived. As of June 2006, the number of missing children in Florida had risen again to more than 640.[13]

Sadly, Florida is doing better than the average state. Nationwide, at any given time more than 2 percent of children are missing from care. Imagine the outrage parents would feel if a program serving their child—a summer camp or school—accepted that two out of a hundred children entrusted to its care would disappear without a trace. The largest group of missing children is children who run away. Children in the child welfare system are twice as likely to run away as children of the same age in the general population. In 2001, some 2 percent of the 542,000 children in foster care—almost 11,000 children—were runaways, part of a larger group estimated at 1.3 million runaway children nationally. Almost 75 percent of runaways nationwide are female. Runaway children face many dangers. They are disconnected from school and community, face high risks of contracting sexually transmitted diseases (STDs) and HIV, of becoming drug involved, and of engaging in survival sex or stealing in order to meet their own most basic needs.[14]

Children who do not disappear or run away are often not provided with things most parents would consider absolute basics. Recall from chapter 1 my description of Brazelton and Greenspan's teachings on the irreducible needs of children? These doctors identified six basic needs: the need for ongoing nurturing relationships; the need for physical protection, safety, and regulation; the need for experiences tailored to individual differences; the need for developmentally appropriate experinces; the need for limit setting, structure, and expectations; and the need for stable, supportive communities and cultural continuity.[15] Deficits in any of these areas are risk factors for future problems, and research on risk factors shows that the more risk factors the more likely a child will develop learning disabilities, behavioral problems, and/or mental illness.

We know that children entering foster care are already at greater risk than the average child. Over 39,000 children, one in five of the children entering foster care each year, is an infant. Low birth weight and/or prematurity affect 40 percent of these babies, and exposure to alcohol or drugs affects up to 80 percent. Fifty percent of children entering foster care have serious physical health problems such as chronic disease, lead poisoning, and asthma. Children entering foster care are four to five times as likely to suffer developmental delays as the average child. Given the situations that brought them into foster care, they are at far greater risk for mental health problems such as attachment disorders. One might assume that, once in state care, they would be sure at least to receive adequate health care, education, and supervision. Most Americans would be surprised to learn that 12 percent of children in foster care have no routine health care, 34 percent have not been immunized, 32 percent have at least one unmet health care need, over 50 percent have untreated dental decay, and only 10 percent, or a quarter of those in need, are receiving treatment for developmental delays. Less than one-third of foster children received mental health services, despite their high level of need, and most of these were older children.[16] Many working-class American parents do not qualify for Medicaid and have no money left for health insurance after they feed, clothe, and house their children. But while all foster children are Medicaid eligible, only 83 percent are enrolled. A recent Department of Health and Human Services audit showed that agencies failed to provide adequate health services in over 30 percent of the cases reviewed.[17] Meeting foster children's emotional needs for nurture and stability is also a special challenge. Multiple disruptions of primary attachments, as occur when children are placed in a series of different foster care settings, can lead to serious mental health problems.[18] One bright spot in foster care reform, as Tony's story illustrates, is the increased emphasis on securing safe and permanent families for children through adoptive placements. But even this positive trend has had negative consequences for families for whom it was not the best answer.[19]

Children who are neither adopted nor reunified with their families face special challenges as they turn eighteen and graduate from foster care. We heard from Tony about his ambitions to earn a college degree and how he wanted to save his money to pay for college. Had he remained in foster care instead of being adopted by Ms. Barnette, he would have faced an uphill battle. A case from the files of North Carolina Legal Services lawyer Lewis Pitts illustrates how an unresponsive system can crush a boy's hopes for independence. John G., who is fifteen-years-old and in foster care, inherited a small house built by Habitat for Humanity when his father passed away and, like Tony, was eligible for Social Security survivors' benefits. The home has been threatened with foreclosure because the North Carolina Department of Social Services officials took 100 percent of John's $538 Social Security payment each month to reimburse the state for the costs of his care. The mortgage on the Habitat for Humanity home is only $221 per month. As John G. told a reporter from the *Charlotte Observer*, the house represents one good thing he has left from a troubled childhood; he wants to live in it after he turns eighteen. "That'd be something I wouldn't have to worry about right then," he said.[20]

John G. will have more than housing to worry about when he graduates from foster care. Every year, approximately 20,000 children "age out" of foster care. The quality of life that young adults discharged from the foster care system experience is grim. Across all sectors of society, we are increasingly seeing young adults living with their parents for longer and longer periods of time. The economic demands of our modern age have led to a rise in young adults staying longer or moving back into the protective nest of their families. But foster children do not have these options. American families spend a median of $44,500 on their children after they reach the age of eighteen, in comparison to about $2,000 available to foster children after age eighteen. The average youth does not achieve self-sufficiency until age twenty-six.[21] The only population that is required to make the transition without a support net in place is youth aging out of the foster care system. These young adults, already with substantial disadvantages, are released from the system to no one but themselves.

A report from researchers at the Chapin Hall Center for Children at the University of Chicago released in 2005 looks at the outcomes of youth aging out of the foster care system.[22] For the approximately 20,000 young adults who age out of the foster care system each year, self-sufficiency and the transition into adulthood are a difficult challenge. These young adults no longer have the support of the state. While many may have longed for this day, it is an overwhelming change from the previous years in which the state was a constant authoritative presence. No longer is the state involved, nor are the foster families or group homes where the young adults lived available for continuing support or guidance Additionally, the study compared their sample of young adults to a nationally representative group of nineteen-year-olds who were part of the National Longitudinal Study of Adolescent Health.[23] The broad implications of the study are clear: young adults discharged from the foster care system are not faring as well as their same-age peers. Within the sample of youths from foster care, the youths who were allowed to remain in care were 50 percent more likely to be employed or in school.[24]

Over one-third of the young adults in the Chapin Hall study had not received their high school diploma, or their General Equivalency Degree (GED).[25] A GED is frequently the only route for young adults in the foster care system to finish their secondary educations because of excessive absences, frequent moving, disrupted school settings, learning disabilities, lack of educational support, and substance abuse. While more than a third of the Chapin Hall study sample had not graduated or received a GED, an amazing 90 percent of their same-aged peers in the control sample of average kids had obtained a high school diploma or GED.[26] Not surprisingly, nineteen-year-olds from the control sample were significantly more likely to be enrolled in an educational program than the kids who had grown up in out-of-home care. While 62 percent of the kids in the national sample were enrolled in a four-year college, only 18 percent of the young adults in the Chapin Hall study were enrolled in a four-year college. Without a high school diploma or GED, these young adults can expect an economic struggle that culminates in poverty and homelessness. Less than half of the young adults no longer in care were employed. A quarter of the young adults did not have enough to eat, and one in seven of those young adults had been homeless at least once. According to the Child Welfare League of America, of the adolescents that age out of foster care each year, 25 percent become homeless, 56 percent are unemployed, and 27 percent of the male children end up in jail.

Because of concerns about the plight of these children, Congress passed the Foster Care Independence Act (FCIA) of 1999, requiring states to provide youth in foster care with help to prepare them for employment, postsecondary education, and successful management of adult responsibilities.[27] But the quality of programs provided under the FCIA often falls short of the mark, and because of lack of funding many eligible children receive no services.[28]

Only 46 percent of the young adults in the Chapin Hall study had a savings or checking account, compared to nearly 82 percent of their peers in the sample from the general population. The nineteen-year-olds in the Midwest study were twice as likely as nineteen-year-olds in the sample to report not having enough money to pay their rent, twice as likely to report being unable to pay a utility bill, 1.5 times as likely to report having their phone service disconnected, and four times as likely to report being evicted. Children exiting foster care were three times more likely to be "disconnected," defined as out of school and out of work, and 25 percent reported "food insecurity," defined as "sometimes or often not having enough to eat."[29]

Ironically, many kids aging out of foster care go back to their families of origin. Most of the former foster youths in the Chapin Hall study maintained relationships with members of their family of origin, with some 35 percent returning to live with parents or relatives at age nineteen.[30] In fact, closeness to at least one family member was one of the factors that increased the likelihood of employment or education for young adults aging out of the system.[31] I recall a social worker I met in New York City in 2000, describing her work with children aging out of care. "I spend most of my time," she said, "reconnecting kids with relatives whose rights were terminated years ago. These kids have no legal claim on their families once a TPR is entered, but when they exit the system these are often the only human resources they can count on."

A child can also easily cross over from the dependency system to the delinquency system. Consider a twelve-year-old boy who was represented by University of Florida law students in our Gator TeamChild clinic. Diagnosed with various learning disabilities, he was transferred from the regular city schools to a special school for children with impulse control problems. Like all learning disabled children, he had an individualized educational plan (IEP). One facet of his IEP dealt with the use of force. This child had been abused and, as a result, would react with panic to any sort of grabbing or rough handling. In the IEP, it was agreed that teachers would use words, not physical force, in dealing with him—he could always be "talked down" from an emotional crisis but, if handled physically, the situation would escalate into chaos. This school had created a "time out" room. This kind of space can play a very positive role in teaching children to control their impulses and to learn to behave responsibly. Usually, it consists of a room with chairs and books or a workspace set apart from the other children. In this school, it was a space about six feet by six feet with a single small window, through which the child could be observed, a door that could not be opened from inside, no furniture, and a drain in the floor. Most of us would call this an isolation cell.

One day this child forgot to bring his lunch to school. He grew emotionally overwrought and began screaming and cursing in the lunchroom. Instead of talking him down, the school resource officers (police officers assigned to keep order in the school) grabbed him. When he began flailing around wildly, they implemented a "take down" in order to hustle him off to the time out room. On the way down the hall, panic-stricken and struggling to get free, he kicked in a glass panel on a door. He was charged in juvenile court with assault on a government official (the resource officers), and destruction of government property. Without intervention by the clinic law students, this would have been the end of his schooling and the beginning of his journey through the juvenile justice system.

Physical force may sometimes be necessary, but routine use of force on children in state custody is a dangerous policy. It provides poor models for handling aggression in dealing with youths who are at risk of becoming violence prone. Use of force in "take down" situations can be fatal. A death in Florida brought public attention to the use of force in state run "boot camps." Boot camps flourished in the 1990s but continued in use long after research evaluations had shown the approach ineffective. In January 2006, Martin Lee Anderson died as a result of a take down in a Panama City, Florida, boot camp. Martin, age fourteen, had been arrested in June 2005 for stealing his grandmother's Jeep Cherokee and sent to the boot camp for violating his probation by trespassing at a school. At first, the state reported his death as due to sickle cell anemia. Originally, officials had said the guards had been restraining Martin using appropriate techniques after he "became uncooperative while doing push-ups, sit-ups and other exercises as part of his physical evaluation hours after being admitted to the camp."[32] But when video tapes of as many as nine guards at a time punching and kicking the boy became public, a second autopsy was ordered and the medical examiner found that he died as a result of the use of force.

The nickname "boot camp" invokes the American values of rugged individualism seen in movies like *An Officer and a Gentleman*, where arrogant and disrespectful boys like Richard Gere are turned into courageous young men through the "tough love" techniques of role models like Lou Gossett. The videotapes of the Florida facility, which can be viewed on various news sites, bear little resemblance to the boot camps of our imagination and none at all to the reality of military training. My son was a sergeant in the U.S. Army and, like his father before him, he went through basic training at Fort Knox, Kentucky. At Fort Knox, two noncommissioned officers trained a platoon of forty recruits without ever using physical force. In the videotape of the Florida incident, however, we see a phalanx of burly uniformed guards standing over kids, one on one, as the kids do push-ups. Later, we see half a dozen guards kneeing and kicking Martin after he has collapsed while running laps. The taped ordeal runs more than five minutes, during which the teenager offers no resistance, and only ends when a nurse who has been observing the scene from the start, listens to his breathing with a stethoscope and calls for an EMT. Martin died the following day as a result of suffocation. During the beating, the guards had shoved ammonia capsules up his nostrils while his mouth was clamped shut.

Martin's death sparked a complete reform of the Florida "tough love" boot camp system. As the legislative inquiry made clear, boot camps were not only dangerous, they were also ineffective.[33] On June 1, 2006, Governor Jeb Bush signed into law the Martin Lee Anderson Act, which eliminated boot camps throughout the state, replacing them with a new program called Sheriffs' Training and Respect, or STAR. "The law forbids guards from using 'harmful psychological intimidation techniques' on children, including threats of violence or efforts to humiliate. It largely outlaws the use of 'pain compliance techniques' and bans altogether the use of weapons such as pepper spray and Tasers."[34] Interventions such as boot camps were designed on a male model and generally there have been far more boys in the juvenile justice system than girls. But girls have become a growing proportion of the nation's juvenile justice population.

Providing robust rights to children in foster care and juvenile systems will not alone transform these systems. But it will help us to hold them accountable when they fail the children they are supposed to serve. Returning to Tony's story, I want some day to be able to assure him that the state cannot deprive him of his legal relationship with his mother without "due process" of law. At a minimum, this must mean the right to notice when such a draconian step is contemplated, the opportunity to state his position, and the right to be represented by a lawyer in any court hearing.[35] I would also like to be able to assure Tony that he cannot be removed from a long-term foster care or preadoptive placement without the same due process protections. His anger at being told to "pack his bag" was wholly justified. What person should be expected to tolerate such arbitrary actions? I want to be able to tell Tony that, when the state convenes a hearing seeking a TPR, it bears the burden of proving that his family ties are truly broken before it terminates the legal relationship. As matters currently stand, a parent has the right to protest termination in every state, yet there are numerous states in which the child has no such right. But suppose Tony's mother lacks the ability to express her own objections. Or suppose the state fails to initiate a TPR when a child like Tony wants to be adopted. I believe that Tony himself should have a voice in deciding whether his birth family should be preserved or whether he should be free to form a new family through adoption.

And why should Tony, because he was born poor, black, and out of wedlock, be deprived of equal protection in his relationship with his father? The law is clear that an unwed father has a right to establish a relationship with his child. Shouldn't the child, too, have a reciprocal right to establish a relationship with his father or mother? Listening to Tony describe the yearning to "know your roots" and "understand where you come from," it would be difficult to deny the power of his argument. But a judge never heard his arguments because he had no voice in the court proceedings that determined where he would live and with whom.

Finally, when the state takes a child into its care, it should be responsible for treating the child as we would like our own children to be treated. Abuse by the state of its physical power over the child, such as the acts that killed Martin Anderson, or neglect by the state of its duty to meet the child's basic needs, such as the failures to provide medical and dental care, housing and supervision, and support in achieving independence, are violations of the child's basic human rights to dignity.

Each of the preceding narratives has illuminated some aspect of children's rights. Frederick Douglass illustrates a core aspect, the right to be treated as a person and not a piece of property. Dred Scott's daughters show how children at the intersection of race and gender may face added barriers to recognition of their dignity and their agency. This chapter, building on narratives of children like Tony and Martin Anderson, shows how systems intended to help children at risk of abuse, neglect, or delinquency, can instead oppress and harm them by robbing them of their human dignity.

Families and societies may differ in their child-rearing practices, but American values surely should not tolerate neglecting the basic needs of children in our care, much less tolerate a system that abuses, loses, or kills them. In the preceding chapters, we explored the experiences of children in slavery and servitude, and saw how the disabilities of slavery were often mirror images of the legal disabilities of minors. Even the rhetoric of parenthood was infected with property metaphors. But, for most children, belonging to a master and belonging to a family were experienced very differently. In stark contrast to slavery, the disabilities of childhood were matched by parents' duties to nurture and educate their young, and parental authority was time-limited and expected to be tempered with love and concern for their offspring.

Privacy and freedom are inextricably intertwined. From a developmental perspective, children's best shot at freedom lies in having deep emotional attachments to strong and authoritative parents entrusted with defining their children's best interests and empowered to defend them. Privacy, for young children, lies in protection of their intimate nurturing relationships. These relationships are essential to the child's survival and are the original template for all the relationships that follow. We should never disrupt these relationships unless it is truly necessary, and once we take children into care, we assume the same moral responsibility to these children as we owe to our own. We must meet their irreducible needs, physical and emotional, so they can make the transition to adulthood safe and whole.

PART II

THE AGENCY PRINCIPLE: STORIES OF VOICE AND PARTICIPATION

CHAPTER 6

THE PRINTER'S APPRENTICE

Ben Franklin and Youth Speech

Whoever would overthrow the liberty of a nation must begin by subduing the freeness of speech.
   —Dame Silence Dogood, *New England Courant* [1722]

Terms like "agency" and "voice" and "self-expression" have a modern ring. Americans might be excused for believing that assertive children were something new, a plague we have brought upon ourselves by failing to exercise appropriate dominion over our young. It is no accident that we, the adults, have tended to cleanse the histories we teach in school of tales of rebellious children and youth. But, as the next two chapters will show, youthful expression and youthful activism have played pivotal roles in American history and in the struggle to perfect our freedoms. Children of all ages have equal claims to agency. But developmental theory tells us that children's agency, while it is present at birth, grows and changes and is asserted in different ways as children begin to interact with and understand the social and political worlds around them.

On a September morning in 1723, a seventeen-year-old boy went to the docks in the colonial port of Boston and prepared to board a sailing sloop bound for New York. With the aid of a teenaged accomplice, he won over the ship's captain with a story that was bound to elicit sympathy from a man of the sea. While he remained in hiding, his friend told the captain that the boy had gotten a "naughty" girl pregnant and was fleeing to avoid a forced marriage. The captain took the money he was offered and looked the other way as the fugitive snuck on board.

In fact, the boy was a runaway apprentice. At age twelve, he had been pressured into signing an indenture that bound him to work for his older brother, a printer, until he turned twenty-one. The older man grew to resent the boy's precocious intellect. As the apprentice became ever more saucy and defiant, the master turned to beatings and humiliation as a means of asserting his dominance. The boy began to fear his body and spirit could not survive his indenture intact.

The boy had another motive for leaving Boston—also stemming from his outspoken nature. He was a political dissident in danger of arrest. As a printer's apprentice, he had mastered the skills necessary to turn words penned by others into printed pages. His master was publisher of a journal called the *New England Courant* that often published readers' essays challenging the colonial government's abuses of power. The apprentice had strong opinions of his own and had begun submitting his opinion pieces under the pseudonym of Dame Silence Dogood.

He had chosen a dangerous pseudonym, one that ridiculed the Puritan cleric, Cotton Mather's religious tracts "Silentarius" and "Essays to Do Good." Targeting Cotton Mather for satire was a dangerous move. Mather, a fierce enforcer of religious orthodoxy who had defended the Salem witch trials, continued to exert tremendous political power in the Massachusetts Colony. The *Courant*'s publisher, not knowing that Silence Dogood's letter was the work of his apprentice, recognized good writing when he saw it and was eager to receive more letters from this source. As one historian later wrote of Dame Dogood, "Silence is irreverent and full of herself, yet she brings most readers—the proud and powerful excepted—into the realm of her sympathy. They laugh when she laughs, and laugh at whom she laughs."[1] The *New England Courant* ultimately published fifteen of Dame Dogood's letters, and she became a minor celebrity for her wit and the bite of her comic critiques.

Dame Dogood's satire was entertaining but it also carried a pointed political message. Dame Dogood strongly endorsed the ideas of free speech and free thought, quoting from great thinkers on the nature of freedom. She also questioned the role of religion in politics. "It has been for some time a question with me, whether a commonwealth suffers more by hypocritical pretenders to religion or by the openly profane." Dame Dogood concluded that the religious hypocrite was by far more dangerous, "especially if he sustains a post in the government."

These letters hit their mark, enraging Cotton Mather and his supporters, and the boy's master was jailed briefly for publishing antigovernment and antireligious opinions. When the master printer was ordered to stop his presses, the apprentice took over his master's role. By this time Dame Dogood's true identity had become known. Now that he was publishing under his own name, the boy feared he would be next in line for a jail cell. Rather than wait for the inevitable, and chaffing under his master's harsh treatment, he determined to leave Boston and find work elsewhere.

The fugitive found no work in New York but headed for Philadelphia where he heard a printer's journeyman was wanted. His Quaker hosts greeted him with suspicion. It was illegal to harbor a fugitive from indenture and the Philadelphia folks who took him in strongly suspected this bedraggled youth, still too young to need a shave, must be a runaway. But there were no telephones to check his bona fides, no newscasts to broadcast his disappearance, or milk cartons to advertise his status as a "missing child." He talked his way into a new job in a new town where he could be free of state censorship and abusive working conditions. He later remarked on one lesson he learned from his master's abuse. "I fancy his harsh and tyrannical treatment of me might be a means of impressing me with that aversion to arbitrary power that has stuck to me through my whole life."[2]

History is written by the powerful. If you recognize the boy in this story it is because he grew up to become a famous and powerful man. His story is so quintessentially American that he has been called "The First American."[3] His name, Benjamin Franklin, is familiar to all Americans, young and old. His signature appears on more of the Founding Fathers' documents than that of any other Revolutionary-era patriot. But most Americans think of him as the old man peering out from behind the bifocal spectacles he invented, not as the headstrong apprentice who took a leadership role in the colonists' fight for free speech.

Children's stories are often overshadowed or simply left untold. Traditional histories typically cast them in the role of supporting players if they are visible at all. When they appear as protagonists, it is only because they grew up to become famous adults. Folk stories of a famous man's childhood, like George Washington's apocryphal confession to cutting down the cherry tree, often tell more about the iconic status of the man than the reality of the child. As a rule, children and youths figure in history as objects of others' actions rather than subjects in their own right, or as passive victims rather than feeling and thinking agents who shape their own and others' lives. Their ideas and opinions are often dismissed as naive or derivative, reflecting the influences of adults or peers and lacking authenticity of their own.

The young Ben Franklin was anything but passive and easily influenced. Even as a small boy, youngest of fifteen siblings, he insisted on being treated as an individual capable of shaping his own future. In his autobiography, written when he was in his sixties, he explained why his formal schooling ended when he was only ten. His father had destined him for the clergy, a future that Ben found appealing. Ben had excelled at his studies in grammar school, skipping grades and moving to the top of each class. But then the elder Franklin abruptly changed his mind. With so many mouths to feed, he could not afford to send Ben to college to study for the ministry. He withdrew Ben from grammar school and enrolled him in a more practical course of study. In a move that modern parents and school counselors would recognize, ten-year-old Ben made his own preferences clear. This future Fellow of the Royal Society and recipient of an honorary doctorate from Oxford University for his accomplishments in the sciences promptly failed arithmetic, twice.[4] So his father had to take him out of school and place him in the family chandler shop to learn how to turn tallow into candles. But Ben had long dreamed of going to sea, and he made plain his distaste for the hot and smelly work of candle making.

> [M]y dislike to the trade continuing, my father was under the apprehension that if he did not find one for me more agreeable, I should break away and get to sea, as his son Josiah had done, to his great vexation. He therefore sometimes took me to walk with him and see joiners, bricklayers, turners, braziers, etc., at their work, that he might observe my inclination, and endeavor to fix it on some trade or other on land.[5]

Ben's father had learned the hard way that this child had a mind of his own.

While shirking at learning candle making, Ben was busy devouring every book in his father's meager library, including *Pilgrim's Progress*, Plutarch's *Lives*, and Cotton Mather's *Essays to Do Good*. Seeing his "bookish inclination," his father decided he should train in the trade of printer.

> I liked [this work] much better than that of my father, but still had a hankering for the sea. To prevent the apprehended effect of such an inclination, my father was very impatient to have me bound to my brother. I stood out some time, but at last was persuaded, and I signed the indentures when I was yet but twelve years old.[6]

His reluctance to sign the indenture papers was understandable, since they bound him to serve one master in one profession for nine long years. What twelve-year-old, even the most bookish, can comprehend all the implications of such a bargain?

While he could not know it then, the move from his father's house to his brother's print shop, while it did not free him to wander the

> When about sixteen years of age I happened to meet with a book written by one Tryon, recommending a vegetable diet. I determined to go into it. My brother, being yet unmarried, did not keep house but boarded himself and his apprentices in another family. . . . [I] proposed to my brother, that if he would give me, weekly, half the money he paid for my board, I would board myself. He instantly agreed to it, and I presently found that I could save half of what he paid me. This was an additional fund for buying books.[7]

Instead of leaving work to go to eat and drink with the others at the boardinghouse, he remained at the printing house to read and study.

> And now it was that, being on some occasion made asham'd of my ignorance in figures, which I twice failed in learning when at school, I took Cocker's book of Arithmetick, and went through the whole myself with great ease. I also read Seller's and Shermy's books of Navigation and became acquainted with the little geometry they contain.

Looking back, the mature Franklin took pains to describe how the books he devoured as an adolescent had shaped his intellectual and social development. Xenophon's *Memorable Things of Socrates* taught him to adopt the tone of "humble inquirer and doubter" in place of the "abrupt contradiction and positive argumentation" that had been his style up to that time. Shaftesbury and Collins led him to doubt various points of religious doctrine that were commonly accepted among his peers and family. Locke's work *On Human Understanding* and the *Art of Thinking* by du Port opened to him the world of philosophy.

Ben may have been a bookworm but he was not a submissive geek. He played pranks, took things that didn't belong to him, and took controversial positions on issues of the day, such as favoring women's education, simply for his own pleasure in being oppositional. He found delight in pulling the wool over adults' eyes, later remembering the "exquisite pleasure" of hearing them speculate about who the real Dame Dogood might be. When his master tried to quell what we might now call Ben's "attitude" with harangues and beatings, he voted with his feet. Like many boys and girls, before and since, he was willing to go hungry and sleep in the street rather than live with verbal and physical abuse.

Ben's life illustrates the role played by American youth, even while under the legal control of parents and masters, in defending the right to free speech and the right to speak out against oppression. With the courage of innocence, young people saw what needed changing and believed in the possibility of change. American adolescents put their bodies on the line to back up their politics. Youths as young as age fourteen volunteered as soldiers in the American Revolution. Children who went to war of their own free will sometimes fought next to children who were sent to war by their masters. In those days, men of means when called to service could send their apprentices and indentured servants in their places.[8] To believe that the right to freedom of speech and expression should apply to adults alone would ignore children's central role in the battle to secure these freedoms.

But how far can this freedom to dissent and to challenge authority extend without destroying the social compact that places children and youth under the legal control as well as protection of adults? While most Americans and the laws of the fifty states now reject beating children as a form of adult control, censorship by parents is an accepted norm. Parents enjoy wide discretion in controlling children's freedom of speech and association. Parents routinely lay down the law of the family on proper speech and expression. As in Ben's day, rudeness or insolence can result in serious restrictions of freedom. "Go to your room, . . . NOW!" "You are grounded, young lady!" "No more car keys, mobile phone, e-mail, instant messaging. And no more iPod, TV, DVD."

Clearly, children in the American family are subject to a level of adult authority that is plainly inconsistent with perfect freedom of speech and assembly. Very few champions of children's rights challenge the authority of parents to enforce reasonable or even idiosyncratic standards of behavior in the home. Even parents who are card-carrying members of the ACLU recognize that equally important values, such as family autonomy, protection of the young, maintenance of public order, educational priorities, and the like, support the imposition of a significant measure of adult control in channeling youthful expression and consumption of expression. When parents place limits on children's freedom of speech and association, they are acting in harmony with modern conceptions of children's human rights that recognize children's rights to intellectual freedom but also recognize parents' duty to guide their children in exercising these rights and to raise children according to individual family and religious values.

But what about opinionated and outspoken minors, like sixteen-year-old Ben Franklin, who enter the *public* debate and find themselves in conflict with *public* authority? What rights do they have when faced with state-sponsored censorship of their speech? By far the most common setting in which children come into conflict with state authority is the public school. Public school administrators and teachers, because they act on behalf of the state, are bound by the restrictions on government imposed by the First Amendment and by the other provisions of the Bill of Rights.[9] When does appropriate pedagogical control cross the line into unconstitutional censorship? In a series of landmark cases construing the application of the First Amendment to school children, the U.S. Supreme Court has attempted to balance values of free speech and press against educational, disciplinary, and protective interests of teachers and administrators. These cases establish that "students in the public schools do not 'shed their constitutional rights to freedom of speech or expression at the school house gate.' "[10] But they also establish that "the First Amendment rights of students in the public schools 'are not automatically coextensive with the rights of adults in other settings,' and must be 'applied in light of the special characteristics of the school environment.' "[11]

Many of the landmark cases on the rights of youth to freedom of expression reflect the reality that children are inevitably caught up in political and social upheaval of their times.[12] Attempts to exert social control over a population often target the young. The earliest cases involving children's intellectual freedom challenged laws, passed in the aftermath of World War I and aimed at Germans and other immigrant minorities, that forbade the teaching of foreign languages to young children.[13] The Court struck down these laws as infringing the rights of parents to educate their children, of teachers to teach, and of children to learn. World War II tensions explained the school authorities' harsh response to the Seventh Day Adventist children in *West Virginia v. Barnette*. The children in this case had refused to pledge allegiance to the American flag because their religion forbade them from swearing any oath other than to God. The Court held they could not be punished for following their consciences.[14] The cold war that followed World War II, bringing fears of communist conspiracy and rising apprehension that the arms race between Russia and the United States would end in nuclear war, sharpened the tensions between free speech and national security. Children as well as adults lived in the shadow of McCarthyism and of the mushroom cloud. I remember that time well. I was only eight years old as I watched the Army-McCarthy hearings with my family, but I could feel the strength of my gentle father's hatred for Joe McCarthy.[15] I knew that many of my own relatives were among those communist sympathizers that McCarthy was trying to expose and destroy. Living not far from Sing Sing prison, I remember the lights dimming on a warm evening in June of 1953 when Julius and Ethel Rosenberg were executed, and feeling sad for their two young sons, who were about the same ages as my brother Charlie and me.[16] I was in third grade when the words "under God" were added to the pledge of allegiance.[17] A favorite ritual of my day became a daily ordeal. I knew from overhearing my parents that the change was intended as a message that all true Americans believed in God. I agonized over whether to say the phrase and deny my parents or not say the phrase and deny my country. I compromised guiltily by mouthing the words. By the time I reached high school, I had developed a greater understanding of my civil rights and a greater capacity to exercise them. The cold war was at it hottest just after the Cuban Missile Crisis, when a shelter drill siren sounded at our school. I felt strongly that these drills led to complacence about the threat of nuclear war. I walked to the principal's office and stated that I could not in good conscience participate. I was suspended indefinitely, without a hearing or opportunity for my parents, let alone a lawyer, to speak on my behalf. Fortunately, a letter from the New York Civil Liberties Union persuaded the school board that indefinite suspension was too harsh a punishment for an idealistic student's peaceful protest.

Today, I teach a course called Child, Parent, and State, in which "the status of children" and their maturation as citizens is a major topic. Many of the cases in the text deal with issues relating to school disciplinary proceedings. Today, school children and their parents take for granted the right to a hearing and to some measure of free speech. But we owe a debt to the students whose cases, unlike my own, *did* end up in court. The most famous such case is *Tinker v. Des Moines Independent Community School District*, which involved three high school students who were suspended in December 1965 for wearing black armbands in protest of the U.S. government's policies in Vietnam. The students' protest was part of a larger organized effort involving their parents and other adults in the community, and the school authorities knew in advance of the students' plan to wear the black armbands during the holiday season. The school adopted a policy that any student wearing an armband would be asked to remove it and, if he or she refused, would be suspended and permitted to return only if not wearing the armband. The students returned to school but they and their parents challenged the school's actions in federal court and argued that the First Amendment protected their right to peacefully express their opposition to government policies. They lost in the federal district and appeals courts but, five years after the case had begun, they won their case in the Supreme Court. Justice Abe Fortas, writing for the majority, held that,

> In order for the State in the person of school officials to justify prohibition of a particular expression of opinion, it must be able to show that its action was caused by something more than a mere desire to avoid the discomfort and unpleasantness that always accompany an unpopular viewpoint. Certainly where there is no

finding and no showing that engaging in the forbidden conduct would "materially and substantially interfere with the requirements of appropriate discipline in the operation of the schools," the prohibition cannot be sustained.[18]

Justice Fortas continued,

> In our system, state-operated schools may not be enclaves of total-itarianism. School officials do not possess absolute authority over their students. Students in school as well as out of school are "persons" under our Constitution. They are possessed of fundamental rights which the State must respect, just as they themselves must respect their obligations to the State. In our system, students may not be regarded as closed-circuit recipients of only that which the State chooses to communicate. They may not be confined to the expression of those sentiments that are officially approved. In the absence of a specific showing of constitutionally valid reasons to regulate their speech, students are entitled to freedom of expression of their views.[19]

These sweeping statements in *Tinker* were the high water mark of student free speech rights. Justice Black raised questions in his dissent in *Tinker* that still resonate today. How can we be sure that children are speaking their own minds and not operating as mouthpieces for their parents? Justice Black clearly believed that the Tinker children, especially the younger ones, were merely parroting the political opinions of their parents. He wrote,

> One defying pupil was Paul Tinker, 8 years old, who was in the second grade; another, Hope Tinker, was 11 years old and in the fifth grade; a third member of the Tinker family was John Tinker, 15 years old, an 11th grade high school pupil. Their father, a Methodist minister without a church, is paid a salary by the American Friends Service Committee. Another student who defied the school order was Christopher Eckhardt, an 11th grade pupil and a petitioner in this case. His mother is an official in the Women's International League for Peace and Freedom.[20]

them. From a developmental perspective, tailoring the First Amendment to match children's situations requires that we respect children's childish expressions so that they can develop self-respect and the capacity to think independently. Parents can and will teach children a family's beliefs, but the role of schools is to teach children respect for their own and others' peaceful *expression* of beliefs.

As always, cases on children's free expression in schools show the stamp of current events. After the Jonesboro and Columbine shootings, schools began to scrutinize children's drawings for signs of hostility toward school or schoolmates. Not surprisingly, they found plenty of material to alarm them. A firm grip on developmental psychology has kept many schools, but not all, from overreacting to kids' fantasies as if they were actual plots.[24] T-shirts and tattoos, prime forms of adolescent expression, have also caused controversy.[25] While courts have been "tinkering" with old First Amendment precedents, communications technology has revolutionized the context of youthful self-expression. In the twenty-first century, to a degree never before imagined, young people can create and publish their own speech and become their own press. In colonial America, Ben Franklin was unusual in having access to a printing press. There is no minimum age limit for Internet bloggers. Unlike Ben Franklin's broadsheets, electronic communication provides a two-way street for instantly disseminating and receiving information in real time. Electronic media also expand the visual and auditory ways in which youth can express themselves. The personal statements made by blue hair and body piercing, by a particular choice of music, or by wrapping oneself in the Confederate flag, can now be broadcast nationally over a blog. If it is difficult to censor what children say, it is even more difficult to censor what they hear and see.

Free expression and free access to others' expression are two sides of the same coin. We saw in chapter 3 how slavery was maintained and slave children were disempowered by denying them access to education and preventing them from obtaining the tools to educate themselves. Recall how young Frederick Douglass was banned from reading, defied his master, learning to read, and eventually used his skills to secure his own freedom. Many modern free speech cases are as much concerned with preventing children from hearing speech adults deem disruptive as they are with preventing them from speaking. Favorite topics for adult censorship include truthful information about safe sex and contraception—information thought to incite young people to sexual action. From a children's rights perspective, it is difficult to justify withholding life-saving information from teens when we know them to be sexually active.[26]

Free expression by children and free access to the expression of others pose dangers as well as opportunities for education and growth. The Internet seems to some older folks like me to have magnified the risks as well as the benefits of access to information. To find out what it was like to have a space of my own on the Internet, I opened an account in the blogosphere known as MySpace. This site and others like it, including Friendster and Xanga, provide a platform for individuals to create their own online identities and to interact with others. They are tremendously attractive to adolescents entering a developmental stage where networking with peers is a primary means of defining one's own emerging identity. A recent study by Cox Communications indicates that 61 percent of thirteen- to seventeen-year-olds have profiles on such sites. Half of them have posted photographs of themselves.[27] While MySpace is supposedly off limits to children under fourteen and all minors' accounts are marked "private," users can easily talk their way into private accounts and lie about their ages, pretending to be older or younger than they actually are. Adult predators, masquerading as teens and looking for vulnerable young people to victimize, have misused the sites. In one small town, MSNBC reports that five teenaged girls were sexually assaulted by males they met on MySpace.[28] Law enforcement and parents who monitor the photographs and self-created profiles have noticed another troubling phenomenon. Even sheltered middle-class youth, perhaps because influenced by a popular culture that uses sex and violence to catch their attention, now compete to portray themselves online with the most violent and sexualized images and personas.

Parents have long expressed concerns about children's access to pornography, and the Internet makes this access far easier and far less amenable to regulation. Under traditional First Amendment law, age plays a very large role in determining access to expressive materials. In a nutshell, the government may always censor obscenity (which by definition appeals only to prurient interests and lacks any redeeming social value). Government may not censor ordinary speech, especially political speech or other protected speech. In the middle lies a realm of images or materials that may not be obscene but are deemed inappropriate for children's consumption—pornography is a prime example. Government may foreclose access to this speech by youth but not if doing so prevents access by adults. In protecting children, government must use the means least restrictive of adults' rights.

Congress has tried several different schemes to limit children's access to objectionable Internet materials, but all have come up against the barrier of adults' constitutional free speech rights. The most recent round of legislation to reach the Court was the Child Online Protection Act (COPA).[29] COPA imposed a fine of up to $50,000 and a prison term of up to six months on operators of Web sites that allow children to access materials that are "harmful to minors." Web sites that established a credit card, pin number, or electronic verification system to verify a patron's age would be protected from liability. In *Ashcroft v. ACLU*, the Court held that COPA's scheme of user verification impinged on adults' access to protected speech. Government would have to show that no less restrictive means existed to protect children. The Court remanded the case, asking the trial court to address whether filters that could be installed by parents provided a less restrictive and yet effective means to achieve congressional goals. In another initiative, Congress tried requiring public libraries to install filters and requiring all patrons to show ID before turning them off. The Supreme Court also struck down this initiative.[30] As these initiatives illustrate, adults are desperately searching for ways to limit children's access to materials that adults consider harmful to minors without thwarting open access to the same materials by adults.

What would Benjamin Franklin make of all this? From what we know of his character as a boy and as a man, I expect he would adore the Internet, learn to use it instantly, and be almost speechless at its possibilities for revolutionizing the spread of knowledge. The images would astonish and, mostly, delight him. He was no prude, but I imagine he would be shocked to the core by some of the materials he might encounter. Would he be so sure that only the young should be prevented from seeing them? I doubt it. If Ben were fourteen today and wanted access to a forbidden site, could he figure out how to get it? You bet!

Looking at free speech and expression through Ben Franklin's eyes reminds us of how difficult it is for adults to keep young people from sharing in the cultures created by their elders. It also reminds us that a bright child worth his salt will be clever enough to circumvent the rickety barriers we erect to keep children from entering a world we insist should be freely accessible to everyone else. In a dangerous world, one option is to empower children to know and to avoid the dangers around them. Both for profit and nonprofit entities provide Internet safety tools that educate children to know and avoid situations that will place them at risk of victimization.[31] Why not build on kids' strengths rather than leave them vulnerable through ignorance? Ben Franklin's example also reminds us that youthful dissent is part of the American heritage and that each generation can be expected to shock and annoy its elders.[32] Kids know this and try to avoid adults' censorious eyes. On the Internet and instant messaging, they have developed a language of their own, but parents can learn to translate it. One common acronym is POS, which means "parent looking over shoulder." In plotting strategies to protect children from access to speech and expression, we should try to act as if we had BOS—Ben looking over our shoulder.

We need robust free speech rights to protect all citizens. But there are real threats to our social well-being from what many have called the "toxic environment" in which we are raising our children. Analyzing these issues as a clash between adults' First Amendment rights and society's interest in protecting children has not produced very useful solutions. In my work I have suggested a different approach.[33] I have suggested that we look at child protection through an ecological lens. We should utilize the latest science to understand the interplay between harmful substances or images and child development, taking into account the child's age and the cultural context. First, we should ask whether we are trying to control children's access to information or images for valid reasons. Can we verify, through objective evidence, that exposure to a bare breast or to information about contraception is harmful to a child of a certain age? What about exposure to images of children having sex with adults? What about exposure to extremely violent images of people killing and raping other people? Adults have been slow to respond to the actual evidence, preferring to focus on harmless nudity rather than volence, when "it is well established by a compelling body of scientific evidence that television violence is harmful to children."[34]

Having sorted out materials that do not actually pose a serious threat, materials that are found to be actually harmful to children, not merely offensive to adults, should not be released into the environment at all without controls. They should be confined to special spaces that adults would have to take affirmative steps to access. We do this when we card people entering X-rated movies or confine strip joints to designated parts of a city or town. We do this when we designate limited smoking areas instead of subjecting all to the effects of secondhand smoke and designating areas where children, asthmatics, and pregnant women can go to escape it. Instead of banishing all minors from the public square, we should reject the idea of living in an environment that is toxic to the young.

Let me emphasize that this discussion is about children's human rights in relation to government, and government-imposed controls on access to various forms of expression. It does not apply to limits set by parents and guardians in the home. Short of conduct that poses an imminent risk of harm (think of using one's children as actors in pornographic movies), families must be free to guide their children's access to media and other forms of speech as they see fit. The presumption that parents act in their children's best interest, the dangers of instilling conformity by standardizing our children, and the high value we place on cultural diversity are three strong American traditions that support giving parents wide latitude to control their children's access to media and other forms of expression. By analogy, while government may prohibit minors from drinking wine in public spaces, many cultural traditions allow children to drink wine at home under adult supervision. Some parents are comfortable with casual nudity in the home and others never appear unless fully dressed. We can trust children to figure these things out. I remember, during one presidential election, commenting that "finally we might get a decent president," to which my four-year-old daughter responded, "Yeah, I'll bet he won't come to breakfast in his underwear." Her father and I laughed but we also cringed.

In this chapter, I have looked at children's agency and empowerment largely in the context of free expression and access to information. We have seen how courts have struggled to balance competing interests, those of children in intellectual freedom and those of society in orderly schools and safe spaces for children. In colonial America, Ben Franklin risked arrest because of his political beliefs—but he participated in creating a system of government that protects free speech not only for adults but also for children. When adults, in their zeal to protect the young, forget these lessons, they risk breaking a young person's spirit as surely as by beating him or starving him. My students and I invoked the spirit of Ben Franklin in a friend of the court brief we wrote in February 2007, on behalf of a boy named John G. You may remember John G. from chapter 5. John G., age fifteen, had been unable to pay the mortgage on a Habitat for Humanity house inherited from his father because the State of North Carolina was taking his Social Security survivors' benefits to fund his foster care. It took an injunction from the court to halt foreclosure on the house. John's case caught the attention of a congressman who proposed a bill to protect foster children's survivor benefits. John was invited to speak to the First Star Bi-Partisan Congressional Roundtable in

Washington, DC, where hill staffers and their bosses would learn about the impact of this policy on children aging out of foster care. At the last minute, the state agency that had legal custody of John withdrew permission for him to attend, explaining that it was not in his best interest to be "an exhibit" in a public debate. John and his lawyer filed a motion to enjoin the state from preventing him from going, and my students and I set to work composing a brief arguing that the state must not interfere with John's exercise of this quintessential free speech right—the right to assemble and petition government for redress of grievances. John was not an "exhibit," he was a person, mature enough to speak about his own experiences and with important information for the legislators to consider. Sadly, our brief was never filed because, on the eve of the hearing, John decided not to go to Washington. He felt "caught in the middle," under heavy pressure to give up the trip, and was so depressed he no longer wanted to talk with anyone, even the judge. In addition to a lawyer, John had a Guardian ad Litem, or GAL, appointed to represent his best interests, who had supported his desire to go to Washington. The GAL's motion, reporting John's change of heart, made clear that an all-expense-paid chance to speak to a congressional roundtable was a wonderful opportunity for a sixteen-year-old, and placed the blame for John's anguish squarely on the state agency's misconduct. It was a sad day for John G. and for free speech in America.

CHAPTER 7

YOUTH IN THE CIVIL RIGHTS MOVEMENT

John Lewis and Sheyann Webb

You see their faces today in history books and nobody knows their names. . . . What ever happened to the little girl who was turned head over heels by those fire hoses?
  —John Lewis, U.S. Congressman from Georgia[1]

I knew that night that being a part of that nonviolent army Dr. King had spoken of was going to be the most important thing in my life. I thought of the stanza in the song We Shall Overcome that "God is on our side." With the depth that only a child's mind could feel, I believed those words, believed them dearly.
  —Sheyann Webb, age 8[2]

In the last chapter we looked at children using their voices and expressive symbols to make their views known and their agency felt. What about children who go beyond expressing their opinions in the public square and challenge injustice in their acts as well as words? One of the proudest achievements in American history was accomplished by young people arrested while engaging in the right to peaceably assemble and petition for redress of grievances. In this chapter, we will look at the involvement of American children in the civil rights movement of the 1960s and 1970s.

The killing in 1955 of Emmett Till, called "America's Anne Frank" by writers at the time, ignited a wave of outrage and disgust within the black community and across the nation. A high-spirited fourteen-year-old from Chicago, he had wanted to impress the country cousins he was visiting in Mississippi with his big city sophistication.[3] He was brutally murdered for taking a dare and flirting with a white woman. As punishment for allegedly uttering the phrase "Bye, Baby" to a white female clerk after making a purchase in a Mississippi grocery store, Emmett was kidnapped, tortured, beaten to death, weighted down with a cotton gin fan, and thrown into a river. Emmett's mother made the controversial decision to display his battered corpse in an open casket. Published in *Jet*, the black national-circulation magazine, Emmett's image mobilized the black community as even the landmark desegregation decision in *Brown v. Board of Education* had failed to do.[4] Turning from the image of the smiling little boy his mother sent down to Mississippi and confronting the sight of the battered, almost unrecognizable body she got back, no one could possibly sanitize or rationalize the brutality of the crime. Its impact on children was profound, as we know from the many movement memoirs that identify Emmett Till's murder as a crucial moment in their education about racism and the personal peril to children like themselves of racial violence.[5] Searching the Web for material on Emmett Till, I found at the Web site of PBS's *American Experience* many moving personal accounts, both from ordinary citizens and famous Americans, recalling the fear, shock, and rage they experienced on seeing these pictures. The boxer Muhammed Ali writes,

> Emmett Till and I were about the same age. A week after he was murdered . . . I stood on the corner with a gang of boys, looking at pictures of him in the black newspapers and magazines. In one he was laughing and happy. In the other, his head was swollen and bashed in, his eyes bulging out of their sockets and his mouth

twisted and broken. His mother had done a bold thing. She refused to let him be buried until hundreds of thousands marched past his open casket in Chicago and looked down at his mutilated body. . . . I couldn't get Emmett out of my mind . . ."[6]

Like Emmett, eleven-year-old Denise McNair, and her friends Cynthia Wesley, Addie Mae Collins, and Carole Robertson, all fourteen, changed the course of history not in their lives but by their deaths in the bombing of the Sixteenth Street Baptist Church in Birmingham, Alabama, on September 15, 1963. They were primping their hair in the restroom when the bomb exploded. "These children—unoffending, innocent, and beautiful—were the victims of one of the most vicious and tragic crimes ever perpetrated against humanity. And yet they died nobly. They are the martyred heroines of a holy crusade for freedom and human dignity."[7] The speaker was a Nobel Peace Prize winner and a martyr himself, Dr. Martin Luther King Jr. The crusade, which came to be known simply as "the movement," was the American civil rights movement challenging segregation of the races and the second-class citizenship of American blacks.

The Civil Rights Memorial of the Southern Poverty Law Center, on its list of forty martyrs of the civil rights movement, includes the names of other children who died doing ordinary things—dancing, primping, riding a bike—that all kids should be safe to do. John Earl Reese, age sixteen, was shot during a campaign of racist intimidation in Mayflower, Texas, in 1955, while dancing in a café. Virgil Lamar Ware, age thirteen, was riding on the handlebars of his brother's bicycle when he was shot by white teens leaving a Birmingham segregationist rally in 1963. These were "innocent" children caught in the cross fire of drive-by shootings and terrorist attacks.[8]

Countless other children were active participants in the movement, and generally they marched, sang, and shed their blood in anonymity. One of the histories that may never be fully told is the story of all the children who served as foot soldiers in the battle for civil rights. John Lewis, now a congressman from Georgia, muses on the anonymity of the men, women, and, especially, the children he used to call the "ground crew":

> They were the rank and file, in Selma, in Americus, in Little Rock, everywhere. You see their faces today in history books and nobody knows their names. That young guy sitting stoically at the lunch counter in Jackson with mustard streaming down his face and a mob of white hoodlums crowded round him taunting and laughing—who is he? Where is he today? The young man whose pants leg is being torn by a snarling German shepherd in Birmingham—what is his name? Where is *he*? What ever happened to the little girl who was turned head over heels by those fire hoses?[9]

Tellingly, looking at the grainy photographs and reading the news accounts to which Lewis refers, we can say one thing for sure about each of the examples he has chosen—they all appear to be teens. Americans do not fully appreciate the enormous role played by children and youth not only as innocent martyrs but also as fully engaged activists in the struggle for justice. When I began researching this chapter I knew already, from photographs and films like *Eyes on the Prize*, that some brave school age children had marched, been tear-gassed, knocked down by fire hoses, attacked by dogs. I did not realize that many thousands of children had been arrested during the civil rights campaigns.

At the time of these events, child psychiatrist Robert Coles spent many months working with many of the children involved—both white and black. His book, *Children in Crisis: Stories of Courage and Fear*, recounted the reactions of children and young civil rights workers to the traumatic events as they unfolded. Although some of Coles's comments may seem dated, his humanity shines through, and the children's accounts also remain vivid and telling. But scholarly attention to the role of children in the movement faded as time passed. Despite its title, David Halberstam, in his book *The Children*, focuses primarily on college students. He tells the story of a group of students ranging in age from about eighteen to twenty-six, who attended American Baptist, Tennessee A&I,

and Fisk—all black colleges in Nashville, Tennessee. The title "Children" is intended to emphasize the youth and innocent idealism of the college kids who engaged in direct action, and to highlight the generation gap between these activists and an older and more cautious generation. The students he profiles launched the first major round of sit-ins at the lunch counters of Nashville's downtown department stores, and their group joined with others to found the Student Nonviolent Coordinating Committee (SNCC). What brought them together was a workshop on nonviolence taught by a man named James Lawson. Lawson, born the same year as Martin Luther King Jr., had enrolled in the Divinity School at Vanderbilt University in Nashville after King urged him to come to the South to teach and preach nonviolence. Lawson had been a student of Mahatma Gandhi and was jailed as a conscientious objector during the Korean War. Lawson's greatest contribution to the movement was persuading the young men and women he trained and mentored of the deep courage, dignity, and efficacy of nonviolent protest.

Lawson's conversion to pacifism occurred when he was ten years old. His mother had sent him on an errand, and a smaller white boy in a parked car had called him "nigger." Without hesitating, he had marched over, reached in, and slapped the child. Expecting praise from his mother when he got home, he was stunned by her response. She said quietly, "What good did that do, Jimmy?" Jimmy was loved by his family and his God, she told him. With all that love surrounding him, how could he be harmed by the stupid insult of an ignorant child?[10] He later described this as a "sanctification experience, a moment when his life seemed to stand still and then change forever."[11] From that day, he never wavered from his commitment to nonviolence. The pacifism preached by Lawson, and put into action by student leaders like Diane Nash and John Lewis, was later disowned by a second wave of more militant leaders like Stokely Carmichael and H. Rap Brown, who took the reins of SNCC in 1966. But at its inception, nonviolence and integration were the core beliefs of the SNCC, and its key strategy was civil disobedience.

With the benefit of hindsight, the nonviolent militancy of the early integrationists looks far less radical than the armed militancy of the leaders who came after them. But there were already deep divisions between the young folks and their elders in the civil rights establishment. John Lewis's memoir provides a firsthand account of one boy's coming of age in the movement and his striving to find a new way to confront segregation head on. As Lewis's story reveals, his generation and the older generation respected each other's motives but shared a mutual distrust of each other's tactics. Future Supreme Court justice and famed NAACP litigator Thurgood Marshall criticized the Nashville students for straying from the path of the law. The victories of the 1940s and '50s had been won in federal courts by lawyers like Marshall. Marshall had himself been trained by Dean Charles Houston of Howard Law School, who drummed into a cadre of elite black students that there was one way only to conquer Jim Crow. Only legal arguments would persuade the Supreme Court to overrule the case of *Plessy v. Ferguson*, condoning the apartheid system of "separate but equal" facilities for whites and blacks. The battle to overrule *Plessy* had been won in the Supreme Court, not the streets, in *Brown v. Board of Education*. Lewis describes how Marshall warned him he was making a mistake by staying in jail and refusing bail, by taking the battle into the Deep South with Freedom Rides and marches in Alabama and Mississippi. "You'll get people hurt, he told us. You'll get people killed."[12] According to their elders, there was a better way. Rather than using tactics of "direct action," involving defiance of the law and mass arrests, they should use the power and majesty of the law to challenge Jim Crow in court.

It struck me as I read Lewis's account that Thurgood Marshall, not to mention the young John Lewis, overlooked or simply took for granted a crucial fact of law that shaped their responses and the methods open to them. The laws that disempowered persons because of their age were so firmly entrenched as to seem natural, even to lawyers and activists bent on challenging laws that disempowered persons because of their color. The education of John Lewis provides a telling story that reveals how the law itself—the disabilities of minority imposed by law—forced the youngest generation of activists to break the law in order to challenge it.

John was born on a farm in Alabama, one of ten children of Eddie and Willie Mae Lewis. He was a strange little boy—living a vivid interior life and relentlessly questioning every premise he encountered. At a very early age, by his own account and by those of his family members, he rejected cotton farming as a form of "gambling" and denounced it as "slavery."[13] He saw clearly that his family was trapped in a never-ending cycle of hard labor, staking its future every year on the weather and getting ever deeper in debt to the white men who ran the cotton mills and warehouses. "Even a six-year-old could tell that this sharecropper's life was nothing but a bottomless pit."[14] Like Frederick Douglass, Lewis found his escape from slavery in education, literally hiding from his mother so he could dash on board the school bus rather than go into the fields to pick cotton. He read everything he could lay his hands on.

> Near the end of my freshman year [in high school], on a May morning in 1954, I read something that stunned me, just absolutely turned my world upside down. The U.S. Supreme Court had finally handed down its decision in the school desegregation case of *Brown v. Board of Education of Topeka*. . . . I remember the feeling of jubilation I had reading the newspaper stories—*all* the newspaper stories—that day. No longer would I have to ride a broken-down bus almost forty miles each day to attend a "training" school with hand-me-down books and supplies. Come fall I'd be riding a state-of-the-art bus to a state-of-the-art school—an *integrated* school.[15]

His joy turned to frustration as he read the boasts of the Alabama politicians who assured their constituents they had no intention of carrying out the ruling. Then in 1955, his frustration turned to fear, anger, and disillusion.

> I was shaken to the core by the killing of Emmett Till. I was fifteen, black, at the edge of my own manhood, just like him. *That* could have been me, beaten, tortured, dead at the bottom of a

river. It had been only a year since I was so elated at the *Brown*
decision. Now I felt like a fool.[16]

But Lewis did not give up on *Brown*'s promise of equal access to
education, and he determined he would challenge the segregated
state university system of Alabama. After finishing high school, he
had obtained a full scholarship to American Baptist College, a
small Bible school in Nashville, Tennessee. Ironically, American
Baptist was an institution created by segregation. Funded by the
"generosity" of white Baptists, its purpose was to prepare "Negroes" to be pastors to segregated churches. While he loved American Baptist, the continuing injustice of his exclusion from his own
state's educational system still gnawed at Lewis's soul. During
Christmas break of 1957, his first year in college, he hatched a
plan to become the test case at Troy State, located just a few miles
from his home in Alabama. He applied to Troy and, receiving no
response, he wrote a letter to Dr. Martin Luther King Jr., then pastor of a church in Montgomery, Alabama.[17] Lewis had heard King
preach on the radio and admired him beyond measure. King sum-
moned him to Montgomery, and, after doing his best to scare the
young man off a path he knew would be hard and dangerous, he
agreed to support him. There was one hitch, however. As a minor,
John Lewis would need his parents' permission.[18] After much soul
searching, his parents refused. Lewis's father worked for the
county, and they feared he would lose his job, be denied credit at
the local feed stores, and lose the land they had worked so hard to
buy. Lewis understood their fears, and he accepted their authority
to veto his plan. But he was deeply disappointed.

When Lewis entered American Baptist, the age of majority in
most of the United States was twenty-one. It took a generation of
activism and the Vietnam War to get an amendment that lowered
the minimum voting age to match the minimum draft age. Given
his status as a minor, even if Lewis had been backed by a powerful
organization with lawyers and war chests for litigation expenses, as
an eighteen- or nineteen-year-old he could not file a civil case to
challenge the validity of a law. But, as Lewis would soon learn, he

could get into court to test an unjust law any time he wanted simply by breaking it. Getting himself booked, fingerprinted, and jailed—a matter of deepest shame to his elders—was the fastest way to the Supreme Court and the only way open to a minor whose parents were too weary or too afraid to confront the status quo. If minors could not get to court as civil plaintiffs, like Linda Brown who had her father's support, they could and did get there as criminal defendants.

Lewis gave up his plan to attend Troy and went back to American Baptist. During his second year at college, he began attending Lawson's workshops and participated in planning and carrying out the first organized Nashville sit-ins. His experiences may have played a role in shaping the direct action tactics of the student movement. Early on, the Nashville students considered a proposal favored by some of the group that students who were minors would only be allowed to participate in sit-ins if their parents had signed releases. The students rejected this idea as wrong and unworkable. Realistically, few parents would have signed. Most of their parents opposed their activism because they were afraid for their children's futures.

When the SNCC students, most of them under twenty-one, dispensed with the idea of asking for parental permission and began to mobilize their fellows to challenge the law through direct action, they crossed a legal line older and more firmly entrenched than the color lines of Jim Crow. The injunction to "Honor thy Father" was deeply ingrained in law and society. In their personal lives, students handled the clash between filial duty and conscience in a range of ways—some hiding the truth from families far away, some defying parental injunctions, and some bowing to adult pressure. Lewis states quite simply that he "lost his family" in 1960 when he was arrested.[19] It was many years before the wounds caused by his disobedience healed and he could truly go home again.

But the civil rights movement was facing a policy crisis as well as a personal crisis. The SNCC leaders' decision to dispense with parental permission raised a larger and more complex issue for the students and for those elders who, like Martin Luther King Jr., supported their strategy. Once the age line of majority had been breached, where would it stop? If an eighteen- or nineteen-year-old was fair game, although still legally a minor, why not a seventeen-year-old or a sixteen-year-old? Middle schoolers were, if anything, more passionate and effective foot soldiers than high schoolers.[20]

Movement leaders understood that children's innocence, idealism, and courage were valuable resources. It was common knowledge among organizers like James Bevel and Bernard Lafayette, who set out intentionally to mobilize the kids of Montgomery and Selma, Alabama, of Albany, Georgia, and of Jackson, Mississippi, that the younger the demonstrator, the greater his or her fearlessness.[21] And the younger the marchers, the more shock value in seeing police or mob violence directed against them and the greater the effects on America's awakening conscience. But was it morally defensible or morally reprehensible to use mere children in this manner?

Like it nor not, the children were already both literally and figuratively at the heart of the movement. Children had joined in the 1957 Montgomery Boycott. They had integrated all white schools in test cases like *Brown*.[22] They were the very reason (so their elders often told them) the struggle was worthwhile.[23] Throughout the struggle, images of children played a central role in the rhetoric of movement leaders and in the motivations of its rank and file. Rereading the letters and speeches of the Rev. Martin Luther King Jr., brought home to me how often the child appears as a metaphor for hope and for humankind at its best. Recall how King used the metaphor of the white child and the black child walking hand in hand, in his famous speech "I Have a Dream." Children play an important role in King's Letter from a Birmingham Jail, explaining to whites who had criticized the movement why the black community could no longer wait patiently for change to come.

> Maybe it is easy for those who have never felt the stinging darts of segregation to say "Wait." . . . [But w]hen you suddenly find your tongue twisted and your speech stammering as you seek to explain to your six-year-old daughter why she can't go to the public

amusement park that has just been advertised on television, and see tears welling up in her eyes when she is told that Funtown is closed to colored children, and see ominous clouds of inferiority beginning to form in her little mental sky, and see her beginning to distort her personality by developing an unconscious bitterness toward white people; when you have to concoct an answer to a five-year-old son who is asking, "Daddy, why do white people treat colored people so mean?"[24]

For a parent faced with explaining a hundred years of Jim Crow to an inquiring child, patience was no longer an option. Viewed through the eyes of their children, insults and indignities that had become routine regained their raw power to wound and their ability to outrage. Elders who had grown weary or fearful rallied to the fight because they knew their children could not wait. The directness of children's questions was matched by the directness of their actions. While their parents needed to earn a living and could be intimidated by threats against their jobs and their persons, children and youths were less encumbered.

In Birmingham in the spring of 1963, when the movement's momentum flagged, Halberstam relates how the young leaders of SNCC and the Southern Christian Leadership Conference (SCLC) pushed Dr. King to agree to their recruiting and training school-aged children to join in the protest.[25] For a time, according to Halberstam's sources, King reluctantly agreed but drew the line at fourteen. The strategy—referred to as the Children's Crusade—was wildly successful. Large numbers of students were recruited and sent to their local churches to see a film about the Nashville sit-in movement so they would understand the principles of nonviolent protest.[26] By the end of the first day, almost one thousand Birmingham children had been arrested and jailed.[27] On the second day, a thousand more children gathered to march. Bull Connor, the vicious police chief who became a symbol worldwide of police brutality, turned high velocity fire hoses and unleashed police dogs on the children. Even TV viewers who had doubts about the confrontational tactics of adult movement activists were appalled as they witnessed these innocents being brutalized by uniformed bullies with clubs, fire hoses, and snarling dogs. *Eyes on the Prize* recounts how one skeptical adult from the black community was instantly converted to the movement's cause. A conservative businessman, he was on the telephone complaining to a movement lawyer that King's strategies were too confrontational. As he spoke, he looked out his window and witnessed the police turning fire hoses exerting 100 pounds of pressure per square inch on a group of children. He saw a little black girl being violently rolled down the street by the blast of water. He hung up and rushed to her rescue.[28] Some of the most dramatic photographs and footage of the movement came from the Children's Crusade. Even in still pictures—like the ones that stuck in John Lewis's memory of a dog attacking a teenage boy and of a little girl in a pleated skirt sent sprawling by a torrent of water—the violence and ugliness of segregation are palpable. In all, an estimated *ten thousand* Birmingham children were arrested and jailed. When the city's jails were filled, they bussed children to a holding pen at the state fairgrounds.[29] The city's resistance was broken.

How did the young people experience being movement foot soldiers? Ellen Levine, author of *Freedom's Children*, wanted to give these children, now adults, a chance to tell their stories in their own words. Of course, by the time she got started, thirty years had passed, so she had her work cut out for her, tracking down and interviewing as many adults as she could find who had participated as children in the major events of the period from 1955 to 1965. Her book reproduces verbatim the spoken recollections of thirty different individuals.[30] While these recollections are filtered through the memories and minds of the grown-ups these children became, their unique perspective as children and teenagers shines through. All were under eighteen when they first became active in the movement and about half were fourteen or younger. These are not the reflections of passive observers—this is no "where were you on the day of the assassination" kind of book. Their stories are vivid personal accounts of marching, arrests, murders, beatings, and bombings. They describe in detail the methods of training for nonviolent action, their own doubts, fears, and triumphs, and their own reasons for being part of the struggle. Ben Chaney, brother of James Chaney who was murdered with two white civil rights workers in the summer of 1964, was arrested more than twenty-one times before he was twelve years old. Multiple arrests were quite typical. Many children witnessed attacks on their families, homes, and churches, and many shed their own blood in the struggle. Some were born into the movement and followed in their parents' footsteps. Birmingham civil rights leader Rev. Fred Shuttlesworth's three children, Fred Jr., Patricia, and Ricky were ten, eleven, and thirteen respectively when their home was nearly destroyed by a bomb. Fred developed a stutter—a symptom of the traumatic effects of the bombing. The next year, the two girls and their parents were attacked by a mob as they tried to register in an all white school. The girls saw their father beaten and their mother stabbed during the mob violence at the schoolhouse and they narrowly escaped injury themselves. Many other children participated in spite of their parents' objections, and even persuaded their parents to join them in marching and picketing. Levine's project documents that many teenaged and preteen children all across the South, not just in Birmingham's "Children's Crusade," wanted to be part of the movement, embraced nonviolence, and were effective in mobilizing not only their peers but also their parents.

Their first-person accounts carry the simplicity and directness of authenticity. Listen to Audrey Faye Hendricks, whose pastor and her mother were both active in the movement. At age nine, she may have been the youngest marcher jailed during the Birmingham Children's Crusade in 1963:

> There was no way for me not to know about the movement. . . . I think my very first recollection of what was going on was at a church meeting. I was about seven. They were going to have a small demonstration. I remember leaving the church and walking out to watch the first demonstrators. There was an elderly black man watching, and a dog attacked him. I was in shock. I just couldn't believe that the police would turn the dog loose on an old man.[31]

Soon, this child began attending mass meetings. "The night before [her arrest in 1963], at a meeting, they told us we'd be arrested. I went home and told my mother that I wanted to go. She just said, 'Okay.' I was in third grade. My teacher knew that I was going and she cried." After Audrey's arrest, "they took me to a room where there were some men who asked me questions about the mass meetings. I was nervous when they first called me in. I didn't know what they were going to do to me. The worst thing I thought was that they might kill me. . . . [I]t crossed my mind. It was a room of five or six men. All white. And I was little."[32] After fifteen minutes of questions aimed at learning which "communistic" outsiders put them up to this and whether the children were forced to march, she was sent back to juvenile hall. She was held for seven days, during which she was prevented from speaking with her parents.

Larry Russell, age sixteen, like many of his classmates, hid his involvement from his parents as long as he could. The teenagers knew when a mass meeting was scheduled from coded messages broadcast each morning by sympathetic radio disc jockeys. Larry recalled the exact day he was first arrested—June 9, 1963. "Once the gate was closed, we were treated like common criminals. We weren't treated like kids. They didn't want the jails filled. They wanted to make it uncomfortable for us so we'd call our parents to come and bail us out." Instead, when he called his mother he told her that, whatever she did, he did not want her to come and get him out. "She was concerned. She sounded tearful on the other end. I said, 'Please, this is what I want to do.' She said, 'Okay.' I was in for ten days."[33]

As Halberstam tells the story of the Children's Crusade, the most ardent advocate of children's rights was James Bevel, a young minister working with Martin Luther King's SCLC in the Deep South. Bevel had been a SNCC founder and had married Diane Nash, SNCC's first chairperson. By all accounts, Bevel was famous for his radical stands and for his joy in what we would now call "pushing the envelope." His arguments were both pragmatic and theological. Were not children the very group that suffered most from racism and had the most to gain from ending it? Wasn't it time to stop sheltering them and involve them in the struggle that could make or break their futures? And if the Baptist church was ready to accept their decisions to give their souls to Jesus, baptizing them as early as age five and six, why were they barred from joining in this holy crusade?[34]

Bevel's arguments were not plucked out of thin air. They were grounded on his own ministry among the children and teens of Jackson, Mississippi, and they were grounded in the Gospel. Bevel talked directly to kids. In some accounts of children's engagement in the movement, children were contacted through elders who mobilized youth in their communities. Youngsters attended mass meetings in churches. But Bevel talked to kids wherever he could find them—in playgrounds and schoolyards and on the street. Playing on his credentials as a Freedom Rider, he helped them convert their anger and their thirst for revenge into a thirst for justice. He would challenge them to show the kind of real courage it takes to stand up to bullies and racists in front of the cops and in the full light of day—without a gun or a fist or a club in your hand. He trained his young recruits in the practices and core beliefs of nonviolence. Bevel respected kids and admired their will to survive without being victimized by the brutal culture of violence around them. Rather than "protecting" them, he issued a challenge. They reciprocated his respect and answered his challenge. The law was not so enlightened. Bevel was charged with seventy counts of contributing to the delinquency of a minor, and it took all his considerable skills in advocacy to get off with a suspended two-year prison sentence.[35]

If Dr. King was ambivalent, as Halberstam's account seems to suggest, the children interviewed by Levine certainly did not sense it. To the contrary, the word pictures they paint of King include telling details suggesting an active outreach to children. Many children and teens recalled the timbre of his voice, the personal notice he took of them, and the comfort of his presence. Myrna Carter, a teenager arrested in the Birmingham Children's Crusade, describes the mass meeting when she decided to commit to the struggle. King asked the students if they wished to commit to the movement, but told them that they had to be able to take an oath to be nonviolent—that if anything happened they would turn the other cheek. Myrna volunteered. When she came to the church the next day for her instructions, King spoke to them again.

> At first I thought I was going to be afraid, but somehow the fear went. The drawing power in Dr. King's voice was like that of no one else who was connected to the struggle. It wasn't that we worshipped him. We certainly did not. He wasn't like that at all. I think that's why he had that power that could make you actually leap and you didn't realize you were leaping.[36]

Fred Taylor was thirteen when the Birmingham bus boycott began. Here is how he describes King's effect on him.

> He would talk about the fact that you are somebody and you are important. This was compared to my orientation of being put down or told, "Boy, you are not going to be anything." A classic example was people would say, "You knotty-head boy, why don't you sit down." But when King started talking, he'd say, "You are somebody." And that began to rub off on me. It was right during the boycott that I began to have a different assessment of myself as an individual and to feel my sense of self worth. Not only did it affect me, but I began to look at my family and how the white community related to them.[37]

Youngest among the marchers was Sheyann Webb, who began marching at age eight. In 1979, she and her friend Rachel Nelson told their story to Frank Sikora, in a book titled *Selma Lord Selma*. A photograph from those days shows Sheyann in a ruffled skirt, the smallest in a human chain of protesters. In one of her earliest memories of Dr. Martin Luther King, he saw the little girls and asked them what they wanted. They answered shyly "freedom," but he kept acting as if he couldn't hear them until they finally shouted the word as loud as they could and dissolved in giggles. " 'I heard you that time,' he says. 'You want freedom? Well, so do I.' We got to be friends from then on. Everytime he'd see us he'd play that little game with us, asking what we wanted, pretending he couldn't hear what we'd say until we were shouting at the top of our lungs, 'Freedom!' "[38]

Like John Lewis, Sheyann Webb was a strong-willed child who refused to heed her parents' fears and rejected their assumption that nothing would ever change. Had King and the other movement leaders come into John Lewis's Alabama town when he was eight, he would probably have done just as Sheyann did—siding with these shining new heroes despite his elders' fears and apprehensions. Sheyann argued constantly with her parents, trying to persuade them to the cause. She snuck out without permission to attend the marches and the mass meetings. Sheyann's mother pleaded with her to stay away from the marches. She was afraid she would lose her job if her white employer learned that their daughter was involved. She held up the scary example of the four Birmingham girls who had been murdered two years earlier, all to no avail.[39] As this independent eight-year-old listened, and especially as she joined in singing the freedom songs, she was drawn into the heart of the movement. "So many black people not only could not vote, but they were even afraid to try to register. I knew that night that being a part of that nonviolent army Dr. King had spoken of was going to be the most important thing in my life. I thought of the stanza in the song We Shall Overcome that 'God is on our side.' With the depth that only a child's mind could feel, I believed those words, believed them dearly."[40]

Sheyann was one of the marchers who gathered at Brown Chapel on March 7, 1965. As she set out on the protest march from Selma to Montgomery with a large group of people of all ages, she did not know that the march would end just a few blocks after it started, on Edmund Pettus Bridge, in the violent assault by Alabama police and state troopers that went down in history as "Bloody Sunday." When Sheyann got to the church to begin the march, "I remember Mrs. Moore telling me that I should go back home, and I was saying that I was going to march. I got in the midway of the march. As usual, we knelt down to pray, and after we had prayed, we began to sing." As the marchers crested the Edmund Pettus Bridge, and were able to see the other side, Sheyann got a child's eye view of a scene that caused shock waves around the world: She looked out and saw literally "hundreds of policeman. The helmets, state troopers, dogs and horses, police cars. I got even more frightened then. I began to hold Mrs. Moore's hand tighter, and the person's hand on the other side of me. My heart was beginning to beat real, real fast. I looked up at Mrs. Moore and I wanted to say, 'I want to go home,' but I didn't. She was looking straight ahead. Then the people began to kneel down and pray again." Within seconds, the first tear gas canisters exploded and the police waded into the crowd of marchers beating them with their clubs and unleashing their police dogs (Fig. 4). The marchers turned and tried to retreat. Dogs and horses were trampling them. She could hear people "screaming and hollering." With the marchers and their attackers surging around her, her one thought was to run back home. Near the bottom of the bridge, Selma civil rights leader Hosea Williams, also fleeing as fast as he could, picked her up. "I told him to put me down 'cause he wasn't running fast enough."[41] Her terrified parents were waiting at the door, and this time they locked her in her room to prevent her from going back to the church. She lay on her bed, sobbing with fright and shock. "I remember taking out a pencil and writing down how I felt and what I saw. Then I wrote down my funeral arrangements because, even with what I saw, I still wanted to go out and fight. And I said if I did that, I would probably die. So I wrote down my funeral arrangements."[42]

Sheyann did not escape unscathed. As late as 1979, she still had nightmares about the horsemen, the masked riders coming through the clouds of tear gas, wielding whips and clubs, and the people screaming. She was often afraid and sometimes, when people she knew were killed or beaten, she almost doubted that the Lord was really going to come to Selma, as she had asked Him to do in song.[43] But Sheyann continued to fight, returning to Brown Chapel for the next wave of demonstrations. By now her parents had joined her. Like many others in Selma and across the land, they had been shocked out of their cocoon of fear, denial, and despair by the sight of peaceable men, women, and children being savagely

Fig. 4. John Lewis on Edmund Pettus Bridge in Selma, Alabama, on Sunday March 7, 1965 (courtesy of the Library of Congress).

attacked by armed militia. In hindsight, the children of the movement had been right all along. They knew that they might die, but they believed the cause was worth the price.

The children of the movement were vindicated by history, and those who marched and went to jail were able to say "I told you so." Towanner Hinkle was sixteen when she defied her parents to join in the protests in Selma in 1965. "[My mother] said, 'I don't want you in jail 'cause you'll have a record the rest of your life.' She was worried I'd get killed. Those kids had got bombed in Birmingham [1963]. I said, 'Mamma, I'm going.'" With the perspective of thirty years, Towanner looks back at the brutality and violence of the whites at the time and believes it is a wonder she and her friends were not all killed. But they *did* survive. And the movement *did* follow them for life, but not in the way their parents had feared. Towanner grew up to be a deputy voting registrar in Selma. "I've had interviews for jobs and they say, 'Have you ever been arrested?' I say, 'Yes, I've been to jail a lot of times.' They look at me real funny. And I say, 'I went to jail for marching with the movement.' 'Oh, don't even worry about that,' they say."[44] They were scared, they were beaten, and they bled. But not one of the thirty children profiled in *Freedom's Children* regrets having risked his or her life, and to a man and a woman they regard the experience as the most formative and inspiring of their lives. Fred Taylor, who grew up to become a minister and a leader in the SCLC, put it this way: "The movement gave me a sense of somebodyness. I was the first person in my immediate family to even finish high school. If the movement had not happened, I don't know where I would have ended up in life."[45] Says James Roberson, "I was blessed to live then. I lived in a poor section of Birmingham, next to a church where a country minister began to say it's time for a change. I would not exchange the experience of living on that street corner and in that section for anything in the world."[46]

Having read many movement memoirs by children and young adults, I believe there is another crucial piece of the puzzle that explains why they seem to have been able to withstand exposure at a young age to such concentrated hatred and ugliness. It was a factor that child psychiatrist Robert Coles identified at the time, in assessing why some children seemed to handle unimaginable stresses so well. At watershed moments in the movement, these children were able to draw strength from the examples around them of hope and belief in nonviolence. They were arrested and beaten, but they did not themselves commit crimes of violence. One might even say that, metaphorically speaking, these children were able to do battle and witness terrible evils without losing their innocence. They were shielded from harm by a deeply held belief in their own goodness as well as in the goodness of their people and the goodness of their cause.

Like Dr. King's child who asked "why do white folks treat colored folks so mean?" many of the children had been baffled at why light-skinned people were so mean to brown-skinned people. When they saw white people beating other white people, attacking "their own," they suddenly understood that the whites who were doing the beating were just mean, hate-filled people. Not all children are tough and resilient as so many of these young folks seem to have been, but many children are. This quality of optimism and resilience, of finding strength in relationships of love, has been identified as a key element in determining how well a particular child will be able to survive traumatic events. One other thing made these children different from others who witnessed or were victims of violence. The children who enlisted as foot soldiers in the movement were not coerced, nor were they swept up as victims of senseless violence—they were volunteers in a battle against violence. Over and over, in many variations on a single theme, they tell us that they were not afraid because they knew they were doing the right thing. I suspect that the very children who were most drawn to the preaching of leaders like Martin Luther King and Fred Shuttlesworth were also the ones most likely to possess the strengths that would bring them through the struggle emotionally intact.

We have known for years about many of the children who were active in the movement through the images of media coverage. The television cameras were rolling in Arkansas when the Little Rock Nine (Jefferson Thomas, Carlotta Walls, Gloria Ray, Elizabeth

Eckford, Thelma Mothershed, Melba Pattillo, Terrence Roberts, Minnijean Brown, and Ernest Green) braved screaming mobs of thousands to integrate Central High School. Anyone who harbors the illusion that their terror and trauma ended when they were escorted up the steps by federal troops must read Melba Pattillo Beals's stark memoir, *Warriors Don't Cry*. Melba and her peers survived nine months of unimaginable violence, harassment, and terror that left them forever changed. All grew up to be successful and respected members of their communities, but only one stayed in Little Rock.[47]

We also know the names of the many other children whose cases are memorialized in Supreme Court decisions. A child's name identifies the most famous Supreme Court case of the twentieth century, that of seven-year-old Linda Brown, lead plaintiff in *Brown v. Board of Education*. Twelve-year-old Spottswood Bolling Jr. is the child behind *Sharpe v. Bolling*, and the list goes on, continuing to this day, in cases brought to vindicate children's rights with the approval and support of their parents. These children, unlike those involved in "direct action," put their names out front and then followed with their bodies. They first obtained a ruling giving them the protection of the law and then challenged the segregationists to violate federal court orders.

Maybe it is inevitable that the rank and file in a movement will march in anonymity. The ambivalence we feel about recruitment of children to serve on the front lines might explain why the names of so many of these children are missing from books like Halberstam's *Children*. But I also found evidence that the legal status of the children as minors played a role in rendering their heroism invisible to history. Children report being arrested and detained but not booked or fingerprinted, because they were under the age of eighteen. I came across a vivid example of how children can disappear from the record. In October of 2000, in honor of the fortieth anniversary of the Jackson, Mississippi, civil rights movement, The Jackson *Sun* produced a series of "news accounts" of the protests, apparently to atone in some measure for the white-owned newspaper's having suppressed coverage of these events when they happened. One article listed the names of 134 of the 144 marchers arrested on November 8, 1960. It must have been a matter of great pride for those 134 marchers of forty years before to see their names in print. But what happened to the final ten names? As the *Sun* reporter explains, these marchers were juveniles, and therefore their names were not preserved in the record and have been lost to history.[48] We owe a debt to Ellen Levine and others who have worked to document the stories of these unknown soldiers.

The story of the movement's children, the youngest martyrs and the youngest marchers, highlights the tensions between our desire to protect children from danger and pain and the reality that children's engagement is inescapable. Whether we like it or not, children will be victims, actors, and citizens in whatever society we have created for them. We continue to have child martyrs, but rarely will the newspapers publish pictures of them as *Jet* published the images of Emmett Till. As an advocate for children, I have heard well-meaning people and state child welfare officials argue that we must protect the privacy of a child who dies because of abuse or neglect. Often, the files that tell the stories of these children's deaths are "sealed" by law. We read in the newspaper harrowing descriptions by neighbors of their torture, but accompanied by images of the victim's smiling face from a happier day. I have long been suspicious that these privacy claims protect the interests and feelings of those who are complicit (directly or indirectly) in these tragic deaths of children, far more than they protect the children. Evidence of the most fundamental invasion of privacy imaginable, the act of murder, these children's stories are censored to protect the innocence of adults. Researching Emmett Till and the other child martyrs of the movement has persuaded me that there is a value to full disclosure to the public of the facts and the images of murdered children.

From a developmental perspective, children's agency and voice should be valued and nurtured, not suppressed. While children should be shielded from exposure to violent images beyond their capacity to understand and place in context, they cannot and should not be cocooned from reality. Harm to children comes not from knowing about the reality of violence, but from seeing it as inevitable and even heroic. Far from disarming our teens with talk of courageous nonviolence, as James Bevel and Martin Luther King did, we seem intent on arming them for revenge. Reading about Bevel's conversations with the kids of Jackson and Birmingham brought to mind a modern-day teacher and hero—Geoffrey Canada. Canada grew up in the toughest section of New York, earned a doctorate at Harvard, and came back to New York to work with kids like himself. His book, titled *Fist Stick Knife Gun*, chronicles the escalation of violence in children's lives and the horrible toll it is taking on young black boys and girls.[49] Like Bevel and Lawson, Canada learned at an early age that "violence is a circle" and violence only begets violence. At our Center on Children and Families conference on "Children, Culture, and Violence" I saw him enthrall an audience with a demonstration of how he used his skill in the martial arts to draw boys into a dialogue that would challenge a culture that makes violence inflicted with fists, guns, and knives into the emblems of manhood.[50]

Children have both needs-based and capacity-based rights to agency and voice. Children need to interact with their social environments, to see and be seen, and to hear and be heard within the microsystems where they live, and eventually in the social environment at large. Rather than fearing children's power and action, parents and mentors can help children find their own voices and exercise their agency in positive and constructive ways.

PART III

THE EQUALITY PRINCIPLE: STORIES
OF EQUAL OPPORTUNITY

CHAPTER 8

OLD MAIDS AND LITTLE WOMEN

Louisa Alcott and William Cather

Too much physical overwork, too much hurried study or worry, or the additional strenuousness of an exciting outside life will result in the complete wrecking of every power which goes to make up perfect womanhood and future motherhood.

 —1903 statement by a female doctor on child rearing[1]

Historically, American boys and girls, whatever their parents' status, inhabited different worlds. Childhood invariably reflects society's expectations for adulthood and, in nineteenth-century America, gender cut a wide swath across every form of cultural expectation. Boys were expected to graduate into manhood, and full political and social citizenship was reserved for men only. Girls were expected to graduate into motherhood. Spinsterhood was an aberration. The great divide between men's lives and those of women widened during the Victorian era, with the growth of a potent ideology of femininity often called the "Cult of Domesticity" or "the Cult of True Womanhood."[2] Modern girls can hardly imagine the oppressive reality of being a "young lady" in the middle-class Victorian household. While Dred Scott's daughters Eliza and Lizzie contended with the effects of race, class, and gender, the girls profiled in this chapter were from the privileged middle classes. These were relatively lucky girls—educated, of English heritage, from "good" families—whose brothers and cousins had the world as their oyster. These girls were often stunned and angry to learn, as they approached adolescence, that gender and gender alone stood between them and their dreams of glory. But, as the stories that follow will show, female children exhibited agency and voice in challenging the dominant gender expectations of their times. In doing so, they changed the shape of womanhood for generations to come.

Ten-year-old Louy was the second of four children. It was well known within the family that Louy was different—marked from birth by "the wild exuberance of a powerful nature" and more "fit for the scuffle" than for civilized society. Louy possessed an innate love of speed and a keen instinct for rough and tumble competition. "I must have been a deer or horse in some former state, because it was such a joy to run." "No boy could be my friend till I had beaten him in a race, and no girl if she refused to climb trees, leap fences and be a tomboy."[3] But Louy's powerful nature, wild exuberance and competitive instincts were seen as liabilities to be overcome, rather than assets to be fostered and admired. This ten-year-old's journal documents a constant battle between a wild and independent nature and the claims of civilization, duty, and obedience. Here are some entries, characteristic of that heartfelt struggle:

> *September 1, 1843* I rose at five and had my bath. I love cold water! . . . After breakfast, I washed dishes and then ran on the hill until nine, and had some thoughts—it was so beautiful up there. . . . We had bread and fruit for dinner. I read and walked and played till supper-time. As I went to bed, the moon came up very brightly and looked at me. I felt sad because I have been cross to-day and did not mind Mother. I cried, and then I felt better, and then said that piece from Mrs. Sigourney, "I must not tease my mother." I get to sleep saying poetry. I know a great deal.

October 8th, 1843 When I woke up, the first thought I got was, "It's Mother's birthday: I must be very good." I ran and wished her a happy birthday, and gave her my kiss. After breakfast we gave her our presents. I had a moss cross and a piece of poetry for her. We did not have any school and played in the woods and got red leaves. In the evening, we danced and sung and I read a story about "Contentment." I wish I was rich, I was good, and we were all a happy family this day.

Thursday, November 29, 1843 It was Father's and my birthday. We had some nice presents. We played in the snow before school. . . . Father asked us in the eve what fault troubled us most. I said my bad temper.

In sharp distinction to the modern notion of a journal as a uniquely private space, Louy's was an open book to Mother, who often read and wrote in it, adding such comments as this one, on the occasion of Louy's tenth birthday. "Go on trying, dear, and each day it will be easier to be and do good. You must help yourself, for the cause of your little troubles is in yourself; and patience and courage only will make you what mother prays to see you— her good and happy girl."

As you may have guessed, Louy grew up to be the Victorian author Louisa May Alcott, who popularized the heroic figure of the exuberant and risk-taking tomboy. Redheaded Jo March, her creation and alter ego, has come to symbolize the American girl, portrayed in countless illustrated books, collector dolls, and Hollywood films. Filmmakers and marketing directors have made Jo conventionally beautiful, but Alcott did not. Here is how Alcott describes her alter ego in the pages of *Little Women*:

Fifteen-year-old Jo was very tall, thin, and brown, and reminded one of a colt, for she never seemed to know what to do with her long limbs, which were very much in her way. She had a decided mouth, a comical nose, and sharp, gray eyes, which appeared to see everything, and were by turns fierce, funny, or thoughtful. Her long, thick hair was her one beauty, but it was usually bundled into a net, to be out of her way. Round shoulders had Jo, big hands and feet, a fly-away look to her clothes, and the uncomfortable appearance of a girl who was rapidly shooting up into a woman and didn't like it.[4]

This description brilliantly captured the awkward situation of a budding female who cannot or will not conform to accepted stereotypes of feminine smallness, softness, and docility.

Many of the differences in the lives of boys and girls, and men and women, that are reflected in Alcott's world were culturally enforced, but many were embodied in written laws. After passage of the Civil War Amendments, the U.S. Constitution, at least in theory, had finally guaranteed all men basic civil rights regardless of race. However, the laws continued to divide people according to gender, assigning the subordinate role to women. Unlike Frederick Douglass's white male playmates, antebellum girls, North and South, could look forward to a sharply limited version of emancipation when they reached adulthood. At age twenty-one, boys became men. Girls, upon marriage, became one person with their husband, and their "very being or legal existence . . . is incorporated and consolidated into that of the husband."[5] A girl who married before the age of majority might pass directly from the status of daughter to that of wife, never achieving the status of a legally empowered individual. Unmarried women were old maids to be pitied because they lacked the protection of males. All adult females, especially married women, remained in a state of perpetual legal childhood—unable to vote, their property rights circumscribed, presumed unfit for jury and military service, barred from professions, and routinely denied educational opportunity.[6] Effectively banished from "public" life, women were confined to the "private" world of the family. Ironically, while women played the primary role in birth and nurture, and their household labor was essential to the family economy, they were assigned a distinctly secondary and legally limited role in family governance as well.[7]

The message imparted to Douglass, that education would certainly "ruin" a good slave, was paraphrased many times over in advice on how to raise daughters. As late as 1903, a *female* physician advised the following regarding the education of young girls, aged eleven to seventeen:

> In the important change taking place at this age (puberty) the whole nervous system is taxed to its utmost in furnishing force to develop a perfect growth of the generative organs and at the same time to maintain nutrition throughout the body. Too much physical overwork, too much hurried study or worry, or the additional strenuousness of an exciting outside life will result in the complete wrecking of every power which goes to make up perfect womanhood and future motherhood. It is not only good hygiene to lighten the strain of study by taking two or three years longer to complete the course, but it is wise for the mother to keep girls out of school entirely for long periods at a time at this age, especially if there is evidence of nervous strain and debility.[8]

An illustration in this same volume, in the section on "Education," depicts two girls of about ten or eleven in frilly frocks, seated at a small table in a Victorian drawing room. They are studying cards in their hands, but they are not gambling, learning the art of oratory, or even practicing for a spelling bee. The caption, "Old Maid," tells us they are playing a card game in which the point is to avoid being left holding the card with the face of an unmarried woman. More powerfully than mere words, such games conveyed the message that remaining unattached and independent was the essence of female failure.

Middle- and upper-class families might coddle and confine their young daughters, ensuring their dependency while protecting their procreative organs, but working-class girls, farmers and immigrants, not to mention girls of color, experienced no such coddling. Listen to the complaint, on the subject of gender discrimination and women's labor, of a North Dakota farmer's daughter growing up around the turn of the century. "[We girls] worked like slaves to build the sod house, barn and other abodes. Plus all the man and house work. After we had grown up and left home, our father gave all the homestead enterprise to his oldest son."[9] Rich or poor, whatever their race or ethnicity, girls were caught in a double bind. For most girls, the ideal of true womanhood would remain illusory. Working their fingers to the bone in home *and* factory, and selling their labor for pennies to keep their children fed, poor women were stigmatized for falling short of the middle-class ideal of perfect motherhood. The "lucky" few who had families affluent enough to keep them in sheltered dependency were denied the education and opportunities provided to their brothers. All girls suffered the inequality of gender discrimination. Whether acculturated to feminine passivity or prematurely worn down by women's work, they were relegated to a subservient status based solely on having been born girls instead of boys.

The title of this chapter, "Old Maids and Little Women," is meant to honor Louisa May Alcott's struggle, beginning in early childhood, to balance the demands of domesticity with her own drive for independence and competitive achievement. Alcott freely chose the life of an "old maid," never marrying and devoting herself to a career that would bring not only fame but also the ability to support her family in comfort. But she could not allow her literary alter ego, the tomboyish Jo of *Little Women*, the same autonomy in matters of marriage and career. Headstrong Jo must be domesticated—must marry and settle down—in order for the book to reach a socially acceptable conclusion. Nor could she allow herself the freedom for which the teenaged Jo had yearned. Alcott's life and her work illustrate the transcendent moral power of domesticity, but also reveal the awful disabilities imposed on growing girls, gently but relentlessly inculcated by devoted mothers and sisters to their destinies as ("little") women. From a very early age, Louy embraced a goal that was inconsistent with perfect freedom. Much as she wished to be free to express her talents, her greatest ambition was to win her struggle to be "good"—and goodness meant being good to and providing for her family. Much as she loved her family, she craved a space of her own. As biographer Cary Ryan points out, when Louisa was finally given a room of her own, it was not only a milestone in achieving some measure of privacy but also a "symbol of passage into womanhood—a fitting place to pledge herself to the duty she would shoulder till her death." And this is exactly what she did. In a diary entry of March 1846, thirteen-year-old Louy writes:

> I have at last got the little room I have wanted for so long, and I am very happy about it. It does me good to be alone, and Mother has made it very pretty and neat for me. My workbasket and desk are by the window, and my closet is full of dried herbs that smell very nice. The door that opens into the garden will be very pretty in summer, and I can run off to the woods when I like.
>
> I have made a plan for my life, as I am in my teens, and no more a child. I am old for my age, and don't care much for girl's things. People think I'm wild and queer; but mother understands and helps me. I have not told anyone about my plan; but I'm going to *be* good. I've made so many resolutions, and written sad notes, and cried over my sins, and it doesn't seem to do any good! Now I am going to *work really*, for I feel a sincere desire to improve, and be a help and comfort, not a care and sorrow, to my dear mother.[10]

Indeed, as Alcott's life and letters demonstrate, she remained true to the promise made at age thirteen, and measured her success by her ability to provide materially and emotionally for her family—from ribbons and art lessons for Sister May to a comfortable old age for her mother and father. But she worked a double shift, as both the wage-earning male and the nurturing female. As bound to the work of hearth and home as any lawful wife, she crammed her writing into the small spaces of time left over from caring for ailing parents, supporting her sisters through their travails, in schooling, childbirth, and widowhood, and raising the orphaned nieces and nephews they left behind. She also made time to support causes such as Abolition and the Woman's Suffrage Movement, but as she wrote to Suffragist Lucy Stone in 1873, "I am so busy just now proving 'Woman's Right to Labor' that I have no time to help prove 'Woman's Right to Vote.'"[11] But she was only being modest. During the last decade of her life, Alcott led a local movement to gain municipal suffrage, staunchly predicting that, once the ice was broken, universal suffrage could not be far behind.

As I learned about the many domestic burdens assumed by the adult Miss Alcott, at first I mourned the passing of the rebellious tomboy Louy. But then it occurred to me that perhaps Louy Alcott had to die in order for Jo March to come alive. Perhaps Alcott was liberated to celebrate the wild tomboy in her mature writings because her capacity to tame this demon was no longer an issue. While she never married and never gave up her writing, she had committed herself to the burdens of domesticity. By the time Alcott wrote *Little Women*, she had already said goodbye to Louy and her headstrong ways, making the choice between freedom and goodness that had been pressed upon her by everyone she held dear, even her devoted mother. For whatever reason, Alcott was able to bring to life, as no other had dared to do, the spirit and daring of a girl who could challenge her assigned destiny and throw aside her needlework to run like a horse and fight like a boy, inspiring little girls everywhere to do the same. While compelled to marry off her first generation of heroines so they and their author could achieve respectability, Alcott refused to bow to public pressure and make Jo into a romantic heroine. As she explained in an 1869 letter to an instructor at Vassar College, " 'Jo' should have remained a literary spinster, but so many enthusiastic young ladies wrote to me clamorously demanding that she should marry Laurie, *or* somebody, that I didn't dare to refuse and out of perversity went and made a funny match for her."[12] By 1886, when Alcott published *Jo's Boys*, the last book in the *Little Women* series, she felt secure enough to send her female characters into careers as doctors and artists instead of to the altar. Alcott's new generation of heroines no longer had to decide between marriage and career. As illustrated by one girl who became a spinster physician and another who married without giving up her work as a sculptress, Jo's girls, like Jo's boys, could finally be happy, fulfilled, and even "good" without sacrificing their dreams of autonomy and individual achievement.

The tensions between feminine duty and masculine freedom that Alcott attempted to finesse in her life and her literature were confronted head on by writer Willa Cather, author of *Song of the Lark* and *My Ántonia*.[13] Unlike Alcott, Cather, who was born in 1873 and died in 1947, is not considered a "juvenile writer." She is recognized as among the greatest of American novelists. I feel a special connection to Cather because my grandmother, Eleanor Ferguson Wolfe, née Nellie Ferguson, worked with Cather when they were both teachers at Allegheny High School in Pittsburgh in the early 1900s. Grandma, who entered college in 1897, was the first person in her family (not to mention the first woman) to attend college—a major leap for any but the wealthiest girls in those days. As the family story goes, Nellie's shopkeeper parents realized their bookish but homely daughter could not count on her face to make her fortune (a euphemism for a "good marriage"), so they decided to encourage her to develop her brain power. They promised her a diamond ring if she graduated first in her high school class. As valedictorian in a class of hundreds of students, she not only got the ring, which I wear on my little finger, she also won a full scholarship to that temple of female excellence near Boston, Wellesley College. Although most of the students were refined upper-class girls, Wellesley also made room for gifted scholarship students. They were housed in a separate dorm and had to clean, cook, and serve at table, which their wealthy classmates did not. Fortunately for me, Grandma did capture a gentleman's heart despite her book learning. She married a widower with six children and of course, once she became pregnant with my mother, she retired from teaching since continuing to work in her "condition" would be unthinkable for a respectable man's wife.

But in 1904, Grandma had just been hired at Allegheny High School—the finest school in the city of Pittsburgh—along with the emerging literary figure Willa Cather. Cather was delighted at this job because it would give her more time to write. One of Cather's biographers reports that the school gave her an assistant, "a Wellesley girl, who eased the burden of reading and correcting student themes and gave her added hours to do her work."[14] Very likely, that "girl" was my grandmother. I knew that she had revered and admired Miss Cather. But I knew little else about the author's life. As with Alcott, I surmised that her work was autobiographical and that her girlhood experiences growing up in Red Cloud, Nebraska, were reflected in her tales of the plains and its pioneers.

Born in 1873, at a time when Alcott's *Little Women* series dominated the market in books for girls, Cather undoubtedly read Alcott. While Alcott wrote of growing up in the northeast, Cather wrote of growing up in the western plains—where girls' horizons, like the sky, were much broader. Born into a middle-class southern family, her earliest memories were of rural Virginia, where she lived until she was nine years old. In 1883, she moved with her family to Nebraska. At first, she was terribly homesick for the green hills of Virginia. Before long, however, she grew to love the plains and later would remark that the absence of natural boundaries and the sweep of the sky gave the spirit a wider range. In contrast to Alcott's mother, a paragon of patient love and strength, historians describe Virginia Cather, Willa's mother, as somewhat vain, detached and distant, and often ill. Partly because of her mother's lack of engagement in her daughter's life, "Willa was allowed to roam at will and it gave her a sense of independence she was never afterward to lose. She discovered, earlier than most, a world outside the home and while she was devoted to them she would always detach herself a little from the other members of her family."[15] Cather's stories in later life would be populated with the Scandinavian and Bohemian immigrants she met in her wanderings. Like Louy Alcott, the young Willa Cather loved to run and jump, and she not only pretended to be a horse, she also roamed for miles across the plains, canoeing and fishing with her two younger brothers, her companions in adventure. She adored books, music, and theater and happily played the male roles, as had Louy Alcott, in amateur theatricals.[16] She hated needlework with a passion, preferred to dissect and even vivisect frogs, and her ambition was to be a doctor.

If she read *Little Women*, as we must assume she did, she would have found much in common with Jo March. Like Jo, Willa Cather loved adventure stories and books of courage and manly virtue (among their mutual favorites were *The Count of Monte Cristo* and *Pilgrim's Progress*). Like Jo, she identified with the male protagonists. As Sharon O'Brien explains in *Willa Cather: The Emerging Voice*,

> It was not unusual for a Victorian girl to read adventure stories or to identify with courageous heroes, but in adolescence most female readers turned their attention to the heroine's story. Although Cather did not succumb to this literary and social rite of passage, she gradually realized that the stories she loved were not intended for women. . . . But until she became more aware of the sexual polarization in adult Victorian society, the young book-lover did not know that she was reading the wrong plot. Identifying with the male heroes who possessed the power and autonomy she wanted for herself, Cather did not at first grasp what she called the "hateful distinction" between boys' and girls' reading: the "fact that I was a girl never damaged my ambitions to become a pope or an emperor."[17]

When Cather finally began to comprehend the split between male and female destinies, in contrast to Alcott, who struggled to dominate her masculine impulses, Cather rejected the feminine role in a most visible and dramatic way. Beginning in 1884, at age fourteen, she took the name William Cather, MD, cut her hair quite short, and began to dress as a boy.[18] "Whereas Alcott accepted, at least externally, and temporarily, the Victorian definition of femininity, Cather's metamorphosis into William signified her attempt to fashion an independent, autonomous, and powerful self."[19] Her performance drew stares and ridicule from the gossips in Red Cloud, but she was unperturbed. She was not passing as a male or impersonating a male. Hers was a conscious and public performance, and she continued this double role, dressing and acting as William but known by all around her to be the female Willa, for almost ten years. Interestingly, during the period of Cather's cross-dressing, she found a surprising degree of acceptance and support from her elders. While some contemporary accounts express shock and disapproval, her parents apparently accepted her metamorphosis and gave her the personal space (including the all-important room of her own that she prized as much as Louy Alcott) in which to dream her unorthodox dreams. Many important people in Red Cloud, like the local physician and the local scientist, took the ambitions of young William Cather, MD seriously, inviting young William to come along on medical rounds and encouraging her interest in science and biology.

When she went away to college, at age sixteen, she went as William Cather, known throughout the university town of Lincoln, Nebraska, as "Billy." But by her senior year at the University of Nebraska, she had established her individuality and had made her reputation as a promising young writer. Now confident that she could access the power and authority she sought despite her gender, she grew her hair and resumed a more feminine dress. By the time she arrived in Pittsburgh, she looked back with amusement on what she called her "Bohemian" period.

I do not know whether my grandmother understood or was even aware of the complexity of Cather's gender identity. Although Willa Cather's most intimate relationships throughout her life were with women, she never openly discussed her sexual orientation. During her years in Pittsburgh, when teaching, she favored a masculine, tailored look, but often surprised her students with striped stockings or other amazing garments. In her leisure time, she loved attending theater and opera attired in brilliant patterns, feathers, and sumptuous fabrics. Perhaps my grandmother—who would have felt naked without her Methodist uniform of lace trimmed shirtwaist and single string of pearls—simply accepted that her mentor was a dramatic and original figure, given to unusual modes of dress. Or perhaps she was aware of and politely did not discuss her mentor's private life. So-called Boston marriages, like Cather's thirty-year relationship with Edith Lewis, were not uncommon among educated women of her day, who found freedom from the hierarchies of marriage by forging relationships of equality with other women.

Cather's years as William, and her ability to bridge gender roles in her imagination, served her well as a storyteller. Her fictional heroes (including those clearly patterned after the author) were both male and female, and she knew how to portray both men and women as full and vivid beings. In *My Ántonia*, her alter ego is a boy named Jim. But in *Song of the Lark*, she tells her most highly autobiographical story—describing the coming of age in Moonstone, Colorado, of an artistically gifted girl who strains against the gendered assumptions about her destiny. Thea, the heroine of *Song of the Lark*, never adopts the dress of a male—instead, she adopts the autonomy and ambition of a male, breaking away from family and forging her own career. Thea grows up in a town much like Red Cloud, but leaves her home and family behind, becoming a world famous opera singer. Initially, her ambition is to be a pianist, but a summer spent riding and climbing in New Mexico liberates her to find her voice as a singer. Thea is following in her author's footsteps, since a summer spent on horseback and hiking in the Southwest with her brother played a pivotal role in Cather's finding her own voice as a novelist. Throughout her life, Cather often visited and wrote about lonely and wild places and characters who dare to explore them. Where Alcott and her heroine Jo March were forced to subordinate their dreams of adventure to the demands of family, Cather's heroine places her striving for glory before family. In one key episode, Thea declines a plea that she leave Europe in order to come to her dying mother's bedside. She has another role to perform—she has been offered a chance to take a leading role in a Wagnerian opera and will lose all she has struggled to gain if she returns home now. Her duty to her art transcends her duty to her family. For a turn-of-the-century heroine this was indeed a radical declaration of independence.

During her years as William, the teenaged Cather sat for a series of formal studio portraits (Fig. 5). The youth gazing at the camera is so natural, open, and relaxed it is easy to see why her new persona was accepted and supported by so many of the good folks of Red Cloud. This child, broad browed and confident, smiling at us from under a jaunty cap perched on close-cropped brown hair, is the very picture of American energy and enterprise. What a handsome child, and how brave! While Cather left no childhood diary or letters, her bold performance as William Cather, MD, tells the story of her coming of age with as much drama and courage as any youthful writings.

Fig. 5. Willa Cather in her youth, dressed as William (courtesy of the Nebraska State Historical Society).

As a teenager, I read *Song of the Lark* with someone named Willa in mind as its inspiration. Now, I went back to reconsider the story with the more complex and dramatic picture of Willa/William in my mind's eye. What a remarkable young person and how vivid and challenging the story she tells of gender, sexuality, and coming of age. I wish I had known her—and him. How could Willa's story, or the story of the American woman and her struggle for equality, ever have been complete as long as *William's* story had to be suppressed? I hope that young readers today, who fly across the plains with Ántonia and soar with *The Song of the Lark*, will be told (as my generation was not) that Willa made her high school graduation speech on "Science and Superstition" in a jacket and a cravat, as William Cather, MD. I look back on the third year of my now grown-up daughter's life, when she took on the identity of her favorite storybook character, Cowboy Pete, and resolutely insisted, against any suggestion by meddlesome neighbors to the contrary, that she was a cow*boy*, not a cowgirl. I am just glad that I understood enough, even back then, to let her be whoever she desired.

As these coming-of-age stories demonstrate, "women's issues" and "women's rights" are also "girls' issues" and "girls' rights." The courage of these two authors in challenging the cramped Victorian definition of womanhood did not suddenly spring forth when they became adults. As children, they were sufficiently clear-eyed to identify the unjust subordination of girls, and they were innocent enough to believe they could overcome it. Their drive to shape a different destiny for themselves began in early childhood and continued throughout their lives. Discrimination against female children often begins at birth (even before, if one considers various forms of sex selection). Even today, girl children cannot escape the pervasive cultural influence of gender stereotypes. Most girls, even as they play with boys on equal terms, will internalize these images of difference during the first decade of life. For many girls, adolescence triggers a lock-down of their potential, as they censor their own behavior to fit within cultural expectations of what it means to be a woman. For many others, as for Alcott and Cather, the struggle against these limited expectations begins in girlhood and can occupy the rest of their lives. Each girl (and boy) resolves the struggle in her own way, but gender is a challenge to all, whether we are fully conscious of it or only vaguely sense its power.

Behind every female "first"—first astronaut, first marathon runner, first female Senator—there is a girl who refused to accept the limitations of the passive female role. I think of Sandra Day O'Connor, the first woman Supreme Court justice. I had the pleasure of serving as one of her law clerks, and she is as feminine as a woman can be. Even now, in her mid-seventies, her mental toughness is matched by physical courage and an appetite for hard work and adventure, lessons she learned growing up as a cowgirl on an isolated ranch in Arizona. Years after I clerked for her, together with her brother she wrote a memoir of her childhood on the *Lazy B. Ranch*, followed by a children's book called *Chico*, about the cow pony who was her companion in adventure. Both are required reading for girls of all ages.[20]

While there have been many female firsts, barriers to full equality and opportunity still remain. Modern girls continue to fight the battle to overcome disabling stereotypes and to gain equal access to male dominated spheres. As a professor of law and law clerk to the first female justice, I have always enjoyed teaching my students about the Supreme Court cases that establish girls' rights to be free of gender discrimination. In the case of the Virginia Military Institute, for example, Nancy Mace won her battle for admission to an elite male school in 1999, defeating the State of Virginia's claim that it could satisfy its constitutional duty by creating a separate but supposedly equal institution for girls. Justice O'Connor and Justice Ruth Bader Ginsburg, both of whom had battled against gender discrimination to reach the highest court in the land, must have enjoyed signing their names to this decision.[21]

But the tyranny of gender stereotypes continues even as the stereotypes themselves change. Katharine Hepburn, a skinny New England tomboy, became an icon of the modern independent woman. Her feisty trouser-clad heroines were a staple in my mother's youth and on the TV screens of my youth. Her role as a female lawyer in *Adam's Rib* is a classic among female law students—neatly capturing the same tensions women experience today between their public and their private lives. Hepburn's first big break came not in the role of a lawyer or doctor but in the role of Jo March. Although much prettier than the real Jo, her beauty was far from conventional, and her boney athletic frame and sharp tongue were true to the original. When George Cukor's film of *Little Women* hit the screen in 1933, the unknown Hepburn was an overnight success, becoming America's second most popular female star—just behind the voluptuous siren, Mae West. As one farewell essayist writing about Katharine Hepburn remarked, "Even if Hepburn looked like the hanger on which Mae West hung her clothes, and seemed as rigid as her own New England scruples, it was she who outlasted every change in the rules of a country that couldn't quite decide whether such women should exist."[22] It seems fair to say that the country has rendered its verdict and that feisty, angular, and ambitious female heroines are here to stay. In fact, tomboy thinness is the new oppressive stereotype. Modern girls with Mae West genes have few positive role models, and many starve themselves to achieve the new culturally imposed image of androgyny.[23]

Many barriers still remain to both boys and girls who challenge gender stereotypes, especially if they are gay or lesbian. Some of the most painful modern American stories of discrimination are those of gay and lesbian youths, harassed and belittled at school or forced to hide their sexual orientation because of very realistic fears of violence and discrimination. The Supreme Court has rejected the notion, in two recent cases, that people may be penalized purely because of their sexual orientation. In *Romer v. Evans*,[24] the Court struck down a Colorado law that attempted to prohibit the enactment of laws or ordinances that would bar discrimination based on sexual orientation. And in *Lawrence v. Texas*,[25] the Court struck down a law criminalizing gay and lesbian sexual conduct, reasoning that the law violated the privacy of the individual to define his or her own intimate relations and personal identity. These rulings have been controversial. Critics from the religious right believe they condone and encourage immorality, while critics from the left believe that they do not go far enough in establishing protections for sexual minorities. But they clearly do set a baseline of fairness that prohibits irrational discrimination against gay and lesbian youth who too often have been treated as pariahs by public schools and other public institutions.

We saw how the ecosystem around William/Willa Cather in the pioneer culture of the American West allowed her to display her masculine self—a step that was as valuable in her present as in her future, as necessary to her giving her valedictory speech as it was to her becoming the writer capable of creating *Song of the Lark*. Her family supported her choices during her earliest years of athletic and adventurous pursuits, and during her adolescence they gave her space of her own and accepted her name change, shorn hair, and masculine mode of dress as an expression of her self and not an assault on their authority. The townsfolk and her peers also apparently accepted her masculinity and respected her individualism and intellectual powers. Perhaps there was no moral panic about female homosexuality in Red Cloud in 1870, or perhaps the power of the macrosystem of the westward expansion, placing such a high value on individual initiative, was strong enough to squelch the push for standardization before it could interfere with her growth into her own mature identity.

Knowing what we do today about the biological influences on sexual orientation, and the ego tasks of a child's emotional growth into a mature and integrated identity, it seems clear that discrimination against gay, lesbian, and transgendered youth is even more pernicious than the traditional gender stereotypes that too long stunted the growth of heterosexual girls and boys. To tell a child, "You cannot become who you want to be," is bad enough. To say, "You cannot be who you *are*," is worse still. Privacy rights for children must include the right to "a psychological room of one's own," a private space in which to construct one's own identity free of distorting gender stereotypes. And equality rights must include the right of both boys and girls to wear clothes that fit their identities, rather than uniforms dictated by gender stereotypes.

How would a modern day William/Willa Cather fare in the schools of my state, the state of Florida? If she were a graduating student at Robinson High in Hillsborough County, Florida, in 2002, even before she donned her graduation robes her wings would have been clipped by the requirement that all female seniors wear a scoop neck drape for their yearbook portraits. One seventeen-year-old student at Robinson High, Nikki Youngblood, wanted to be photographed in a tuxedo. The school desired a "standard" for senior portraits and the standard dictated that boys wear a jacket and tie and girls wear scoop neck drapes. "I don't understand why this is such a big deal to them. This is how I dressed in school every day. I even wore a tuxedo to a school dance. This is 2002, not 1802. No female student should be deprived of the right to be in a yearbook because she does not want to wear a frilly drape."[26] Nikki sued, with the help of the National Center for Lesbian Rights, and in September 2005, her case was settled while pending before the U.S. Court of Appeals for the Eleventh Circuit. The Hillsborough School Board agreed to do away with any sex-differentiated dress codes.

In February 2005, another Floridian, Kelli Davis, of Fleming Island High School in Clay County, showed up for her senior yearbook picture in a tuxedo, and refused to be photographed in the "revealing frilly scoop neck drape" the girls at her school were required to wear. In the offending picture, Kelli is smiling into the camera, her body concealed to the chin in a black tuxedo, white shirt, and black bow tie. With Nikki's case as a precedent, Kelli's was resolved more quickly. In September 2005, Clay County agreed to change its senior portrait policy, add sexual orientation to its nondiscrimination policy, and provide diversity training to all junior and senior high schools. Said Kelli, who had already started college when the settlement was reached: "I'm just relieved it's over and that no other student in Clay County will have to go through the embarrassment, humiliation and frustration I went though. I hope the new policies will help the faculty understand it's their responsibility to intervene when kids are being picked on because they're gay or because they don't meet society's stereotype of how they are supposed to look or act." [27]

Time magazine chose as its cover story for October 10, 2005, "The Battle over Gay Teens."[28] The thrust of the article is that, as gay teens are gaining more acceptance, the struggle for their souls has sharpened. It profiles two organizations that seem to offer opposite philosophies. Exodus Youth is a Christian group that hosts conferences and provides support for youth seeking to break free of homosexual tendencies. The Point Foundation gives college scholarship and mentoring to deserving youth who are marginalized because of their "sexual identity, gender expression or gender identity." Brittany Bjurgstrom, a scholarship recipient attending Wellesley, writes: "I am committed to creating a world where such current divisions as sexual orientation, race, religion, and gender identity can be expressed openly and honestly, bringing out the best in humanity's diversity. There is too much work to be done to allow our differences to hinder real progress. When we lose sight of ourselves, we lose hold of our potential"[29] As this quote suggests, the heart of the equality principle is genuine respect for difference. All young persons who struggle to define their own identities, those profiled in the *Time* magazine's piece on Exodus Youth as well as those profiled in Point Foundation, deserve acceptance and respect wherever their journey takes them.

Looking through a developmental lens at the stories of these girls and their historical counterparts, Louy/Louisa and William/Willa, we can see what happens when a child encounters and is asked to internalize gender stereotypes. Clearly, historical time and place play a large role in when this encounter takes place and how it is negotiated. Alcott was indoctrinated almost from birth in dominating her tomboyish tendencies. Cather, a child living on the frontier in a family that took a lax approach to child rearing, reached adolescence before it dawned on her that she was expected to act like a girl and become a woman. Developmental science tells us that nature and environment play interactive roles. For some children, the masculine suit or frilly dress, and the expectations that they embody, fit fairly comfortably. But for others the pressure to conform involves abandoning an emerging and yet deeply felt sense of self. The phrase used by the Point Foundation, "sexual identity, gender expression or gender identity," captures the ways in which gender, identity, and sexuality are intertwined and yet distinct. The self a child struggles to define may involve a sexual identity, defined as an attraction to those of the same rather than opposite sex. Or it may be a gender identity, the sense of fit between the stereotypical sex role and one's own personality and aspirations. Or it may be a particular expression of self that challenges the straightjacket of gender roles, like Willa's shorn head and Kelli's and Nikki's tuxedos.

The equality principle tells us we should not impose on either girls or boys a script for becoming adults that is dictated by stereotypes that feel confining and alien to them. This is not to deny the reality of gender differences. As a former nursery school teacher and mother of a son and a daughter, I can say from firsthand observation that boys and girls *are* different, each in his or her own way. Human rights principles of equality, but also of individual dignity, privacy, agency, and protection, require that we respect and support our children in becoming themselves.

As these stories show, girls played an unsung but crucial part in the battle for gender equality. In order for women to inhabit active roles in the public sphere, they first had to rehearse them in the privacy of imagination, in the room of one's own so important to a girl's coming of age. Iconic women—those female "firsts"—like to say that they got where they are by "standing on the shoulders of other women." It is time to acknowledge another and equally important debt. Modern women are standing on the slim but sturdy shoulders of girls.

CHAPTER 9

BREAKING THE PRISON OF DISABILITY

Helen Keller and the Children of "Greenhaven"

I knew then that "w-a-t-e-r" meant the wonderful cool something that was flowing over my hand. That living word awakened my soul, gave it light, hope, joy, set it free!
—Helen Keller, *The Story of My Life*[1]

Although there are differences between males and females, we generally assume they are born with equal if different capacities. What about children who are not born equal or suffer traumas that render them unequal? Whether we call them handicapped, exceptional, disabled, or differently abled, many children must face obstacles due to differences that cannot be regarded as primarily culturally or legally imposed. Looking at the lives of children with disabilities forces us to think more deeply about the meaning of equality as well as other human rights principles such as dignity and empowerment. Here is one such story, already familiar to many readers as a drama about a gifted teacher, but revisited from a child-centered perspective as the story of an exceptional child.

Helen Adams Keller was born in 1880 in the small Alabama town of Tuscumbia. Her father was a prosperous man, editor of the regional newspaper. Her mother was a gentle and affectionate woman. Both doted on this first child of their marriage and watched her grow into an active toddler with joy and pride. At eighteen months of age, Helen nearly died of what was probably scarlet fever. Although she survived, she was never again able to see or hear. Robbed of the powers of hearing and sight, she soon lost her small toddler vocabulary. In the terminology of the time, Helen was "blind, deaf, and dumb."

Most readers will have encountered Helen Keller in the play, later made into a film, called *The Miracle Worker*. The title refers to Helen's gifted teacher, Annie Sullivan. The "miracle" of the title refers to Annie Sullivan's success in breaking through the prison of darkness and silence. She did it by spelling words into the six-year-old child's hand using a form of sign language developed for the deaf and blind. Here is how Helen, at age twenty-two, recalled her world on the day of Annie Sullivan's arrival in Tuscumbia.

> Have you ever been at sea in a dense fog, when it seemed that a tangible white darkness shut you in, and the great ship, tense and anxious, groped her way toward the shore with plummet and sounding-line, and you waited with beating heart for something to happen? I was like that ship before my education began, only I was without compass or sounding-line, and had no way of knowing how near the harbour was. "Light! Give me light!" was the wordless cry of my soul, and the light of love shown on me in that very hour.[2]

The Miracle Worker portrays Helen, before Annie Sullivan's intervention, as a little animal running wild in the household and wreaking havoc wherever she went. But Helen's own biography and Annie Sullivan's letters tell a different story. The story they tell, of avid exploration and intense frustration, will be familiar to the parent of any small child pushing against boundaries he or she cannot comprehend. Helen was desperate to be a part of the world she could neither hear nor see. She used her senses of touch and smell—feeling the faces and lips of people, playing with dolls and pets, tasting and smelling good things from the garden—to engage the world around her. She used her sense of motion—acting out motions like churning ice cream and cutting bread, running, skipping, jumping—to communicate her needs and desires and to feel real in the dark and silent world. By age five, she had learned to fold the laundry and to identify her own clothes. Her developing brain struggled to make sense of the world she was exploring. In one striking passage, Helen describes her father, the newspaper editor:

> My earliest distinct recollection of my father is making my way through great drifts of newspapers to his side and finding him alone, holding a sheet of paper before his face. I was greatly puzzled to know what he was doing. I imitated this action, even wearing his spectacles, thinking they might help solve the mystery. But I did not find out the secret for several years. Then I learned what those papers were, and that my father edited them.[3]

As Helen grew, her desires for voice and agency outstripped her body's resources. "The few signs I used became less and less adequate, and my failures to make myself understood were invariably followed by outbursts of passion. I felt as if invisible hands were holding me and I made frantic efforts to free myself. I struggled—not that struggling helped matters, but the spirit of resistance was strong within me; I generally broke down in tears and physical exhaustion."[4] Helen came very near to death in her determination to function as an equal in a sightless world. One day she spilled water on her apron and spread it on the hearth to dry, as she had known adults to do. Frustrated at the slowness of this process, she flung the apron nearer to the fire and caught fire herself.

In her dark and silent world, Helen understood far more than she could express. Long before Annie Sullivan's arrival, Helen knew that she was different from other people. With her hands and body, she could feel them interacting in mysterious ways that were closed to her. "Sometimes I stood between two persons who were conversing and touched their lips. I could not understand and was vexed. I moved my lips and gesticulated frantically, without result. This made me so angry at times that I kicked and screamed until I was exhausted."[5] Helen developed relationships with those around her through touch and signs. She nestled in her mother's lap, seeking refuge from her own storms of frustration. Her constant playmate was a little black girl named Martha Washington who understood her signs intuitively and was her accomplice in mischief. The two had free range of the house, kitchen, and barns and helped to milk the cows, to groom the horses, and to make the family meals.

From an early age, Helen felt keenly the special significance of having eyes. When six-year-old Helen was traveling by train to Baltimore to consult a famous doctor, her aunt improvised a doll out of towels to keep her occupied. The doll lacked nose, mouth, ears, and eyes. "Curiously enough, the absence of eyes struck me more than all the other defects put together. I pointed this out to everybody with provoking consistency, but no one seemed equal to the task of providing the doll with eyes."[6] Helen solved the problem herself, by tearing two large beads from her Aunt's traveling cape and insisting that they be sewed onto the doll's face where her eyes should be. She recalls being transported with joy when she felt the eyes in their proper place, but immediately losing interest in the doll.

The adult Helen wrote that in the still, dark world in which the child lived, there was no strong sentiment or tenderness. Yet her recollections prove this was not true. Modern readers, conversant with theories of child development, will see the full range of the child's natural feelings, from tenderness to fury, from affection to searing jealousy. Helen had one special doll that she later named Nancy, after she learned to give names to things and people. Nancy had a cradle and Helen would rock her tenderly in the cradle for an hour at a time. One day, she discovered her baby sister Mildred asleep in the cradle. She rushed at the cradle and overturned it in her fury. She looked back on this episode with sorrow and insight. "Thus it is that when we walk in the valley of twofold solitude we know little of the tender affections that grow out of endearing words and actions and companionship. But afterward, when I was restored to my human heritage, Mildred and I grew into each other's hearts."[7]

I have dwelt on Helen Keller's life before Annie Sullivan to show that the story told in *The Miracle Worker* of a wild child civilized by adult intervention is far from complete. In fact, the six-year-old Helen was an avid seeker of truth and knowledge and a full participant in the journey out of darkness and silence. Helen's fits of temper and her acts of desperation spurred those around her, who did truly love and value her, to respond to her need for stimulation and to search for some avenue of educating this terribly handicapped child. To build a developmental foundation upon her sensations and emotions, she needed words. The climactic moment of *The Miracle Worker* is when Annie Sullivan holds the struggling Helen's hand in the stream of water from a garden pump. Helen suddenly understands that "w-a-t-e-r," as it is being spelled into her other hand by her teacher, means "the wonderful cool something that was flowing over my hand. That living word awakened my soul, gave it light, hope, joy, set it free!"[8]

This one moment has overshadowed the rest of the story of Helen Keller's childhood. Few who know the story of *The Miracle Worker* are aware that within less than one year of this first word, Helen had mastered a rich vocabulary and was writing letters in her own hand. Annie Sullivan arrived in Tuscumbia on March 3, 1887. The breakthrough described above occurred on April 5.[9] On June 17, she wrote her first letter, using a pencil and frame designed to help blind people write letters to sighted people. A few months later, in November 1987, Helen wrote a letter to Alexander Graham Bell, who had examined her a year earlier in Washington DC and had encouraged her parents to hire a specialized teacher for her. In a few short months, Helen had learned to report events from her past and present life, and to express complicated concepts like guilt and innocence.[10]

> Dear Mr. Bell.
> I am glad to write you a letter. Father will send you picture. I and Father and aunt did go to see you in Washington. I did play with your watch. I do love you. I saw doctor in Washington. He looked in my eyes. I can read stories in my book. I can write and count and spell.

Good girl. My sister can walk and run. We do have fun with Jumbo. Prince is not a good dog. He can not get birds. Rat did kill baby pigeons. I am sorry. Rat does not know wrong. I and mother and teacher will go to Boston in June. I will see little blind girls. Nancy will go with me. She is a good doll. Father will buy me lovely new watch. Cousin Anna gave me a pretty doll. Her name is Allie.

Good-by,

Helen Keller[11]

By October of 1888, the eight-year-old Helen was writing letters that demonstrated a full command of English idiom, rules of grammar, and a beginner's skills in several foreign languages, including French and Greek.

As a child, Helen Keller met and corresponded with many famous people of the day. At nine years of age, she wrote a letter to John Greenleaf Whittier, in admiration of his poems "My Playmate" and "In School Days," and they began a written correspondence. The same year, she visited Dr. Oliver Wendell Holmes, the prominent Boston poet and essayist, who was the father of the great Supreme Court justice of the same name. They began an active correspondence that continued for many years. In a reply to Helen's letter of July 1890, Holmes expressed astonishment at the mastery of language Helen had achieved.[12] Indeed, the ten-year-old's letters read like the graceful missives of a little Victorian lady. She quoted from famous poets and asked searching questions about the nature of God and the meaning of life. At age eleven, she actively engaged in fund-raising so that other blind and deaf children would have the opportunity to study as she had, at Perkins Institution. She wrote to Dr. Holmes seeking contributions for little Tommy Stringer, softening up the old poet before the pitch for funds with these artful words of thanks: "I think that you will be glad to hear that [your] poems have taught me to enjoy and love the beautiful springtime, even though I cannot see the fair, frail blossoms which proclaim its approach or hear the joyous warbling of the home-coming birds. But when I read 'Spring has Come,' lo! I am not blind any longer, for I see with your eyes and hear with your ears."[13]

A close reading of the autobiography and childhood letters of Helen Keller, together with the letters of her teacher, Annie Sullivan, reveals not only her astonishing brilliance of mind but also the way she utilized her remaining senses to make sense of the world. Helen could feel the wind and sunshine on her face, feel and smell a storm coming as the sun went behind a cloud and her skin grew cooler. She could identify place and season through the fragrance of plants and flowers, and she could feel sound in the throats of purring cats, barking dogs, and speaking people. She also identified, in describing her experience of the world, a keen sense of motion. Throwing herself into the waves, flinging herself onto a toboggan, cantering on her pony, all thrilled her beyond measure. Most highly developed, however, was Helen Keller's "sense of think." I refer to that process of experiencing the flow of ideas in abstraction from objects.

Here is how Helen described the dawning of her awareness of this sense of think, this internal conversation with the intangible. Her teacher, Annie Sullivan, had spelled the word "l-o-v-e" into her hand, in thanking Helen for the gift of some freshly picked violets.

> "What is love?" I asked.
>
> She drew me closer to her and said, "It is here," pointing to my heart, whose beats I was conscious of for the first time. Her words puzzled me very much, for I did not then understand anything unless I touched it.
>
> I smelt the violets in her hand and asked, half in words, half in signs, a question which meant, "Is love the sweetness of flowers?"
>
> "No," said my teacher.
>
> Again, I thought. The warm sun was shining on us.
>
> "Is this not love?" I asked, pointing in the direction from which the heat came, "Is this not love?"
>
> It seemed to me there could be nothing more beautiful than the sun, whose warmth makes all things grow. But Miss Sullivan shook her head, and I was greatly puzzled and disappointed. I thought it strange that my teacher could not show me love.

A day or two afterward I was stringing beads of different sizes in symmetrical groups—two large beads, three small ones, and so on. I had made many mistakes, and Miss Sullivan had pointed them out again and again with gentle patience. Finally, I noticed a very obvious error in the sequence and for an instant I concentrated my attention on the lesson and tried to think how I should have arranged the beads. Miss Sullivan touched my forehead and spelled with decided emphasis, "Think."

In a flash I knew that the word was the name of the process going on in my head. This was my first conscious perception of an abstract idea.

For a long time I was still—I was not thinking of the beads in my lap, but trying to find a meaning for "love" in light of this new idea. The sun had been under a cloud all day, and there had been brief showers; but suddenly the sun broke forth in all its southern splendour.

Again I asked my teacher, "Is this not love?"[14]

In simple words Sullivan explained that you cannot touch love but, like the sun, you feel the sweetness that it pours into everything. And suddenly, Helen writes, "The beautiful truth burst upon my mind—I felt that there were invisible lines stretched between my spirit and the spirits of others."[15] Utilizing her newfound power of think, Helen had unlocked the secret of life's most important mysteries (Fig. 6).

Annie Sullivan's contemporaneous letters describing her pupil's progress are consistent with Helen's recollections. All of the developmental theories of Piaget and Erikson, not yet "discovered" in 1887, can be seen in Helen's interactions with her environment and her growing understandings of her physical and emotional world.[16] Agency, voice, will are all present in abundance. In one letter, written in May of 1887, Annie Sullivan writes, "Since I have abandoned the idea of regular lessons, I find that Helen learns much faster." Instead, she lets Helen's thirst for learning inspire the lesson. She describes how that day Helen had come running, urgently spelling into her hand "dog-baby," pointing to her own five

Fig. 6. Helen Keller (front) with Annie Sullivan (courtesy of the Library of Congress).

fingers one after another and sucking them. Annie was baffled, until Helen led her to the pump house where five newborn puppies were suckling. In rapid sequence, after Annie teaches her the word for puppy, Helen signs "eyes—shut" and "sleep—no," and Annie confirms her observation, spelling into her hand that the puppies' eyes are shut but they are not sleeping. Touching the runt of the litter, Helen signs "small" and Annie responds by signing "very small." Annie observes,

> She evidently understood that *very* was the name of the new thing that had come into her head; for all the way back to the house she used the word "very" correctly. One stone was small, another was "very small." When she touched her little sister she said "Baby—small. Puppy—*very* small." Soon after, she began to vary her steps from large to small, and the little, mincing steps were "very small." She is going through the house now applying the new words to all kinds of objects.[17]

By July, she had reached the "question stage" of her development. "It is 'what?' 'why?' 'when?' especially 'why?' all day long. . . . The 'why?' is the door through which [a child] enters the world of reason and reflection. 'How does carpenter know to build house?' 'Who put chickens in eggs?' 'Why is Viney black?' 'Flies bite—why?' 'Can flies know not to bite?' 'Why did father kill sheep?'[18] Sullivan followed Helen's lead, answering as fully as she could even though Helen might not comprehend every word she spelled into her hand. She compared Helen's questions to those of a bright three-year-old, and felt she would learn best when her curiosity was aroused by direct experiences with the things and people around her. It was important that her education be dictated by her unique needs and capacities, rather than by some standardized curriculum.

Helen went on to study at the Perkins Institute in Boston, where she was astonished to find that there were many other girls who could not see or could not hear yet played happily and communicated in their own language. Helen, however, insisted on learning not only to sign but also to speak—an accomplishment many had believed was impossible. Still blind and deaf, by the age of eleven she was no longer "dumb." She could communicate directly with those around her in the world of the sighted and the hearing. Helen's struggle for equality presaged the modern movement favoring mainstreaming of children with disabilities. Eager to compete with her peers, she used sign language and Braille as a bridge to skills such as typing and speech that would allow her to communicate with the hearing and sighted. She persisted in the face of testing methods that exacerbated her inequality. Her entrance exams for Radcliffe were spelled to her by strangers speaking different forms of sign language, she was given no extra time, and she was not allowed to have the papers she typed read back to her before they were submitted.[19] When she passed the exams, she insisted against great opposition from Radcliffe that she could and would do the work to earn her degree, side by side with other girls. And she did. The adult Helen Keller became a pioneer in the struggle for disability rights, promoting access to education for all disabled children and subsidies of new tools like the talking book.[20]

In 1975, almost one hundred years after Helen Keller's birth, the U.S. Congress passed the Education of All Handicapped Children Act.[21] Under this federal law, expanded in 1990 and renamed the Individuals with Disabilities Education Act (IDEA), all children are entitled to a free appropriate public education. But what does "appropriate" mean? Like new words in a child's vocabulary, laws can only be fully explored in context. Following in Helen's activist footsteps, one little girl tested the meaning of "appropriate" in court. I knew Amy Rowley long before her court case, when she attended nursery school with my son. Amy was the youngest child of hearing impaired parents, Cliff and Nancy Rowley. Quick, bright, and willful, she played happily with the other children although she had little residual hearing. At age four, she already communicated very effectively, using a combination of sign language, lip reading, and speech. What sticks in my mind about Amy is how often she would run to her mother to get an explanation in sign language of something that puzzled her—so like the process Annie Sullivan and Helen describe. When she was in first grade, the Hendrick Hudson

School Board decided she did not need a full-time sign language interpreter with her in class since they had provided a hearing aid, part-time interpreter, and tutoring. Amy was performing above average and passing from grade to grade. But her parents, Cliff and Nancy, believed that she could never reach her full potential if she could hear only about half of what went on in class. They won their case in the federal district and appeals courts, but lost at the Supreme Court. In the words of Justice Rehnquist, while the IDEA was intended to create a basic floor of opportunity for the handicapped child, the state "satisfies the [free appropriate education] requirement by providing personalized instruction with sufficient support services to permit the child to benefit educationally from that instruction."[22] Justice White, joined by Justices Marshall and Brennan, disagreed.

> The Act requires more. It defines "special education" to mean "specifically designed instruction . . . to *meet the unique needs* of a handicapped child. . . ." Providing a teacher with a loud voice would not meet Amy's needs and would not satisfy the Act. The basic floor of opportunity is instead . . . intended to eliminate the effects of the handicap, at least to the extent that the child will be given an equal opportunity to learn if that is reasonably possible. Amy Rowley, without a sign-language interpreter, comprehends less than half of what is said in the classroom less than half of what normal children comprehend. This is hardly an equal opportunity to learn, even if Amy makes passing grades.[23]

Amy had not attended the oral arguments of her case. Her parents wanted to shield her from the intense news coverage. But two years later, when I was clerking at the Court, I invited Amy for a "behind the scenes" tour. Actually, it was *she* who gave the tour as I watched in amazement. She blew into the empty courtroom like a small cyclone, running behind the bench and calling out the name of each justice without pausing to look at any of the brass labels on the chair's backs. "Here is where my lawyer sat, and here is the red light that told him when to stop and here is where the interpreter stood." The only thing that surprised her about her visit was seeing that the Supreme Court basketball court, often referred to as the "highest court in the land," had a wooden floor. "What did you expect?" I asked her. "I thought it would be marble like everything else." Amy was well aware she had "lost" her case—but she certainly gained in voice and agency from having fought it.

As Amy's case shows, many of the crucial questions of modern education law were foreshadowed in Helen Keller's childhood. Consider Helen's delight at meeting and playing with other blind girls and signing with other deaf girls, and her determination to compete on an equal footing with sighted and hearing girls in a regular college setting. We are still asking whether it is better that children be mainstreamed—educated with "normal" children whenever possible—or placed in settings where they can learn side by side with others like them, who know and appreciate the experiences of a shared difference.[24] Contrast the good start made possible by the freedom Helen experienced in her earliest years to roam and play with the different kind of learning made possible by the more structured studies that followed. Consider the misery Helen suffered when well-meaning people and institutions imposed a rigid set of standards and testing methods, ignoring the reality of Helen's difference. We are still working to define the proper balance of universalized measures and individualized learning that will help children of varying abilities and disabilities to learn and grow.

I thought of Helen and Amy in 2001, when I first visited a public school for special children located in a leafy part of a large southern city. I shall call it "Greenhaven School" to protect the privacy of students and teachers. The school is a cheerful place with brightly colored artwork on the walls and a staff of caring and competent people. It has been in operation for about fifty years. As I paged through albums of photographs from years past, I saw for myself what the principal had told me. The school's population has changed radically over the past twenty-five years. In the 1970s, its students (many of them moderately retarded Down syndrome children) were wearing penny loafers, going to sock hops, and acting in plays in the auditorium. Today, of the seventy-odd students, all but a handful arrive in high-tech wheelchairs. Most have been diagnosed as either severely or profoundly retarded and have multiple handicaps.

A casual observer paging through the albums and comparing them with Greenhaven's classrooms today might think that American children have grown more medically fragile and more disabled in the past quarter century. True, some disabled children now survive who might have died as newborns. But the major reason for the change in this population is that mildly and moderately retarded children who attended Greenhaven in the past are now learning side by side with "normal" children in regular classrooms. Even many severely retarded children have been transferred out of Greenhaven and into specially equipped classrooms located in ordinary primary, middle, and high schools

This change in the school's population is the result of three interlocking concepts that have shaped modern educational policy for disabled children. First is the drive to de-institutionalize. Beginning in the late 1960s and early 1970s, reformers argued that too many children were growing up in institutional settings when they could be growing up at home with their families or in family-like settings. Responding to the rallying cry of "least restrictive environment," states and localities closed down their large residential facilities and sent the children home. Second, a series of federal laws, including the IDEA, have mandated a free appropriate education for even the most seriously handicapped. Children who were previously thought to be too disabled to benefit from education now have detailed individualized education plans, or IEPs, that set out specific goals tailored to meet that child's special circumstances and range of abilities. Finally, concepts such as "inclusion" and "mainstreaming" have challenged the notion that children should be segregated in specialized schools with others who share their special needs. To the maximum possible extent, disabled children are to be integrated into the regular classroom. For those who cannot be mainstreamed, the trend is toward housing their special classes in separate rooms in regular neighborhood schools.

In some ways, Greenhaven is an endangered species—a public day school devoted solely to the needs of developmentally disabled children. At Greenhaven, the school day begins when the teachers arrive around 7:30 a.m. to prepare their classrooms. But the highpoint of the morning comes at 8:15, when the children arrive in a line of bright yellow school buses that stretches out of sight around the circular drive. Each bus discharges its precious cargo of four to six children, lowering them in their wheelchairs one by one to the sidewalk, using the bus's special lifts. A few children are mobile—those who are autistic are often *too* mobile and require a lot of chasing and catching! But most pupils are wheelchair-bound and many have feeding tubes or oxygen cylinders that bear witness to the medical issues that complicate their learning disabilities. For many, their disabilities were caused by oxygen deprivation at birth or other birth or genetic complications. For a few, head trauma is the culprit, but it is common to see mental disability accompanied by conditions such as blindness, hearing impairment, respiratory or gastric difficulty, and cerebral palsy.

Despite the severity of their disabilities, the scene as they arrive at Greenhaven is the opposite of gloomy. The bright voices of the teachers and aides as they greet the children by name and comment on new barrettes and new T-shirts, the bright colors of the children's clothing and diaper bags slung over the wheelchair handles, and the evident joy in many children's expressions as they respond to these greetings brought me back forcefully to my years as a nursery school teacher. There is a lot of hands-on love, with teachers and aides affectionately patting students' hair and cheeks, holding the children's hands, and placing their faces inches from the child's own, the better to communicate. When all the students have arrived, they are wheeled to their classrooms. The classrooms, with brightly colored decorations, toys, and posters, look much like an ordinary grade school room, except for the absence of desks and the presence of a number of specialized contraptions made of wood, metal, and plastic.

Greenhaven children spend as little time as possible in their wheelchairs. Long wooden Rifton Boards that pivot from horizontal to vertical are used to hold children upright, relieving stress on their skin, bones, and organs. Bright blue plastic Tumble Forms, resembling large baby seats with webbed safety harnesses, hold the children securely for feeding and learning. Wooden and plastic tray tables fit over these Tumble Forms to provide play and learning spaces. Padded tables, the size of a doctor's examining table, allow teachers and aides to change diapers and clothing. Foam floor mats and beanbag chairs provide places for children to recline and play. A large wading pool filled with soft-colored foam balls, called the Ball Pit, provides a safe and tactile environment for children to stretch and exercise.

Each child's IEP outlines specific learning goals. For example, a child may have the goal of "indicating a choice by responding with a signal to spoken cues." This jargon describes the teacher's goal of teaching a child who cannot speak how to communicate that he prefers chocolate milk instead of juice, or is wet and needs to be changed. A number of specialized devices are used to help children communicate. Head switches mounted on wheelchairs allow a child to signal by bumping the switch with his head. Pictures of objects on a Velcro storyboard allow the child to express preferences or needs. You can gaze at the picture of a cup to show you want to drink or at a radio to show you want music. You can even communicate more abstract information. I saw a child gaze at a picture of a playground swing in response to "Where did you come from just now?" But every IEP goal must have a functional payoff in the child's daily life. As one teacher remarked, "We are not here to teach them clever tricks. It takes us a year to teach these children a new skill and it better be something worth knowing."

As you already have guessed, you will not find a Helen Keller or an Amy Rowley in this school. Children of their intellect, even with multiple severe handicaps, will be studying in a regular school or in a specialized class with other high functioning children. But you will certainly find their grit and determination at Greenhaven, and you will find miracles being worked every day by dedicated teachers and by children who are driven by the universal human need for self-expression and autonomy.

Let me describe one classroom and the children learning there. Classroom 312 has six students, but one was absent the day I spent there and one is home bound. The teacher was a bouncy and up-beat woman in her fifties whose cheery demeanor and gift for making silly faces hides a deep determination to teach these children all they can possibly learn. As I began searching for a pseudonym for her, I came up blank. I realized it was because her students do not call her either "Ms. Sutton" or "Susan" since they lack the power of speech. They cannot form the sounds of a name although most understand their own names and some of what is said to them. Two teacher's aides, Carol and Mary, were assigned to her class in 2001, because of the class size and the special needs of the pupils.

Ms. Sutton's pupils (whose identities are disguised to protect their privacy) all arrive at school in their own specially adapted wheelchairs. All are legally blind. Most have some hearing impairment. All have neurological and motor difficulties. The first to arrive is James. An African American child of eight, he lives at home with a doting mother and grandmother. He has a radiant smile and enjoys being cuddled, but he suffers frequent seizures and his medications make him sleepy. Samantha is a large round pale-skinned child of ten with a placid moonlike face and long brown eyelashes. She is sweet tempered and undemanding. Her foster mother has braided her smooth brown hair into Pippi Longstocking pigtails that fall almost to her waist. One of Samantha's IEP goals is to "respond to voice cues" by focusing on the speaker. What this means in practice is that her teacher crouches by her chair and calls "Sammy, look at me," placing her face close to the child's and stroking her cheeks. She waits intently for a full minute until Samantha's eyes have found the teacher's face and focused on her eyes. Samantha breaks into a glorious grin of recognition and is lavishly praised. She has worked hard to fight her way out of the shroud of her disability and has accomplished a difficult but worthwhile task. Her ability to connect with caregivers will enhance her life and make those around her more responsive to her needs.

Mitzy is an adorable child of six with glossy brown skin. She is the most medically fragile of the children in this classroom. In addition to a feeding tube in her abdomen that allows nutrition to be fed directly into her stomach, she receives oxygen through a tracheotomy in her neck. The oxygen tank accompanies her everywhere she goes, in a rack on the back of her wheelchair. A spare is recharging in the classroom. Mitzi is perhaps the most responsive and engaging of all the children. As she struggles to vocalize despite the "trach," she smiles and reaches out her hands and arms to touch and be touched. Her thick dark hair is parted and fastened into topknots with bright-colored barrettes. In her gay yellow dress and matching canvas shoes, with a crocheted white cardigan in her diaper bag, she is clearly well cared for by a devoted foster mother. Although details of a child's case are confidential, I can guess that she came into foster care because of abuse and neglect, of which she still bears visible scars.

Today, Mitzi, usually so cheerful, seems to be in some distress. The teacher's aide, Carol, who loves to groom and pamper the children, starts brushing Mitzi's hair and discovers that her neck has been scraped raw by the band that holds her trach tube in place. The nurse is called, and makes the first of half a dozen unscheduled visits to Ms. Sutton's classroom to tend to children's medical needs. The trach is cleaned and a soft new padded band is put in place, and Mitzi seems much more comfortable. She has three respiratory treatments scheduled during the day, to ease her breathing difficulties. At one point she will precipitate a mini-emergency by pulling out the button securing her feeding tube and will need to have it reinserted. Her hands constantly roam restlessly around her face and body, and one of her IEP goals is to redirect all this tactile activity away from the tubes to a set of fuzzy objects that dangle on her wrist.

Mitzi, her teacher tells me, has true grit. I can see that for myself. Her tears of pain have dried and she is cheerful again. This child's will to love and thrive is astonishing. Brushing off discomfort that would drive most adults and many other children to withdraw into a shell of isolation, Mitzi reaches out eagerly to form relationships. She is a living testament to the fact that "quality of life" is a peculiarly individualized concept, and that children are active agents in creating and defining the quality of their own lives.

The fourth child in class today is Mara, age nine, an immigrant from the former Soviet Union. A pretty waif with blue eyes under fluttering eyelids, she is dressed by her mother in a pink sweatshirt and knit slacks, and her straight blond hair falls loosely around a pale delicate face. Mara uses a borrowed wheelchair with another child's name on it because she is not eligible for Medicaid due to her immigrant status—another gap that Greenhaven manages to bridge. When Mara arrived at Greenhaven two years ago, it was her first contact with formal schooling. She is completely blind, seeing at most some differences between a bright light and total darkness. She is further disabled by cerebral palsy and various other physical and neurological deficits. She cannot form words. Mara provides a case study in the values of a Greenhaven education. Two years ago, she could not feed herself nor could she effectively express her needs. She would thrash her head, bite her hand, and scream shrilly for hours at a time for no discernable reason. A child with such habits is not only unhappy but also hard to love. One of Greenhaven's objectives is to identify the function of such behaviors and to help children replace them with more appropriate behaviors. Ms. Sutton soon realized that Mara's screaming was a sign of her high sensitivity to touch and sound and her intense frustration.

Today, Mara interacts very differently with her world. Instead of screaming, she has learned to place a hand on her abdomen to show that she is wet or dirty and needs to be changed. I saw her do this and wait patiently for her teacher to notice, praise, and change her. Mara understands such cognitive concepts as "object permanence"—her teacher practices this skill, placing a cracker on her tray and hiding it under a napkin. Mara removes the napkin to find the cracker. She can now feed herself, drinking juice from her own cup and choosing with her fingers from an array of foods on her table which foods she wants to eat. Bananas are a favorite food, which she carefully picks up, brings to her lips, and consumes with pleasure. Other foods are not so welcome—she eats the meat out of her hamburger and consigns the bread to the empty world beyond her tray. One of Mara's IEP goals is to learn to keep her things within the physical boundaries of her table. She must learn to put aside things she wants to discard, rather than tossing them into the void where caretakers will have to pick them up.

Mara loves music, but she has very distinct likes and dislikes. Instead of screaming for her favorite songs (or in protest against her least favorite songs) she now listens to music using headphones connected to a tape recorder. The tape recorder is timed to stop playing every fifty seconds, and Mara must press a large yellow button on her tray to turn it back on. These motor tasks are not easy for Mara who must struggle to get her hands to do what she wants them to do. This morning, her teacher rewards her for working hard on her IEP goals with a music break. While the teacher turns to another child, Mara is happily engaged in listening to a favorite tape, periodically searching for and pressing the button as the music stops and she starts it going again. She is showing her capacity to understand "cause and effect"—she is using her precious sense of think.

At noon we go to the cafeteria and see many children like Mara who are working diligently to learn to feed themselves, and many others who are being fed by the teachers and aides, but are being taught to signal their wants and choices as they eat. Children who are being tube fed go as well, to enjoy the socialization of a large room filled with conversation and to watch a brightly colored cartoon. The ugly phrase "useless eaters" pops into my mind. This was the term the Nazis used to describe those defective persons, many of them children, whom they considered so useless to society that they should be put to death for the common good. Many such defective children were first subjected to medical experimentation. Their brains and organs remained in jars in an Austrian laboratory until they were finally buried in 2002, half a century after their brutal murders.[25] Ethicists often pose the question of whether the cost of educating children like Mara, James, Mitzi, and Samantha outweighs the meager economic benefits to society. No one here wants to talk about the cost of these children's education. With a physical plant that is clean and inviting, a staff including exercise and speech therapists, nurses, and nurses aides, and its faculty of teachers and teacher's aides, Greenhaven is clearly expensive. Yet it seems plain to me, as I watch these children learning to eat, that the moral cost to America of declaring such children "ineducable" or "useless eaters" is simply unacceptable. None of us knows whether the babies we or our sons and daughters bear or beget will be "perfect" or "defective." We can either come together to ensure all our children a life of dignity, or decide that some children are expendable. The Nazis made many such judgments about the value of human beings, and the price they paid for their choices was the destruction of their dreams of greatness and a well-earned place in infamy. Americans, too, embraced a eugenics movement that resulted in sterilization of many deemed "mentally defective." The son of Helen Keller's literary friend, Oliver Wendell Holmes Jr., authored an opinion in 1927 in a case called *Buck v. Bell* holding that sterilization policies did not violate any fundamental right and that "three generations of imbeciles are enough."[26] But the Nazi experiments showed us the slippery slope that leads from eugenics to genocide, and *Buck v. Bell*, although never overruled, fell into disfavor.[27]

The issue of costs and benefits is still an important one. Talk of how to fund services without breaking the bank came up in several contexts during my day at Greenhaven. I heard concerns expressed that closing institutions and sending children to live at home and attend day school has its drawbacks. It is surely cheaper for the state to close these institutions. And it is better for children to be raised by parents who love them. But what if the parents are overwhelmed by the daunting task of caring for a severely disabled child? Are they receiving sufficient assistance from the state to make their burdens tolerable? Some are forced to make their children wards of the state when a relatively small expenditure could keep them at home.[28] Two Greenhaven mothers, when asked what the system could do better, say, in unison, "Pay for vans with wheelchair lifts!" Wheelchairs are covered by Medicaid, but a van with a wheelchair lift costs $40,000, more than these working mothers can pay. As their children have grown heavier, these mothers have reached and exceeded the limits of their physical strength. They are suffering dislocated shoulders and herniated disks lifting their children, who now weigh upwards of one hundred pounds, in and out of beat-up old cars. Not all parents cope well, even with the burdens imposed by smaller children. Not every child arrives neat and clean and with properly administered medications or hygienic feeding tubes. Not every child has a parent reliably waiting at the bus stop when the school day is over and the driver takes him or her home. Greenhaven's bus drivers, social workers, teachers, aides, and nurses must struggle to close the gaps between what children need and what they get.

The most sobering thought of all, however, is what will happen when these children become adults. At age twenty-two they are no longer entitled to be in school. Parents and teachers alike understand that these children will never be independent. Most will continue to live at home, with aging parents who are less and less able to care for them. What kind of supports will be in place for these families? Many such worries about the future keep parents and educators awake at night. But these somber thoughts of tomorrow are put aside for today, so that we can concentrate on the children's present needs.

In the afternoon, we join another class on the playground. The teachers and aides put their physically disabled pupils on specially designed swinging ramps that hold wheelchairs, or place them into chair-swings and other child-safe playground apparatus. The children love the sense of motion and the feel of the wind on their faces and in their hair. Swinging and gliding gives these children the physical practice at balancing and shifting equilibrium that other children gain through running and jumping. As we learned from Helen Keller, motion also provides a wonderful sensory experience. Apparently, all of the Greenhaven children love to swing, especially Mara. I push her high in the air and sing out her name as she swings. Up in the sky she goes, with her hair streaming and a quiet smile spreading across her face. It is a cool spring day, and as the sun comes out from behind a cloud she turns her smiling face and pale eyelids to its warm and bright caress.

As I watch this child, I am powerfully reminded of Helen Keller's struggle. Like Helen, Mara has a strong will and very distinct wants and needs. She does not have Helen's brilliant mind, but her mind sparkles in its own way. The fact that this child, raised for her first six years in a Russian-speaking family, has learned to understand English indicates a higher cognitive ability than is readily apparent. Mara will have difficulty learning to sign—while she is not deaf, she is completely blind, has some mental impairment, and her motor control is severely limited. She is learning to smile for "yes" and shake her head for "no," and she is working on the signs for "more," "enough," and "hungry." Her teachers practice these signs by moving the child's hands in sign language adapted to her limitations, while speaking the words and demonstrating their meaning. This is how Ms. Sutton taught Mara to sign that her diaper was wet. That one sign took a year to learn. But even if Mara never learns to sign fluently, as Helen Keller did, she has already learned how to convey her wants and needs in very important ways. Once she was a captive in the dark shell of blindness, robbed of speech, unable to express her autonomy except through screaming, thrashing about, and inflicting pain on her self. Now she is an active participant in relationships with those around her and able to communicate her sadness, discomfort, pleasure, and displeasure in constructive ways. This small measure of control is the essence of human dignity and something each child, however limited his or her abilities, needs and deserves. For Mara, the payoff has been immense. As I watch her swing, I know that her life is worth living and that witnessing her struggle and her small triumphs has made my life more worth living.

I returned to Greenhaven four years later, in the spring of 2005, to visit again with Susan Sutton, who was now teaching a sixth grade class. Mara was no longer at Greenhaven. Her mother had strained her back and could no longer carry Mara up and down the two flights of stairs from their walk-up apartment to the school bus. Her education was over. When I asked after the other children I had met, I learned that many of them were still there. Samantha, by coincidence, was once again a student in Ms. Sutton's class. Now fourteen and weighing over 130 pounds, Samantha was the same dreamy moonfaced girl with Pippi Longstocking braids that I knew from before. She still needed to be lifted in and out of her wheelchair, to be coaxed into responding to voices, her diapers still needed to be changed, and now that she was menstruating, she also needed sanitary napkins. Seeing the changes in Samantha reminded me how fearful parents of disabled children become as their daughters pass through puberty and become fertile. Ms. Sutton's class today had four children—three in wheelchairs and one who was a "walker." The walking child, whom I shall call Naomi, was a Greenhaven success story. Although she suffered severe cognitive deficits, her vision and motor skills were less impaired. For six years, one of the goals on her IEP had been "learn to walk." The teachers had set aside time each day for her to walk, propping her in a standing position and encouraging her to move, but for six years she had seemed unable to take a step. Then one day, she began to walk. Now she walked everywhere. The day of my visit, we went on a field trip to the city's botanical garden, and Naomi walked and walked and walked, her nostrils flaring, as she smelled the moist air of the hothouses and enjoyed her mobility.

But all was not well with Ms. Sutton. Once so upbeat and optimistic, she was now counting the days until her retirement. She was still cheerful and vivacious with the children but her eyes and body language showed her fatigue. When I asked her what had changed she rolled her eyes and said, "No Child Left Behind." It was not just the endless paperwork (she had complained at my first visit of the mountains of paperwork for which she was responsible). Most Americans connect the phrase No Child Left Behind with mandatory standardized testing.[29] I was curious to know how this could affect the children at Greenhaven. The legislation, signed by President George W. Bush in 2002, requires schools receiving federal funds to measure the progress of all of the students in every public school. Schools where pupils fail to achieve "adequate yearly progress," may be given failing grades and may lose their funding. I knew that schools with significant populations of learning disabled students had been complaining that the same standardized testing was being imposed on the learning disabled students as on the students without learning disabilities. Having raised a learning disabled child, I knew the broad spectrum of students covered by the term, from children who have difficulty reading and writing (dyslexia and dysgraphia), to those who have difficulty with concentration (attention deficit and hyperactivity disorder). The rationale for including learning disabled children in the same pool with other students was as much ideological as practical. Grounded in the same philosophy that mandates color blindness in the area of race, a guiding principle of No Child Left Behind is that "all students, including students with disabilities, be held to the same challenging content and achievement standards."[30]

Surely an institution like Greenhaven, where so many children could not see or hear or hold pencils or read Braille, would be exempt from No Child Left Behind. The teachers at Greenhaven had always identified goals for their students in the IEP. But as No Child Left Behind was being implemented, they were required to set annual benchmarks for progress toward these goals. Children must be tested and would have to achieve 80 percent of their goal in order for the school to receive a passing grade. I saw this process in action in Ms. Sutton's classroom. Samantha had a new curriculum designed to mesh with the statewide standards—tasks like, "Illustrate the concept of subtraction using groups of objects." Samantha had demonstrated this skill sporadically by removing objects from her tray, but today was not a good day for her. Despite repeated attempts by her teacher and the aides to interest her in the objects on her tray, she was unable to illustrate anything at all with them. She received a zero on her chart. And so it went throughout the day. Each zero dutifully recorded on the chart seemed to sap some of Ms. Sutton's cheer and verve, although she worked hard not to communicate this to Samantha.

A check of the Code of Federal Regulations confirmed what Ms. Sutton had told me. In fact, a new requirement had been added that, in addition to following children's individualized plans as required by the IDEA, teachers of disabled students must now demonstrate adequate yearly progress for each student in each area of the state's *standardized* statewide curriculum for reading, language arts, and mathematics. Educators were to identify a "continuum of 'entry points' at which a student with disabilities can access the content at an appropriately challenging level." As the regulators explained,

> [a]lternate achievement standards must be aligned with the State's academic content standards, promote access to the general curriculum, and reflect professional judgment of the highest learning standards possible for the group of students with the most significant cognitive disabilities. In practice, alignment with the State's academic content standards means that the State has defined clearly the connection between the instructional content appropriate for non-disabled students and the related knowledge and skills that may serve as the basis for a definition of proficient achievement for students with the most significant cognitive disabilities.[31]

What I had witnessed was the effects of putting this theory into practice.

The model of "adequate yearly improvement" in skills dictated by a standard statewide curriculum was all wrong for Greenhaven children. Many of the Greenhaven students were never going to improve beyond a certain level. It was all the teachers could do to maintain the child's skills. And, as Ms. Sutton explained, many of the children were suffering from degenerative conditions that would likely end in an early death. No matter how skilled the teacher or hardworking the child, ground would inevitably be lost as the disease progressed. Defining success for these children, and for their teachers, required understanding the child in context.

Applying the No Child Left Behind model to Greenhaven children also created a perverse incentive that surely had not been intended. Instead of raising their expectations, teachers were forced to lower them. Greenhaven's successes stemmed from the willingness of the teachers to set high but individualized expectations and to work tirelessly toward these expectations, year after year, when others might have been discouraged. Recall that it had taken Ms. Sutton a full year to teach Mara to signal she needed her diaper changed. And Naomi, the child who walked so tirelessly through the botanical garden, had put in six years making zero progress toward the goal of walking—not one single step. After No Child Left Behind, no teacher could afford to fail so visibly, day after day and year after year. Better to set a modest goal with the hope of achieving 80 percent of it than to set an ambitious goal and be penalized for failing to reach it within the prescribed time.

It should come as no surprise that No Child Left Behind was failing the children at Greenhaven. According to many critics, from Red States as well as Blue, No Child Left Behind has been failing children all over America. The accountability imposed by the Act was supposed to close the achievement gap between poor and wealthy, black and white, and there has been some success in this regard. Parents of many students with learning disabilities support the legislation's strong commitment to educational equality.

But I believe its basic premise is flawed. Instead of focusing our assets and energies on each child as an individual and his or her capacity to learn, the legislation has forced our public schools to treat children as if they were all the same. Schools with poor children from struggling families must compete with schools in affluent neighborhoods. Children for whom English is a second language must be tested along with native speakers. All but the most severely disabled children are measured by the same yardstick as children who have no disabilities.[32] Parents can take their child out of a school that does not make a passing grade and the school will lose funding. Eventually, the only children left behind in the "failing" schools will be those students whose parents are unable or unwilling to take an active part in their education.

In thinking about how the principle of equality applies to children, we must recognize that children are not equal to adults or to one another, or even to themselves at various stages of development. Equality for children must mean something other than identical treatment. The dissenters in *Rowley* were right. The heart of equality for children is the child's right to an equal opportunity to achieve his or her natural potential. Helen Keller's story, as well as those of Mara and Naomi, shows us how the child's natural drive to engage her surroundings and experience her world can surmount seemingly insurmountable barriers. But these breakthroughs were possible because adults respected the children's innate capacities, however different, and encouraged them to grow. By applying standardized measures to our disabled children we ignore their dignity as individuals and deprive them of the equal opportunity to excel in their own ways.

I would go further and argue that the disabled child is the miner's canary, signaling what is wrong with current educational policies. Policies like No Child Left Behind, which focus solely on outputs rather then on the process of learning, violate the rights of "normal" children as well as those who face exceptional educational challenges. Children may have varying abilities to process information, but each child has what Helen Keller called "a sense of think." Forcing all children to think and learn in the same ways, and measuring all children's achievements by the same narrow set of criteria, violates their developmental rights to be treated as unique and valuable individuals. While the injury to children in the general population may be subtler, all children suffer when their individuality is subsumed in order to standardize the child as the end product of an educational system.[33]

This concept is a bedrock principle of American constitutional law on education. In cases dating back to the 1920s, such as *Meyer v. Nebraska* and *Pierce v. Society of Sisters*, the Supreme Court rejected the standardization of children as fundamentally un-American. These cases involved laws passed in response to the perceived crisis of immigration and the rise of communism. In *Meyer*, children were prohibited from learning foreign languages, and in *Pierce* they were required to attend only public schools. In those days, the rights at stake were identified primarily as rights of parents to educate their children as they saw fit. But the underlying rationale remains highly relevant to thinking about children's rights. In a democracy, education should not be used to impose uniformity of thought on all children, even in the name of national goals of unity and progress. Children should be allowed to develop in ways that reflect the diversity of their families and their diversity as individuals. Of course, some standardization is necessary in order to hold educators accountable for educating the young. But when the goal of standardization displaces the individualized processes of children's learning, I would argue it has gone too far. In curricular design, as well as in testing, children should have a right to a useful education fitted to their needs.

The reality of children's difference from adults and from one another pushes us to construct a deeper and more complex meaning for the idea of equality.[34] Given children's diversity, mandating equal outcomes seems like a rather shallow way to measure a child's or a teacher's success. Looking at equality through a developmental lens, it seems that Brazelton is right—all children have an irreducible need for experiences tailored to individual differences. At the same time, Helen's story illustrates children's needs for structure and limit-setting if they are to achieve their full potential. Spending time with Mara and Naomi also reminds us that the human dignity of each child transcends her impairments. In addition to teaching us about equality and dignity, the stories of children like Helen and Mara vividly illustrate the importance of the agency principle, for this is what unlocks the child's sense of think. We can also see the key role of children's own agency in the process of learning and growing. It is easy to imagine a disabled child's needs-based rights—in fact, the educational polestar at Greenhaven has been identifying and meeting the students' most basic and pragmatic everyday needs. Placed in context, we can also see the roles of capacity-based rights, even in the lives of severely disabled children. We can only teach when we accept the child as a partner in learning and respect the child's developmental needs above our yearning for order and accountability.

Annie Sullivan, back in 1877, captured the folly of allowing testing to displace teaching:

> I am convinced that the time spent by the teacher in digging out of the child what she has put into him, for the sake of satisfying herself that it has taken root, is so much time thrown away. *It's much*

better, I think, to assume that the child is doing his part, and that the seed you have sown will bear fruit in due time. It's only fair to the child, anyhow, and it saves you much unnecessary trouble.[35]

Sullivan had the luxury of working one on one, in a less technological era with an exceptional and affluent student. In the modern world of public education, we cannot simply stop testing. And standardization of course content is a necessary tool of education policy. But there must be limits on government's freedom to impose its will on students, and teachers, in the name of educating the young. Looking at education policy through the prism of children's rights should sensitize us to the risk of abusing our power over children to advance adult ideologies and adult agendas. While it is hard to draw abstract lines separating valid from invalid policies, in other rights-based contexts we hold government has overstepped its authority when its policies are arbitrary and capricious or fail to advance legitimate state interests. Under this standard, the most blatant examples of abuse in the name of education would speak for themselves.

In her latest e-mail message to me, the ever-cheerful and creative Susan Sutton described how she developed a unit on "The Bill of Rights," complete with individual assessment portfolio, to comply with the requirement in No Child left Behind that she teach and test her class of four severely disabled thirteen-year-olds—who could neither read nor write nor speak, and who had so many more important things to learn—on the first ten amendments to the U.S. Constitution, as mandated by the statewide standard civics curriculum. "It was not so bad," she told me.

> Here's what I did. I took three amendments, 1, 4, and 5, and we made a sign for our bulletin board, "Bill of rights just for me." Then we went to the polls (rerun election in the cafeteria) with a survey. The kids asked people which was their favorite amendment of the three, by using voice in-putted speaking devices. We are going to take an age appropriate doll around the building in a toy wheelchair and build ramps where there are stairs (to illustrate the Americans with Disabilities Act and simple machinery for science).

> We are going on a field trip to the state capital next month, and
> will do something interesting there.

As you picture these activities, recall that these children are all se-
verely and profoundly retarded with multiple physical, developmental, and neurological handicaps. It takes a year of hard work
to teach them a fundamental concept, like signaling Yes or No.
Ms. Sutton closed this description of a gifted teacher laboring to
teach her students in the face of an arbitrary and capricious educational policy with a final observation on the burdens of testing.
"These portfolios we need for the new assessment require 38
pieces of paper per child. Wow. Glad to be retiring."

PART IV

THE DIGNITY PRINCIPLE: STORIES OF RESISTANCE AND RESILIENCE

CHAPTER 10

HIDE AND SURVIVE

Anne Frank and "Liu"

Ours was not the usual kind of hiding: we were not in an attic
or underground; we were in plain sight.
    —Holocaust survivor Renee Roth-Hano[1]

Children everywhere, in common with the young of
many species, instinctively know and love to play the
game of "hide and seek." I remember the delicious suspense of hiding with my best friend Sally, packed like sardines in a kitchen
pantry and suppressing our giggles, while the big boys prowled the
house, bragging that there was no place we could hide that they
could not find us. We knew better—eventually they gave up and
admitted we had won. Like much of the play of children, this game
had a very serious purpose. Hide and seek has its roots in a primitive world where survival of the small and weak depends upon the
ability to hide in absolute silence while a predator stalks nearby.

Nature often provides special camouflage to the young, equipping them to blend into their surroundings, remaining still and
quiet, while their parents must leave them unprotected to hunt for
food. Human children have used these hiding strategies in times of
danger, sometimes by hiding out of sight and sometimes by hiding
in plain view, by denying their identities so they might blend into

hostile or dangerous surroundings. Uncounted numbers of children have hidden their religion, ethnicity, and sex in order to escape a genocidal enemy. During the Holocaust, Jewish boys pretended to be girls, to avoid exposing their circumcisions. Jewish girls mimed Catholic confession and communion in order to blend in with the Catholic girls in convents where they were hidden. Sophisticated city children pretended to be illiterate peasants. This deadly serious game, played in Europe during World War II, was played also by Muslim children in Bosnia, urban children in Cambodia, Tutsi children in Rwanda, African American children during Jim Crow, and "wetback" children in the American Southwest. All have been forced to hide their family and their identity in order to survive.

The most famous of hidden children did not survive (Fig. 7). She was betrayed and captured, and died in the Bergen-Belsen Nazi concentration camp at the age of sixteen. She left behind a written record of her time in hiding that remained hidden in the drawer of a desk in Amsterdam until after the war was over. The book we know as *Anne Frank: Diary of a Young Girl*, was first published in 1947 as *Het Achterhuis* (*The House Behind*). It has become the most widely read account of the Holocaust, translated into almost every language and assigned reading for school children around the world. When I wrote *Hidden in Plain Sight*, on children's rights and American values, I included Anne's story because, although she was not an American child by birth, her story is that of so many children who came to America as refugees from persecution. Anne Frank's story is so deeply embedded in American consciousness and so powerfully shapes American children's understanding of injustice it could not be left out of the narratives included herein.

However, few of the American children and adults who read the diary, or see the films and plays it inspired, understand that they are reading a carefully crafted piece of writing. I assumed, when I first read the diary as a teenager, that it was a naive series of daily reflections such as any teenage diarist might have created to while away the time while in hiding. In fact, Anne wrote several drafts of her diary, revising and analyzing her own work as she perfected her

Fig. 7. Anne Frank on a West German postage stamp, 1979 (with permission of The Granger Collection).

craft. Fifty years after her death, her biographer Melissa Müller analyzed all of Anne's surviving writings to better understand what motivated her to write. Here are some key excerpts.

> I have made up my mind now to lead a different life from other girls and, later on, different from ordinary housewives.[2]

> Oh yes, I don't want to have lived for nothing like most people. I want to be useful or give pleasure to the people around me yet who don't really know me. I want to go on living even after my death! And therefore I am grateful to God for giving me this gift, this possibility of developing myself and of writing, of expressing all that is in me![3]

You've known for a long time that my greatest wish is to become a journalist someday and later on a famous writer. Whether these leanings to greatness (or insanity?) will ever materialize remains to be seen, but I certainly have the subjects in my mind. In any case, I want to publish a book titled *Het Achterhuis* after the war, whether I shall succeed or not, I cannot say, but my diary will be a great help.[4]

If God lets me live . . . I shall not remain insignificant, I shall work in the world and for mankind.[5]

These are the reflections of a young author who is determined to make her mark. As Müller puts it,

The Nazis had taken from Anne her freedom to make decisions and choices in so many routine matters of life. But until a few months before her death in Bergen-Belsen, her interest in life, the hope that interest gave her, and her will to live did not desert her. Under the pressure of persecution she created for herself—much earlier than many young people do—her own place in life and insisted on setting specific goals for herself and working toward their realization.[6]

Anne's ambition to become a journalist and speak out against the Nazi regime was an integral part of her resistance to oppression. In March of 1944, she heard a radio address by an exiled Dutch leader urging Dutch citizens to keep diaries to document their courage and suffering for future generations. Anne took this charge very seriously, revising her earlier writings and giving pseudonyms to those who helped the family hide. "I can shake off everything if I write, my sorrows disappear, my courage is reborn."[7] While her prayer for a long life was not answered, her ambition to be a "famous writer" who would "work in the world for mankind" was realized to a degree she could hardly have imagined. Anne Frank is undoubtedly the most famous and widely read "journalist" of the Nazi Holocaust. Royalties from her works continue to fund the Anne Frank Foundation, whose mission is to foster relationships between youth of different faiths and nations and to fight against intolerance.

Anne Frank is unique among young writers in yet another way. Students of Anne Frank and her work cannot treat her childhood as a mere preface to her adult life—they must treat her story as a life story, with a meaning and integrity of its own. Unlike Fred Douglass and Ben Franklin, she did not live long enough to write a book that looked back on her teenage years. She wrote about them as she lived them, with intensity and honesty. She was changing even as she wrote. We know that the fifteen-year-old Anne thought some of her reflections penned a year or two earlier were naive. We will never read what Anne would have approved as her final draft for publication. But the work that survives is a classic that stands on its own without need for apology or revision.

More than fifty years after Anne Frank's death, Melissa Müller published the first comprehensive and carefully researched biography of Anne Frank—to my knowledge, it is the first serious biography of any child or adolescent. Anne was born into a fairly affluent Jewish family in Germany. Her family left Germany in 1934, when the Nazis first came to power, hoping to find safety in Holland, a country with a long history of tolerance and a well-established Jewish community. But six years later, the Germans invaded Holland. The Nazis targeted gypsies, homosexuals, disabled people, and many others in addition to Jews for persecution and extermination. But before I visited the Anne Frank House in Amsterdam I had not realized that the Nazis specifically targeted children. This fact was driven home to me as I made my pilgrimage to the narrow row house beside the canal at 263 Prinsengracht. Anne's house has become a stop on the network of canal boats that transport citizens around the town. Today, visitors can tour a carefully researched replica of the "Secret Annex." Forty years ago, the building was rescued from demolition and restored to its wartime appearance. The hiding place of the Frank family consisted of several rooms entered through a door concealed behind a cupboard on a stair landing in the rear portion of the commercial building that housed Mr. Frank's business. Otto Frank had signed the business over to loyal gentile friends and workers who would protect the Frank family if they were forced into hiding. In these rooms, Anne and her family, as well as another family of three, were hidden from July 6, 1942, until August 4, 1944. On that day, an anonymous caller reported to the Gestapo that there were Jews hiding in the building, and they were captured and deported.

As the docent who conducted my tour of the Secret Annex explained as the tour was ending, Anne Frank had celebrated her fifteenth birthday in the Annex just a few months before she was sent to Auschwitz. Children were useless to the Nazi war machine, except as guinea pigs in medical experiments. On arrival in Auschwitz, the males were separated from the females. This would be the last time Anne would see her father. Then the captives were sorted into two lines, on the right were those capable of working and on the left were the old, the young, and the ill, who were to be immediately exterminated. Children under age fifteen or sixteen were generally sent to the left. Anne's diary shows how she struggled to be accepted as an adult and resented being treated as a child—this time, she got her way. On the cusp between childhood and adulthood, she was sent to the right with the women, and survived this heinous process of "Selection."[8] As I listened to the docent tell this story, I realized for the first time that the one and a half million Jewish children murdered in the Holocaust were murdered not only because they were Jewish but also because they were *children*.

Before long, Anne and her sister were separated from their mother and shipped to Bergen-Belsen. Her biographer provides a detailed account of the horrors of Anne's last months that is almost unbearable to read. Separated from both her parents, weakened by typhus, starvation, and grief, Anne died in Bergen-Belsen in March 1945 only a month before the camp was liberated.

For Anne Frank, unlawful imprisonment, forced labor, untreated illness, and starvation were only the final chapters in a long story of persecution. Many of the harms inflicted on Jewish children were uniquely designed to destroy the growing child's freedom, spirit, and sense of identity. Shortly after the invasion, books by Jews were ordered removed from school libraries in Holland. In January 1941, Jews were banned from movie theaters—a change that was keenly felt by Anne, who adored movies and movie stars. In May 1941, just in time for the school holidays, Jews were banned from beaches, pools, parks, spas, and hotels.[9] In September 1941, as a new school year was about to start, Anne had to say goodbye to the Montessori school she had always attended and was exiled from all her gentile friends. All Jewish children were ordered to attend a separate Jewish school hastily constructed in a former factory. Strangely, the children remembered this school as a warm and friendly environment, a place of respite from the growing persecution outside its walls. In April 1942, all Jewish adults and children over six years of age were forced to wear a yellow cloth star. Now easily identifiable, Jews were prohibited from shopping in stores, associating with non-Jews, or going freely in the public streets. Their bicycles were confiscated. They could not use public transportation. A curfew kept them inside their homes between 8:00 p.m. and 6:00 a.m. Jews were forbidden to play any sport, from tennis to soccer. As Müller notes, "For the children, these restrictions were painful experiences of isolation, humiliation, and rejection, a noose that was pulled tighter and tighter each day, leaving them less and less room to breathe."[10]

Jewish parents grew increasingly desperate with each of these new restrictions, and their fears could no longer be hidden from their children. One of the early entries in Anne's diary, which had been a gift for her thirteenth birthday on June 12, 1942, concerns Otto Frank's terror and anger when Anne came home five minutes late, violating the Nazi curfew. She was distraught, because she had made her gentle father so angry. Finally, an event they had dreaded sent the family into hiding in June of 1942. Anne's sixteen-year-old sister Margot received an order to report for transportation to a labor camp in Germany. The family was determined to stay together and hiding seemed their only option.

As this litany illustrates, Anne and other Jewish children in Holland were systematically persecuted from the moment of the Nazi invasion, deprived of the crucial freedoms of education, association, and speech and even the freedom to play. The Nazi objective was destruction of a race, which could only be accomplished through

destruction of the dignity of the individual and of family ties between parents and children, wives and husbands. In September
1944, Anne suffered her greatest loss. She was separated from the
person she most loved, her father Otto Frank, and soon after, she
was separated from her mother. At the time of her death, it was
Anne's belief that both of her parents were already dead. A school
friend who was the last to speak with her in the camps reported, "It
was so terrible. She immediately began to cry and she told me 'I
don't have parents anymore.' " Anne did not know, when she spoke
these words, that only a few days earlier the Russian Army had liberated her father Otto Frank from Auschwitz. As her school friend
observed, "I always think that if Anne had known her father was
still alive, she might have had more strength to survive."[11]

Anne Frank is the most famous of the hidden children of the
Holocaust, but there were many thousands more. Initially, most
child survivors remained silent, feeling a mixture of gratitude and
guilt at having lived when so many others died. In 1991, at the
First International Gathering of Children Hidden during World
War II, 1,800 of these survivors met in New York City. Jane Marks
gathers twenty-three of their stories in her 1998 book *The Hidden
Children: The Secret Survivors of the Holocaust*. The Hidden Child
Foundation continues to gather and disseminate the stories of their
suffering and their courage, and it provides narratives, speakers,
and teachers' guides so that modern children can learn about their
experiences.[12]

Strangely, while many of their memories are harrowing, other
memories involve cherished moments of intimacy with parents
who made them feel loved and safe in the midst of unspeakable
brutality and hardship. Nicole David recalled hiding in a ditch as a
four-year-old during a strafing by enemy planes while her parents
lay on top of her to shield her body. "When the bombing stopped
and not everyone got up, I realized how lucky I was to have my
parents to protect me. I was certain that, as long as I had them,
nothing bad could happen to me."[13] Richard Rozen, recalling his
family's many months in hiding in a box the size of an armoire,
says "one great thing about this odd existence was that I got to see

so much of my father for the first time in my life! He taught me the alphabet and counting to one hundred by writing on the palm of my hand and silently whispering in my ear. I was challenged and fascinated."[14] These were precious memories that sustained him even after his father was killed.

After thirteen months, the Rozen family was forced to leave its hiding place and flee into the night. As dawn arrived, he recalls, "something extraordinary happened: the color of the world began to change from pitch black to the pinks, reds and oranges of a sunrise. I was dazzled!" Having known only darkness for one quarter of his life, he saw the world as painfully and achingly beautiful. Such moments of beauty, intimacy, and hope were rare but precious to all the hidden children.

Now, the Rozen family's only hope for survival lay in hiding their Jewish identity. Captured by German soldiers, their secret was revealed when the soldiers ordered Richard and his father to drop their trousers and expose their circumcised penises. Sent to the ghetto, they once again escaped. This time, Richard hid with his mother in a Polish village by masquerading as a Christian girl. As a girl, he would not be asked to expose his private parts for inspection. Soon, he rejoined his father who was with a band of partisans, tending to their wounded. When he was nine, Richard was given the job of "feather boy" by the partisans, which involved holding a feather under the noses of ambushed German soldiers to insure they were really dead. In yet another strategy of the children's deadly game of hide and survive, he forced himself to suppress the empathy he felt for the soldiers who begged for mercy, because he knew it was kill or be killed.

After the war was over, ten-year-old Richard found that his skill at survival was now a liability. His father had been killed when Russian bombs destroyed the partisan field hospital. Now Richard and his mother returned penniless to a Poland that did not welcome its exiled Jews. It became important to survival for Richard to hide his past. His mother was unable to deal with the full extent of the horrors he had seen. "One day we came across a Jewish man who had been shot. He was lying in the street. My mother saw me looking and she pushed me away. She said, 'You can't see those things. It's not for little children.' I said to her, '*Little children?* I spent a year and a half as a partisan. What's another dead person?' She was horrified." For as long as she lived, mother and son avoided speaking about it.

After wandering from place to place, they thought they had found refuge with relatives in France. But during the first evening in this bourgeois home, Richard was caught hiding slices of roast beef under his shirt at the dinner table. His horrified aunt thought him so savage she insisted he be sent to an orphanage to protect her little girls from his bad influence. He spent four years in this orphanage while his mother scrabbled for money to emigrate. Finally, a full decade after he had first gone into hiding in the Polish farmer's cellar, he and his mother were able to join an uncle in Australia. He was terrified that he might make a fatal mistake, as he had in France. He hid his hunger and thirst. He remembers the joyful moment when his aunt assured him that he could pour himself a full glass of milk without risking rejection—it was the first full glass of milk he had drunk in twelve years.

Here is how Richard Rozen sums up his experience as a boy who played and won the game of hide and survive:

> What's the bottom line for me? To survive the war made everything else seem easy. On the positive side I have a lot of willpower, determination to succeed at all cost, the ability to work hard and avoid the pitfalls, and also the ability to put on a good act. On the negative side I've had difficulty learning to trust and to love people enough. Have I been successful in my life? Yes! Am I happy? That is still a question mark.[15]

As I read the narratives of the hidden children both online and in books, it seemed that the children who had remained with their parents, even under horrific circumstances, had suffered less emotional trauma than those who were separated from their parents. The Hidden Child Web site includes an analysis by a child psychiatrist of the lasting psychological trauma of separation from one's family and how it affected children hidden with gentile rescuers or in convents and orphanages. Children who hid in sewers or in hay stacks, who were kept in cellars or in attics, relate their experiences of running, hiding, being tormented by rats, illness, and cold, but their accounts are free of the searing loneliness and self-doubt that marks so many of the stories of children who passed the war years with strangers, hiding in plain sight.

Meanwhile, the desperate game continues around the world, wherever children are persecuted because of their race, tribe, religion, birth status, gender, or simply because they are children. Jewish organizations continue to assist not only Jews but also people of every nation who are fleeing from persecution. I learned the story of one such child from my longtime friend Judith Bernstein-Baker, who serves as executive director of HIAS and Council Migration Service of Philadelphia. HIAS of Philadelphia (which stands for Hebrew Immigrant Aid Society) began its work as early as 1882, under the name of Association for Protection of Jewish Immigrants. While HIAS and Council Migration Service of Philadelphia continues to assist Jewish immigrants, its case load includes refugees and asylum seekers from every part of the world, including Africa, Asia, Eastern Europe, Russia, the Middle East, and Latin America. HIAS Philadelphia's symbol is the Statue of Liberty and its motto is "helping to reach the dream." Its mission is "to advance the fair treatment and protection of the rights of immigrants and refugees, and to educate [the] larger community about the positive economic, social and cultural contributions made by new Americans."[16]

I called Judy, who had been a lawyer for children before she joined HIAS, because I wanted to be able to tell the story of a modern-day hidden child. Judy had many such stories to tell, of children from Russia to Rwanda. Especially poignant was the story of a Chinese girl I shall call Liu. Born in a small village in Fujian Province, Liu was the oldest of three children. She and her siblings were persecuted throughout her childhood because her parents had violated the one-child policy. The family was always poor but its troubles began in earnest when Liu was about two and her mother became pregnant with a second child. The family wanted a son, but the new baby was a girl. "In China," Liu writes in her affidavit,

we have a term known as "black child." This is a child who has no
identity papers because the family violated the one-child policy. In
my parents' case, they wanted to have a boy. This is a very strong
tradition in China, especially among the Buddhists. My family is
Buddhist; my mother goes to a Temple to pray and we have a
statute of Buddha in my home in China. I often accompanied my
mother. When my sister was born, although a second child was
permitted, my parents did not report her birth.[17]

As a "black child," Liu's sister was without identity papers and
her family had to shoulder the entire burden of raising her, including paying tuition for her at school. When Liu's mother became pregnant again, she was hoping to bear a son. To hide her
condition, she was forced to move to another village where she
stayed until the child was born. Four-year-old Liu must have
missed her mother terribly. This time the baby was a son, but the
government soon found out about his birth and the family was
punished with a heavy fine. Already poor, they were unable to
pay the fine and were driven from their home. When Liu was
seven, her mother again became pregnant. This time, the woman
was forcibly sterilized. When Liu was ten years old, her father
had to leave the country in search of work, and the family was
forced into hiding to avoid the government officials who were
still pressing for payment of the fine, which this poor farming
family could never hope to pay. They were even stigmatized and
persecuted by their own relatives.

Liu hoped to gain an education and be able to help her family
rise out of poverty. Although Liu was second in her high school
class, she was forced to leave school to care for her mother, whose
health had been destroyed by stress and malnutrition. Then, when
Liu was seventeen years old, she took a very serious risk. One
might think that she had been taught a lesson by the authorities
and would know better than to help someone else violate the one-
child rule. But Liu was arrested for hiding her pregnant cousin in
her home. Her cousin was forced to have an abortion, and when
Liu protested she was fined and imprisoned.

With her mother's blessing, she decided she must escape from China. Her relatives had saved money to pay agents to smuggle her across the border to Vietnam and to provide her with false papers. She made her way to Vietnam and then to the United States. When Judith met her, she was living with her aunt and uncle in Philadelphia, and had applied for asylum in the United States. Here is how she summed up her case in a statement titled "Why I Seek Asylum":

> Although I left China after the police were trying to find me, I am afraid to go back to China because my family and I have suffered for many years. Because of the one-child policy, my family was stigmatized and plunged into poverty. We were never rich to begin with, but we became destitute. We even had to sell chickens that were given to us for food. The only way out of this is through education. But due to pressure exerted on my mother from the one-child policy she became ill and I was forced to leave school. I am unable to have a life in China. If I return it would be even worse. I would be fined and jailed because I left China without proper papers. I realize that the way I entered the United States was against the law. But there was no other way to escape from China.[18]

China's one-child policy punishes children simply for being born.[19] It has forced many pregnant women and their babies into hiding. It has led to widespread abandonment of newborns, especially girls, and to high rates of infanticide. So-called black children are denied basic rights to a name and identity, and their rights to equal treatment regardless of birth status are violated systematically. It is a testament to her spirit that Liu, whose childhood was scarred by this form of persecution, would risk jail by helping her cousin and would leave behind everything she knew in order to spare her own children from persecution.

Under international law, a refugee is someone who was the victim of persecution or has a well-founded fear of persecution, based upon religion, nationality, political opinion, race, or membership in a particular social group. Economic hardship does not qualify as a basis for seeking asylum. Under U.S. immigration law, a refugee must also have completed all the required paperwork and processing prior to entering the United States. Liu has a well-founded fear of persecution, but she does not qualify for refugee status because she entered the United States without having completed an application—this would have been very difficult since, given China's policies and her troubles with police, she was unable to obtain a valid passport or travel document. Although she arrived illegally, she immediately applied for asylum. On the very day she arrived in the United States, she told the Immigration and Naturalization officer in the airport that she had no papers and that she had fled from China and was afraid to go back. If she is granted asylum, she will be eligible after one year to apply for permanent resident status. If not, she will be deported. Especially in this post-9/11 world, her chances of success are extremely slim.

Emma Lazarus, in her poem "The New Colossus," described Liberty as the "Mother of Exiles." She gave voice to the destiny of America as a new world of refuge from persecution:

> "Keep, ancient lands, your storied pomp," she cries with silent lips.
> "Give me your tired, your poor, your huddled masses yearning to breathe free, the wretched refuse of your teaming shore. Send these, the homeless, tempest-tost to me. I lift my lamp beside the golden door!"

Despite this glorification of America as a haven for refugees, the United States has often been slow to open its doors in times of crisis. During the period when Anne Frank's family was in hiding, the United States was slow to credit the evidence of mass murders of Jews, and thousands of Jewish refugees were turned away and refused asylum.[20] American values represented by the metaphor of a lamp beside the golden door are at greatest risk when most sorely tested. In the aftermath of 9/11, admissions of refugees fell abruptly from an annual average of 76,000 to less than 29,000 in 2002 and 2003.[21]

As Anne's and Liu's stories remind us, even very young hidden children and youthful refugees are able to keep hoping and fighting for a better life despite persecution that has shattered the hopes of the adults around them. The dramatic stories of hidden children in foreign lands should serve as well to sensitize us to the situation of hidden children closer to home. At various times and in various places, children in America have faced extreme pressure to deny their family, religious, racial, or ethnic identities.

Perhaps the most public example in American history of children being forced to abandon their identities occurred in the Indian Boarding Schools in the late 1800s and early 1900s. Well-meaning reformers within the federal Bureau of Indian Affairs (BIA) believed that it was possible, if training began early enough in childhood, to teach "primitive" peoples such as the American Indian to assimilate into "civilized" mainstream culture. Beginning shortly after the Civil War, thousands of Native American children were taken from their families and sent to BIA boarding schools that were explicitly designed and intended to train them out of their Indian ways and to fit them for industrial work in modern society.[22] Children were forbidden to speak their native languages or observe native customs. Many ran away and, when caught, were severely punished. These policies were abandoned and federal laws now protect Native American children's culture and heritage and establish preferences for adoptive and foster care placements of Indian children within their own tribes.[23] But several generations of Native American children suffered under this policy of separation and forced reeducation. Survivors of the Bureau's initiative have had to struggle to recapture their cultural and linguistic heritage.[24]

Before 9/11, few Americans gave much thought to another group of hidden children—the thousands of undocumented alien children hiding in plain sight in the United States. Estimates of the numbers of undocumented aliens currently in the United States vary widely, but some place the number as high as 12 million. Anxieties about job security and declining wages, as much as fears that terrorists will penetrate our "porous borders," have caused many Americans to favor harsh sanctions against immigrants who entered the country without proper documentation. The issue spilled into the streets in 2006 after the House of Representatives passed a bill making presence in the United States without proper documentation a felony.[25]

The bill also imposed criminal penalties on persons who hid, fed, or otherwise aided and abetted undocumented aliens in trying to avoid detection and deportation. These policies sharply divided the population as well as the Congress. Tens of thousands of people across America, many of them undocumented aliens but many of them citizens and voters, marched in protests. In a rare prime-time message, President George W. Bush spoke to the people of the United States suggesting a compromise immigration plan. Bush proposed sending the National Guard to seal our border with Mexico and renewed his plan for a guest worker program so aliens could enter and work legally without becoming permanent residents. When the Senate, a few weeks later, backed an immigration bill that avoided criminalization and included avenues for legalization of undocumented immigrants, the battle lines became clear. Here was a situation that challenged American values, but which American values? Many Americans resonated to rhetoric portraying immigrant parents as coming to America to "make a better life for their children." But many Americans also resonated to the rhetoric portraying undocumented aliens as lawbreakers willing to gain unfair advantage and jump their place in line, by sneaking across the border. It was fascinating and painful to see Americans struggling to balance deeply rooted values of fairness and tolerance and equally deeply rooted sentiments of respect for law and feelings that America owed its primary allegiance to Americans.[26]

Amnesty became a dirty word, avoided by both major parties, yet if the immigration problem was to be solved something had to be done about the 12 million so-called illegals presently hiding in plain sight. Should all of them be arrested and deported? Should some of them be given a chance to become legal, green-card-carrying immigrants and, eventually, citizens? If so, who and under what restrictions or penalties? At this writing, it is unclear how these tensions will be resolved or whether sufficient consensus will emerge to allow passage of any legislation at all.[27]

Children's rights and American values about family and childhood are central to these debates. Children serve a key symbolic role on both sides of the divide. To supporters of amnesty, they provide a cleansing metaphor excusing illegal entry as an act of selflessness done by parents for their children. To hard-liners, immigrant children figure as competitors with their own young, vying with native-born children for a share of scarce public resources. According to one Web site, immigrant workers take food from the mouths of poor American children by depressing wages, and their children take places in American schools and colleges that should go first to Americans.[28]

As we grapple with immigration reform, Americans are facing a moral dilemma. A basic value of American law is that innocent persons should not be punished. The Supreme Court applied this concept in the 1982 case of *Plyler v. Doe*, striking down a Texas law that denied access to public education to undocumented alien children. The Court held that it was wrong to punish innocent children for the deeds of their parents and irrational to create a permanent underclass of people who would have no education and no prospects for contributing to society.[29] Since that time the children of illegal alien parents have been able to attend school. Recall that Mara, the Russian child I met at Greenhaven, was not eligible for Medicaid because she was an undocumented alien. But she was eligible to attend school and to receive special education targeted to her severe disabilities.

Each year, approximately 65,000 undocumented alien children who have lived in the United States for at least five years graduate from U.S. high schools. These are kids who have grown up in America, and speak and write English. They graduate into limbo. They drive without licenses and work off the books. They have grown up with the American dream, but suddenly all roads seem closed to them. Most come from poor families but they are ineligible for Pell grants or in-state tuition at public universities and they have no way to legalize their status. Buried in the pages of the huge and complex Senate bill of 2006 was a proposal called the DREAM Act.[30] The Development, Relief, and Education for Alien Minors Act, was first introduced in 2001. The DREAM Act would apply to students of good moral character who have lived in the United States for at least five years and who entered at age fifteen or younger. Upon high school graduation or acceptance at college, students would be eligible to apply for conditional permanent resident status. After six years, if they had successfully completed two years of college or military service and had continued to be model citizens, they would be eligible for permanent resident status.

Of the 65,000 students annually who are theoretically covered by the DREAM Act, only a small fraction would ultimately qualify. Yet undocumented young people all over the country know all about the DREAM Act. The information superhighway, where kids can drive without a license, has helped spread the word. When I visited it in May of 2006, it was buzzing with talk among kids who are waiting and hoping. Listen to Victor, who posted this message in December 2005:

> If the Dream Act becomes law, it will greatly influence my opportunities to acquire a better job, drivers' license, and maybe financial aid. I'm currently attending college—although it's very tough coming up with $ to pay because it's hard to get a job in this situation—but I'm trying & don't plan to give up. I graduated as top 15% of my class. How can they possibly think that we pose a threat to America and want to treat us as CRIMINALS! I agree that there's a lot of immigrants that don't have good moral standings—but the government has a way of finding them and getting them out, but us . . . we shouldn't be treated like criminals when we are not!!! We didn't choose to come here, although we greatly appreciate it, and for most of us, returning us back to our country—a place we don't know, where we have no family, where we have no life, alone—it's just very unfair.[31]

Pamela, posting on March 26, 2006, took courage from reading others' stories:

> I thought I was in my own little world with my own set of problems; however, that is not the case, as all of you out there know how complicated our life's are because we are "illegal aliens." However, I also believe that together we can make a difference!!! I graduated from high school with high honors, was member of the

volleyball team, track and field team, leadership, president of Latino Club, and many other community service clubs. I was accepted to every university I applied to. One day a cruel reality stomped all over my dreams; my parents were not able to pay for my college tuition and I was not a candidate for financial aid. All my doors shattered, but my scholarships for which I am so thankful for helped me tremendously. Now I am getting ready to transfer to a university again. I fear the same story will repeat itself.

Young people seeking passage of the DREAM Act have taken a page from the history of the civil rights movement of the 1960s. They have been visiting the offices of politicians, gathering signatures on petitions, and picketing. Some have gone on hunger strikes.[32]

What do Anne and the hidden children of the Holocaust and Liu and the refugees from China have in common with these undocumented alien children? In all of these cases, through no fault of their own, children have been forced to hide who they are in order to survive. They have been taken from one world into an unfamiliar other world, faced with assimilating new languages and new customs. Their mesosystems, those places where microsystems overlap, have been fractured and fraught with tension among their status as family members, their status as students, and their status as illegal aliens. Their resilience has helped them to survive difficult circumstances and, in many cases, to thrive. From a developmental perspective, dropping these students into a legal void just as they reach young adulthood seems cruel and counterproductive. We have educated them to become Americans and they feel themselves to be Americans.

These stories also carry another meaning, separate and apart from children's relationships to their identities and their ecosystems. The dignity principle tells us that it is the birthright of each human being to be treated as an individual. During the Holocaust, and in times of sectarian strife and social collapse, many children around the world have been swept up in unjust laws that classified them as expendable or as nonpersons because of their racial identity or simply, as in Liu's case, because they were born. Many learned to hide in order to survive. Many came to the United States as refugees to start new lives. From the children's perspective, whether their parents crossed the border fleeing political persecution or fleeing starvation is immaterial. They are caught in a bind between their legal status as aliens and the fact that they have become, in every other sense of the word, Americans. Treating these children with dignity means looking at them as individuals, not as members of a class defined by the conduct of others. Are they to be punished as lawbreakers because they were smuggled over the border by their parents? We can choose between two unsavory approaches: treating them like contraband human property, or punishing them for the sins of their elders. Each of these approaches has been rejected as contrary to American values that require each individual to be treated according to his own actions and not as chattels or symbols of otherness.

Of all the groups having a valid claim to "earn their way" to citizenship, the claims of this group of "illegal" immigrants strikes me as the most persuasive. They provide a modern-day example of children's stories being subsumed in the stories of adults. Critics of "amnesty" have not paused to make a distinction between adults who knowingly broke our laws and children who were brought here or sent here by parents. Educated in American schools with American tax dollars, they are now on the cusp of adulthood and ready to take up a role as citizens. The dignity principle tells us they have a right to be treated as individuals and not punished for their ethnicity or for crimes we attribute to their parents. To paraphrase the children of the 2002 United Nations Summit, "They are not the sources of problems; they are the resources that are needed to solve them. They are not expenses; they are investments. They are not just young people; they are people and citizens of the world."[33] The jury is still out on whether they will be eligible to become citizens of this country.

As this book was going to press, a news story about Anne Frank hit the headlines. After half a century in the spotlight of history, we thought we knew all there was to know about Anne and her family. But a file of letters written by her father had just been discovered in a New Jersey warehouse.[34] These letters should resonate powerfully in a post-9/11 America that has all but closed its doors to refugees from the ethnic cleansing taking place in Iraq.[35] In Otto Frank's letters, written during the year before the family went into hiding, he pleads with friends for help in navigating the maze of red tape and finding the money to pay a $5,000 bond so he can bring his family to safety in the United States. Despite strong support from powerful people, the doors to life in America remained firmly shut against Anne and her family. Confronted with a humanitarian crisis, Americans' anti-Semitism and their fear of Nazi spies entering disguised as Jewish refugees, carried the day. We all know how the story ended.

CHAPTER 11

CHILDREN AT WORK

Newsboys, Entrepreneurs, and "Evelyn"

As Christian men we cannot look upon this great multitude of
unhappy, deserted, and degraded boys and girls without feeling
our responsibility to God for them.
  —Charles Loring Brace[1]

The [newsboys] gave speeches and passed a cigar box for
contributions to the strike fund. To a *Sun* reporter, they vowed
that their fight could last forever because "We ain't got no wifes
and families."[2]
  —Susan Campbell Bartoletti, *Kids on Strike*[2]

Dignity is not an abstract right but a developmental dialogue between the child and his or her environment.
In the first months of their lives, infants learn that they are individuals through interaction with those around them. "The ability for
self-observation comes from the ability to observe oneself and another in a relationship."[3] Children's individuality both requires and
grows from the meeting of their basic needs for nurture. As children
mature, they interact with a larger world. The dignity principle requires that their needs for protection be met, but it also requires
that their capacities for autonomy be respected and supported. The

stories that follow are stories of children at work. Some are stories of exploitation, but others are stories of achievement and pride. All are stories about children's dignity and resilience.

In New York City, in July of 1899, a bunch of kids shut down the two most powerful publishers in America. William Randolph Hearst, publisher of the *New York Journal*, and Joseph Pulitzer, publisher of the *New York World*, relied on a network of newsboys, or "newsies," to distribute their papers to an avid public. The newsies, mostly boys age eight to fifteen, were entrepreneurs not employees. They bought papers from the publisher at 50 cents for a hundred, and they sold them for a penny each. A newsboy could make a tidy profit if he sold all his papers, but he also bore the risk of loss if any papers remained unsold. Over the decades, the newsboy trade had become highly if informally organized, and an elaborate system of territoriality and seniority allowed a boy to start at the bottom and work his way up to the best street corners in town. But in 1899, profits began to flag for the publishers. Pulitzer and Hearst had grown tired of competing against each other by cutting prices on their papers. But if they raised their prices, they feared that readers would switch to other cheaper papers. So they decided to increase their profit margins by raising the price they charged the newsboys from 50 to 60 cents per hundred. With this scheme, the consumer would continue to pay the same price, but an extra 10 cents per hundred would remain in the millionaire publishers' coffers.

"The difference was only ten cents, but if ten cents meant that much to millionaires like Hearst and Pulitzer, it meant even more to the newsies. The angry newsboys demanded that the owners roll back the price increase—or they would boycott the *Journal* and *World*."[4] When the publishers refused, the newsboys made good on their threat, and soon there were no newsboys selling the *World* or the *Journal* in Manhattan, Harlem, Brooklyn, Long Island City, or Jersey City. The publishers brought in bands of scabs—bigger boys and men who were sent into the streets to peddle the papers. Gangs of newsboys banded together to attack the scabs with stones and buckets of water. They kicked them and tripped them and shredded and trampled their bundles of papers underfoot. Susan Campbell Bartoletti tells this amazing story in pictures and words in her book *Kids on Strike.*

The newsies' collective action had all the hallmarks of a classic labor struggle—greed, violence, betrayal, and, eventually, compromise. At one point, Hearst and Pulitzer managed to buy off the newsboys' spokesman, a boy named "Kid Blink," by bribing him with a new suit of clothes and setting him up with a huge stash of papers. He called off a march and claimed he had settled with the papers. But the rank and file soon figured out they had been double-crossed. They took matters into their own hands, attacking the turncoats and destroying over six thousand papers in one mass demonstration. After two weeks of the boycott, the publishers offered a deal. The newsboys would still pay 60 cents a hundred but they would be able to return unsold papers to Hearst and Pulitzer for a refund. Naturally, the victory of the newsboys over Hearst and Pulitzer made headlines on the front pages of all the competitor newspapers. They knew good copy when they saw it, and they knew what stories would sell best—the man in the street loved seeing a newsboy come out on top almost as much as he loved seeing a millionaire brought low by a little kid.

This narrative suggests that the newsboy represented a simple concept—kids banding together against oppressive adults. But the reality was more complex. Sometimes an image, like an individual, comes to represent all those who share a similar story. The image of the newsboy came to occupy an iconic status in American culture. To the nineteenth-century observer, the figure of the newsboy instantly called to mind the social problem of children displaced by the industrial revolution and surviving by their wits in a dog-eat-dog environment. In the middle 1800s, a new "genre" school of painting emerged; the works romanticized and sentimentalized images of working-class immigrant children, called "street urchins" or "street Arabs" in the popular press. This type of genre painting achieved an immense popularity during the latter part of the nineteenth century.[5] The newsboy's iconography captured a delicate balance between American myths of innocence and dependency, which defined childhood, and equally powerful myths of rugged individualism and survival of the fittest, which defined American manhood. Much of this symbolism is captured by William Penn Morgan in his oil painting the *New York Newsboy*, reproduced in this volume as the frontispiece. The newsboy in the frontis is only one among hundreds of similar romanticized images of "street urchins." Morgan, an artist who emigrated as a boy from England to America and worked primarily in New York, painted this picture around 1870. We see a sweet-faced dark-haired child of about eight or nine, perched on an overturned barrel with a broom in his hand. Modern viewers at first glance might classify this vignette with a hundred *Saturday Evening Post* images—Norman Rockwell evocations of a carefree childhood that seems timeless. Look carefully, however, and you will see the stirrings of a social and legal revolution in the brush strokes of this seemingly innocuous painting.

We can date the setting from the child's old-fashioned clothing and the shadowy horse carriage in the background. While the child's image may be softened and romanticized, his surroundings are bleak. Note that the scene is set in the dead of winter, and the ground is blanketed in dirty ice. The boy's clothing is thin, his boots are without laces, his hands are bare and chapped with cold. He seems entirely alone, abandoned in the frigid, ice-bound streetscape. An elegant marble building, perhaps a bank or investment house, with the shadow of a rich man's carriage drawn up in front, serves as a backdrop for his isolated figure.

This charming genre picture was a political statement. The intended buyer, most likely a middle-class wife and mother looking for a work of art for her Victorian parlor, would have recognized in this painting a sharp if sentimentalized commentary on the plight of the poor urban child. This painting would have reinforced a sense of maternal solicitude for the children of the poor, and would have told the visitors to her home of an emerging social issue that loomed almost as large to her as abolition of slavery had to her mother's generation. It spoke of a nascent movement to guarantee a newly discovered right—the right to childhood. Modern critics who have taken the nineteenth-century artists and their patrons to task for romanticizing poor children miss the potent symbolism and cultural reconstruction of childhood conveyed in pictures such as these. Far from distancing the observer from the reality of the child's life, these appealing images served to diminish the distance between poor children and the average middle-class American. The boy in this picture is calculated to draw upon the viewers' sympathies. His thoughtful pose and wistful smile were designed to evoke a sense of empathy with his condition. He brought together two key cultural strands that otherwise defied interweaving—the sacralization of the individual "innocent" child and a deep-seated fear of children—especially poor, nonwhite, or immigrant children—as a class. The newsboy bridges the social divisions between middle-class American society and the hordes of a new generation whose failure to assimilate threatened to strain the American social fabric.

In the 1860s, Horatio Alger's portrayals of Ragged Dick, who rose from shoeshine boy to banker, and Mark the Match Boy, who starts selling matches and ends with a fortune, captured the reading public.[6] Dick was the archetypical self-made man, beginning his life with few resources beyond his own ingenuity and drive to succeed. His success against the odds held out the promise of success for any child, no matter how humble, who was willing to work and struggle for a foothold on the ladder to success. Journalist and photographer Jacob A. Riis, in his famous 1890 book *How the Other Half Lives*, devotes an admiring chapter to "The Street Arab" of Newspaper Row. He is talking about the boys who so effectively managed a boycott that stopped the Hearst and Pulitzer presses. "Vagabond that he is, acknowledging no authority and owing no allegiance to anybody or anything, with his grimy fist raised against society whenever it tries to coerce him, he is as bright and sharp as the weasel which, among all the predatory beasts, he most resembles."[7] Riis admired such children's "sturdy independence, love of freedom and absolute self-reliance," and he was not alone. Many joined him in praising the efforts of those reformers who found ways to help the newsboy, and his brothers the sweeper, rag picker, and boot black, in their battle for survival, without quashing their culture of self reliance.

Most famous of the street children's civic institutions were the various shelters that came to be popularly known as "the newsboys lodging houses," operated by the New York Children's Aid Society. Horatio Alger stayed for a period in one of the newsboys lodging houses, gathering material for his popular fictional accounts of self-reliant youths who rise from poverty to riches.[8] They offered homeless boys willing to abide by rules against smoking and swearing a dormitory bed and meals for a nominal sum. The boys were free to come and go as they pleased.

> Recognized as an independent trader, capable of and bound to take care of himself, he is in a position to ask trust if trade has gone against him and he cannot pay cash for his "grub" and his bed, and get it without question. He can even have the loan of the small capital required to start him in business with a boot black's kit, or an armful of papers, if he is known and vouched for; but every cent is charged to him as carefully as though the transaction involved as many hundreds of dollars, and he is expected to pay back the money as soon as he has made enough to keep him going without it.[9]

Girls were also sheltered in a separate home, where they learned to support themselves with sewing, but images of autonomous girls challenged the cult of domesticity. Alger's one female heroine, Tattered Tom, was not a success.[10]

Why did the image of the newsboy capture the Victorian reformer's imagination, and what does he tell us about the early movement for children's rights? The newsboy is a child without home or family. He is on his own. This image of the child as isolated individual was a critical step toward conceptualizing children as a separate class of persons bearing some form of individual rights distinct from their status as dependent members of a patriarch's household. He is a working child. We know from contemporary accounts that children of the urban poor earned their own bread, often in "the street trades," peddling newspapers or rags, singing and dancing for pennies, and asking money from passing ladies and gentleman in return for sweeping the pavement.[11] Working children had been the American norm. But in the early nineteenth century, family life and children's lives had undergone a number of subtle changes that placed children's work in a new light. With the industrial revolution, the family had lost its centrality as a unit of economic production. Children who formerly learned adult trades as apprentices or worked with adult supervision in intimate household settings, now found themselves hustling for their living on city streets or working with gangs of other children in huge textile mills and factories at jobs that would be closed to them when they reached puberty.[12]

The reality of labor in a mill was driven home to me when I visited the historic restoration of a textile mill near the Vermont border. I stood among the now silent dusty looms in a barnlike wooden building and tried to imagine the roar and clash of these ranks upon ranks of machines running full tilt for twelve to eighteen hours a day. As the docent explained to us, the workers here were forcibly retired by age eleven or twelve. Children were only useful as long as they remained small and nimble enough to dart between the treadles of the huge clattering steam-driven looms. Many were maimed or killed. Even such dangerous work was difficult to find and highly sought after. The development of ever more efficient machines meant a reduction in calls for skilled factory work in textile, shoe, and clothing manufacture. Training in such skills as fine needlework, which formerly prepared a girl for adult wage earning, was no longer enough to insure self-sufficiency.[13]

With the influx of immigrants to urban industrial centers such as New York, Philadelphia, and Boston, the numbers of vagrant and destitute children left to fend for themselves because of parents' poverty, illness, death, or neglect swelled to alarming proportions. Added to this were the dislocations caused by loss of breadwinners who died or were wounded in the Civil War. By the end of the war, Boston reported six thousand vagrant children living in the streets, and New York reported estimates of thirty thousand.[14] The mechanisms of indenture and apprenticeship that previously served as a safety net, no longer met the growing needs for socialization and

care of displaced children. In addition, a new generation of reformers sensitized by their opposition to slavery, began to feel uncomfortable with the notion of an enforceable contract that bound
children to remain with employers, whether they wished to or
not.[15] By the turn of the century, photographers were beginning to
document the lives of children laboring in textile mills, sugar beet
factories, canneries, and coal mines. These images began to reshape
the way Americans talked and thought about children's work. A
photograph from the early 1900s of young garment workers in
New York City marching in a labor protest and wearing banners
emblazoned with the words "Abolish Child Slavery" shows that
working children themselves began to make the comparison between exploitive labor practices and the evils of slavery (Fig. 8).[16]

Like these Yiddish-speaking garment workers, the newsboy in
Morgan's painting was most likely a foreign child. In choosing
models for paintings like the *New York Newsboy*, artists gravi-
tated to children with dark hair and dark eyes. The stereotype
evoked in the Victorian mind was that of an immigrant child—
Irish, Italian, or Eastern European. In the relatively homogeneous
and localized society of colonial times, displaced children had been
absorbed into the household economies of their more affluent
neighbors. During the nineteenth century, however, urbanization
together with sequential waves of immigration were rapidly changing the demographics of America's children. A new class of alien
urban poor congregated in vast slums, ate strange foods, and spoke
in foreign tongues, and seemed to defy assimilation into American
society. These foreign children both fascinated and frightened the
native-born middle classes. In the nineteenth century, Irish, Slavic,
and Italian peoples were explicitly classified as fundamentally infe-
rior nonwhite races—barely a step above the "Negro" and the
"Oriental."

Middle-class Americans became increasingly worried about these
hordes of foreign children swarming in alleys and tenements, settings that were condemned as a breeding ground for criminality and
vice. Anxiety about juvenile crime widened the gulf between the
middle-class American and these alien "other peoples' children,"

Fig. 8. Young workers march, carrying signs reading "abolish child slavery," in the early 1900s (courtesy of the Library of Congress).

who were as likely to excite fear as sympathy.[17] This social ambivalence was reflected in other, more complex images of street children. Street urchins were pictured not only as individual icons of innocence but also as symbols of decadence—gathered in gangs, to gamble, smoke cigarettes, and drink beer.

Poor, black, and immigrant children elicited not only sympathy but also fear, because they posed a triple threat of anarchy. They were guilty of corrupting the notion of innocent childhood while resisting assimilation to white American language, culture, and morals and also to law-abiding adulthood. Further widening the chasm between poor children and their wealthier neighbors was the fact that middle-class parents were under great pressure to prolong the period of their own children's dependency. As professions and trades became more complex, children needed more education and technological skills to maintain their standing in the new social order.[18]

Society's failure to deal with the street urchin's poverty was difficult to square with the cult of childhood and its concept of children as sacred treasures. "Christian duty demanded that children of the indigent classes be given not only a chance to survive, but to experience childhood as society had defined that phase of life."[19] The street urchin's detachment from family and his mode of street-smart survival was equally difficult to square with the cult of childhood and its depiction of children as helpless and guileless, as empty vessels and blank slates ready to be filled with Christian American values. Yet these images of incapacity and malleability, always problematic descriptions of childhood, were necessary to prolonging the middle-class child's period of dependency and to justifying the cult of domesticity that kept middleclass women at home in the role of mother.

The romanticized figures of newsboys served to mediate the tensions between conflicting images of childhood that troubled and perplexed our great-grandparents, as they perplex us today—children at play and at work, children as sacred promises and as looming threats to the social order, children as inherently dependent and as destined for self-sufficiency, as belonging to parents but also to themselves, members of families but also of the body politic, aliens and citizens, objects of adult concern and agents of their own destinies. The image of the poor child as potential American success story, a hero capable of remaking his own destiny with some help from his Christian friends, also provided early reformers with a concrete plan of action for American society, one that promised to address its worst fears and further its best aspirations. As Joseph Hawes observes, "Children became more sentimentalized (and sacralized) at the end of the nineteenth century because people believed that by saving the children they could improve the future."[20]

In the mid-1800s, children's aid societies and home missionary societies formed in cities like New York, Boston, and Philadelphia, and began to address the problem of poor urban children. At first, their agenda was largely pragmatic. There were no federal welfare programs, few if any regulations on child labor, no Head Start or Medicaid plans. The condition of destitute children, the exploitation of children working in factories and on factory farms, and the ravages to children and families caused by alcohol and domestic violence were all burning issues for the Victorian reformer and her peers. Reformers preached, lobbied, and marched for laws regulating child labor. They pressed for laws granting women the rights to custody and child support upon divorce from an abusive husband.[21] They formed Temperance Societies favoring regulation or prohibition of alcohol, seen as the single largest threat to the welfare of dependent children and their mothers. Despite his role as a catalyst for these interventions, the "street urchin" icon had serious limitations. These limitations, ingrained in the American ethos of rugged individualism, continue to figure in American policy to the present day. By focusing on the child, in isolation from his family's material circumstances, the figure of the street urchin failed to provide a bridge to the adults and communities that constituted the child's family and neighborhood. William Penn Morgan's painting is typical, in that the viewer's empathy is confined to the child. Separated from his community, presented unadulterated by the complexity of his parents' poverty, we do not see him in ecological context as a refugee from a family in trouble or a society in crisis, nor as one small part of a larger social problem of adult joblessness and dislocation. Instead, he is a clean page upon which a Horatio Alger story may yet be written. He cannot be blamed for his poverty, but his parents, his neighbors, and his ethnic or racial community can.

Not surprisingly, the response of many nineteenth-century reformers to the street child was to remove him from his surroundings. Like a seedling stunted by infertile ground and crowded conditions, he would certainly thrive if transplanted to a better environment. The newsboy depicted here would have been a prime candidate for one of the reformers' most striking attempts to address the problem of street children—an initiative called the "orphan trains." One of the earliest projects of the New York Children's Aid Society, starting around 1853 and continuing for more than seventy years, trains departed regularly for rural towns in the North and West, to resettle destitute and vagrant children. The word "orphan" was a euphemism that covered all kinds of displaced or needy children, many with parents who were too poor or too mentally or physically disabled to care for them.[22] Before the movement ended in the late 1920s, at least two hundred thousand infants and children were transported from the slums of Eastern and Midwestern industrial cities to rural communities. They left their parents and families behind, and often lost their siblings as children from the same family were placed out separately along the route. Many arrived at their destinations with only a cardboard suitcase to connect them to their past lives. Affluent families legally adopted a few lucky ones, but most were put to work by farmers, in exchange for room and board and basic education. Some were happy, others miserable. Many of these children never saw their families of origin again.

Only a few of the last passengers on the orphan trains, and even fewer of the farmers who took them in, are still alive. Their stories inspired the documentary "The Orphan Trains," broadcast on public television as part of the series the *American Experience*.[23] Thanks to these oral histories and to research in the records of the Children's Aid Society and other archives, we can hear the voices of the children, expressing their grief at parting from parents and siblings, their sense of helplessness at never knowing what the next morning would bring, their anger at being treated as if they had no feelings or wishes of their own, and the hopes that prompted many of the children to volunteer for the journey—hopes of finding a better life, free of the material and emotional deprivation or physical abuse they suffered at home or in juvenile institutions.

These long-ago children's voices, and the stories they tell, bring a distinctly different perspective to our assessment of the social and legal policies that shaped their experiences. These real children's voices defy many of the stereotypes of children harbored by their elders. These children were not innocent, passive victims, or tabula rasa. Many noticed every minute detail. Their voices and their acts speak clearly about their agency. One old man recalls biting and kicking a potential foster parent who seemed to want him only as a laborer and smelled bad. His act of defiance saved him and he was ultimately adopted by a doting childless couple who loved him tenderly. A woman tells of running away from a home where she was expected to serve as scullery maid. Placed back on the market, she refused to go with the "new" father who selected her until he solemnly promised never to beat her. She recalls proudly, "And he never did." The oldest of three brothers tells of his sense of responsibility for his siblings and his desperate, but fruitless, efforts to keep the family together on their journey West, and to preserve a "pink envelope" that was their only connection with the father they left behind. Some children condemn long dead parents who beat or abandoned them, while others remember tearful partings with parents whom the children, even then, understood had been overwhelmed by circumstances beyond their control and were trusting their children to the train as one might place a child in a lifeboat, hoping for the best.

As early as 1870, some had begun to question the morality of separating children from their families rather than reforming the living conditions of the families themselves. By the turn of the century, work with the poor, formerly a branch of Christian charity, had become a branch of scientific professionalism, as universities began to offer degrees in social science and social work. Economically motivated out-placement and coerced adoption came to be seen as a violation of parents' rights to custody and control of children and, eventually, as a violation of the children's rights to maintain their home and family ties. Gradually, the emphasis shifted away from relocation of children. "The Cult of the Child remained a strong force in American thought, but the ways in which children of poverty were to reach that ideal changed. . . . A holistic approach that included entire families came to be the way of things in social welfare."[24] Following the lead of reformers like Jane Addams of the Settlement House movement, charities and government agencies now stressed kindergartens, day nurseries, home relief, foster care, and other means of alleviating child poverty without permanently removing children from their families.

While the iconography of the newsboy and street urchin, and the strategies of the "child savers" who sought to help them, now seem highly problematic, we must view them in the context of their times. These early advocates for children helped establish awareness of children as individuals. By extending the "Cult of Childhood" to the children of the poor—in effect, acknowledging a moral right of all children "to experience childhood as society has defined that phase of life"—reformers like Charles Loring Brace opened a bridge that ultimately reached from children to children's caregivers, in the reforms such as the New Deal and War on Poverty. The child savers were also revolutionary in their focus on each child as a person of unique potential, defined by his own abilities as much as by the class into which he was born. While reformers may have romanticized childhood innocence, they also showed a striking belief in children's toughness and adaptability, and recognized that children were capable of shaping their own lives. Also remarkable was Brace's insistence that the children ought to be free to leave homes where they were not treated properly or were simply not happy, without being bound by legally enforceable indentures. Neither fully independent adults nor fully dependent children, their ambiguous status challenged the principle that every child must be at all times under the legal control of some adult. The idea of emancipated children was almost as unsettling as the idea of emancipated slaves. This lacuna in the systems for social control of children did not go unnoticed; the Children's Aid Society attracted criticism for leaving children's status in limbo. In later years, the Society moved toward encouraging, although not requiring, adoption. But the Society's support of lodging houses and other direct aids to children continued, and like the image of the newsboy, helped establish the idea of children as persons in their own right, sometimes more capable of directing their affairs than the adults around them.

But honoring children's autonomy and capacity for work and their needs for education is not an easy balancing act. If children can work, why not let poor children earn their own keep, as we did in times past, rather than providing welfare subsidies (now called TANF for Temporary Assistance to Needy Families)? As an economic matter, putting children to work on a large scale would depress adults' wages and make parents ever less able to support their families. As a society, we have found it hard to draw the line between giving children autonomy and taking away needed protections. We have also found it hard to draw the line between encouraging children to become contributing members of society and exploiting their labor without concern for their futures.

A few years ago, traveling north from Pennsylvania on my way to visit my daughter in Ithaca, New York, I drove by miles of abandoned textile mills by the rivers' edges. I was thinking of the mill girls and their working conditions as I arrived in a small town and checked into a bed and breakfast. By the next morning, I had forgotten these working girls as I sat at breakfast chatting with Violet, the innkeeper, a pretty brown-haired woman of about thirty-five. She asked me, "What do you teach?" and, when I replied "children's law," she pounced upon my answer. "Tell me, is it child abuse for a nine-year-old to have her own business?"

Here is the story Violet told me. She had two daughters, about two years apart in age. About a year earlier, the older daughter had asked to help out with the inn and was paid a small sum by her mother to do easy tasks, such as putting fresh soaps and little bottles of conditioner and shampoo in the guest rooms. The younger daughter, whom I shall call Evelyn, wanted to earn money too, and Violet had given her two guest rooms as her own. But Evelyn repeatedly forgot to refresh the supplies and there were complaints. "So I fired her," said Violet. "I explained that I was sorry to have to do it, but I was running a business and could not afford to have workers who were not reliable." Evelyn accepted the justice of her termination, but her pride was stung. So far, to my expert ears, there had been no child abuse. Just some well-executed parenting.

Violet told me that a few weeks after the firing, she and Evelyn had stopped to chat with a friend who owned the bistro on Main Street. I had seen the bistro, with its red-checked tablecloths, and it looked like a lovely spot for lunch. But Evelyn had looked around and remarked, with third-grade bluntness, "Your windows are very dirty." The owner responded, "I know, but it is hard to find anyone reliable to clean them." "I can clean them," Evelyn volunteered. "OK," said the bistro owner, "if you'll clean them, I'll pay you." Evelyn asked, "How much?" "How much do you think the job is worth?" With some coaching from her mother, Evelyn figured out what she thought her time was worth and then added in the cost of supplies. Since the idea of using a ladder was vetoed by her mother as unsafe, she figured she would need to buy window cleaning solution, a bucket, and a squeegee with a long handle. So the deal was struck between Evelyn and the owner of the bistro that she would clean the bistro windows once a week during the summer season. Her mother advanced her the capital to start her business, and she bought her supplies and washed the bistro windows that afternoon.

Knowing her prior work record, Violet was surprised when Evelyn took to her new role as entrepreneur so quickly and so well. They opened a bank account for Evelyn's earnings and the balance began to grow. Neighboring storekeepers were impressed with the quality of her work and her reliability, and asked her to clean their windows too, and she soon had an entire block on her customer list. After six months, she had more work than she could handle on her own so she hired her older sister to help out with the business. This time, it was the older sister who proved unreliable and she had to be let go. Evelyn thought over her options for expanding the business and decided she should stay with the small group of storeowners she could handle on her own. But the coming of winter posed a new problem. She could still clean the insides of the windows, but the outsides were too cold—the water would freeze. Evelyn reasoned that there must be something to add to water to keep it from freezing—otherwise the water for cleaning windshields would freeze on the wipers. Her father told her about antifreeze, and Evelyn figured in the extra cost and charged more for winter jobs than she had for summer jobs.

By this point, Evelyn had been running her business for a year and had saved quite a lot of money. She wanted to learn how to ski so she decided to use her savings to buy a ski package at the local ski area, including a lift ticket and lessons from a ski instructor. One day Evelyn came home from skiing very upset and told her mother that the ski instructor thought she was telling a fib. He had made some joke about her parents' "getting their money's worth" out of the lessons and she had responded, "I paid for the ski package myself." He had laughed at her in a patronizing way. "Yeah, sure!" he said, "with money from your allowance." She insisted she had earned the money herself, washing windows, but he seemed unconvinced. When she told him how much money she had in her bank account, it was clear he thought she was lying. When Violet took her to the lesson next week, the ski instructor asked if the story about the window washing business was true and Violet confirmed it. Evelyn was very insulted and hurt by his assumption that she could not have earned money of her own, though she liked the young instructor enough to forgive him.

About the same time (just a week or so before our breakfast table conversation) something more troubling happened. Evelyn was washing the inside of the bistro windows with her squeegee when a teacher from the public school she attended passed by. She came into the bistro and asked Evelyn what she was doing there, and Evelyn proudly explained about her window washing business. That evening, the teacher called Violet at home and warned her that she and the bistro owner were violating the child labor laws by permitting a minor to work without a permit and especially in a place that sold alcohol. Violet explained that the business had been Evelyn's idea from the start, that Evelyn was self-employed, she kept all her earnings, the work was not dangerous, and she was never at work when the bistro was open and serving customers. But the teacher was adamant. She would have to report Violet if the child continued working at the bistro. (In her defense, teachers are mandatory reporters under the laws of most states and are subject to criminal penalties for failing to report a reasonable suspicion of child abuse.)

"So," Violet asked me again, "is it child abuse?"

"First of all," I replied, "I want to tell you what a wonderful job I think you are doing raising your daughter. She is learning such important lessons from you about pride in your work, about responsibility, about running a business. I really admire the way you encouraged her to think through her decisions, to calculate the costs and benefits. But, yes, I must tell you it is, probably, technically speaking, child abuse. I don't think anyone would question Evelyn's having her own business—what could be more American pie than kids' running lemonade stands, babysitting, lawn mowing, and car washing to earn money? But I suspect that state law does bar minors from working in places that sell alcoholic beverages. Arguably, both you and the bistro owner may be violating the law."

"But she isn't an employee; she's an independent contractor. And she doesn't serve the wine; she just cleans the windows," protested the mother. The problem with that argument, I pointed out, was that it created too big a loophole. If restaurant owners could hire minors to tend bar or even sweep floors, as long as they brought their own equipment and weren't on the payroll, it would be much too easy to get around the child labor laws.

Violet found herself in a dilemma. She was proud of her daughter's work ethic, she felt she was doing a good job raising her child, but, technically, she was guilty of child abuse. Should she tell Evelyn she could no longer run her business? What would happen if the teacher made good her promise to report this as child abuse? We discussed the options and the risks involved. Evelyn was clearly a happy child and an A student. Her parents were respected business owners in a small town. It seemed unlikely that the folks at child protective services would consider the window washing business abusive and, even if they did, they would probably do no more than issue a warning of some sort. Violet concluded that she would talk to Evelyn and if Evelyn wanted to continue her business, they would take the risk. But maybe, I suggested, it would be prudent if she only cleaned the outsides of the Bistro windows from now on.

What a difference race and class make, I thought, as I recalled a case I had handled many years earlier when I was an attorney in New York. I had received a call from a woman my firm had represented pro bono in a class action to force the city to stop putting homeless families into SROs, those single room occupancy hotels that had become infamous as "welfare hotels." These welfare hotels were a terrible place for mothers with children, who had to keep the children cooped up all day because of the unsavory characters that frequented the SROs. The former client was an articulate African American mother of three—so articulate and charismatic that she had caught the attention of a wealthy benefactor who saw her speaking to the television cameras about her situation. This anonymous benefactor had paid for her to move into an apartment in Queens, the borough next door to Manhattan. She was calling me because she had been served with notice that the city had filed a petition charging her with child abuse, and child protective services was about to remove her children from her care. A city welfare worker had reported her because she was sending her six-year-old to school in Manhattan on the subway in the care of her thirteen-year-old. The mother was unable to accompany the children herself because of a medical condition that temporarily limited her mobility. She had a home health aide assisting her during her illness, but they did not get along, and she suspected he had been the one to call in the report. I suggested sending the children to local schools and she exploded. She had fought like a tiger to get them into their Manhattan schools where each was doing well. The thirteen-year-old was in a "prep for prep" program at a private school, and was clearly on track for college. She had gotten the six-year-old into a "gifted and talented" program at one of the city's best public magnet schools. In the mother's opinion, they were both a lot safer riding the subway to these schools that would give them a future than they would have been walking the ten blocks to some dead end school in a bad part of Queens.

I went to her apartment and spoke with the mother and her children. The thirteen-year-old seemed very comfortable with his role as escort during his mother's illness, and the six-year-old appeared

n do have a right to meaningful work, just as they have a
· protection from exploitative work. The thirteen-year-old I
ed above, entrusted with his brother's care, was providing a
gful service to the family and to his brother. Both children
ernalized their mother's message about the importance of
g up for themselves and of working toward a better future.
ed strange that the same authorities who had placed these
n in an SRO next door to drug addicts and prostitutes
prevent them from traveling to and from school.

n, in her very different rural environment, was engaged in
gful work of a different kind, but work that she enjoyed
t gave her a sense of pride. Should she be forced back into
American society increasingly assigns to its young—as pas-
nsumers of products and services advertised on TV?

not suggesting that child labor laws be abolished. Abusive
bor continues to be a problem in America, despite the laws
books. Too many undocumented alien children work in
ure. Too many kids work in fast food restaurants where
n be burned or scalded, at jobs where they learn very little
are them for life. Too many boys and girls work in an un-
nd sex and pornography industry that harms and exploits
'oo many teens are working at jobs that interfere with their
on, just to buy consumer goods they see advertised and are
to "need." And too many American children in poor fami-
working at jobs that interfere with their education, just to
d on the table. These are abuses that must be addressed. But
nes it seems as if the pendulum that brought these laws into
as swung too far in the other direction. At the risk of
g as if I am talking about some mythical "good old days,"
· lifetime I have seen a decline in opportunities for Ameri-
dren to engage in meaningful work in the wage economy.
n have been recast as consumers, and are courted by mer-
ers selling junk food, clothing, media, and all sorts of
hat children are being taught are necessary to their survival
-respect. For poor children, these messages are destructive
umanizing, defining them as defective because they cannot

mature enough to understand that he |
brother. I contacted the city attorney,
the mother's story about the basis for
suggested other options to the city auth
children or finding funding to send tl
caretaker to go with them. All opti
mother was adamant she would go to c
to remove her children from the school
so hard to find for them. At the time,
York, but never enforced, set age four
which a parent could leave a child t
open to a charge of neglect.

Even today, this story makes me a
hired twelve-year-olds to babysit and
twelve. My twelve-year-old son regul
Morningside Heights to his school ii
sional Caucasian woman, I was never
to trust my son with this level of resp
and class played a large role in this so
ashamed. Meanwhile, as we haggled
hung tough and the children continue
utes without incident and to do well i
took me several weeks and many hou
suade child protective services that thi
suing. But they realized a judge wou
protective services for pushing a case
Mom when so many other children we
intervention. It took me an additiona
port of child abuse, which would have
holding many types of employment,
child abuse registry.

When I first proposed this book,
thought that the heading about a sec
work" must be a typo. But, looking
work in America, and examining hum
centered and developmentally sensiti

childr
right t
descri
meani
had in
standi
It seen
childr
would
Eve
meani
and th
the ro
sive co
I am
child l
on the
agricu
they ca
to prej
dergro
them.
educat
taught
lies are
put foo
someti
being
soundi
over m
can ch
Childr
chandi
goods
and se
and de

buy the things they see, and pushing them into illegal acts to earn or get money. For middle-class children, they lead to jobs that are not meaningful and habits of consumption that are unsustainable.

Respect for children's agency requires that there be room within the laws that protect children for work that empowers children. Children who want to work, and whose parents approve, should be able to engage in age-appropriate, meaningful work.

From a child-centered, developmentally attuned perspective, meaningful work is the very definition of childhood. Play is work. Getting along with peers and family is work (for parents as well as for kids). School is work. In fact, in trying to decide how to define children's eligibility for federal disability benefits known as SSI, lawmakers concluded that the process of growing up was work and a child who had serious disabilities that interfered with that process should be eligible for assistance, the same as a disabled adult. Equality of opportunity in a modern society is achieved by supporting poor children so they do not need to work at exploitative jobs in order to eat. In the international human rights community, scholars have pointed out that, as a practical matter, we cannot pick and choose which rights of children we will honor and which we will ignore. When parents cannot meet children's needs for food and shelter, child labor laws and laws forbidding human trafficking are unenforceable.[25] For children in an affluent society, looking at the principle of human dignity through a developmental lens, I would suggest we should respect children as workers—in school, in the community, and in the economy—and we should look hard at the developmental consequences of current trends discouraging children from engaging in meaningful work while exploiting them as consumers.

I stayed at the same upstate New York inn a year after my first visit, when we were gathering for a family reunion. Evelyn, now ten years old, was still enjoying her status as an entrepreneur. There had been no abuse and neglect report made to the hotline or, if a report had been made, the authorities had not pursued it. When I saw Evelyn, I said I was glad her business was going well and I complimented her on the sparkling windows on Main Street. She just smiled and nodded, but it was clear she was pleased. And when I bought a post card in the drug store and took my family to the bistro for dinner, I made a point of complimenting the store owners on their lovely clean windows.

PART V

THE PROTECTION PRINCIPLE: STORIES OF GUILT AND INNOCENCE

CHAPTER 12

TELLING THE SCARIEST SECRETS

Maya Angelou and "Jeannie"

He leaned over, his whole face a threat that could have smothered me. "If you tell . . ." And again so softly, I almost couldn't hear it—"If you tell." . . .

The only thing I could do was stop talking to people. . . . If I talked to anyone else, that person might die too. Just my breath, carrying my words out, might poison people and they'd curl up and die like the fat black slugs that only pretended. I had to stop talking.

—Maya Angelou, *I Know Why the Caged Bird Sings*[1]

I have kept the protection principle for last not because it is less important but because I fear the focus on protection of children viewed as "victims" plays too dominant a role in American child policy. Removing children from their families is always far easier than creating an ecology of childhood in which they can grow up healthy and strong. The systems we have created to protect children from harm at the hands of their parents may benefit many children, but they often end up doing as much harm as good. The harm is rarely intentional. Instead, it comes about because we see children in isolation from the world in which they live, and therefore neglect the other dimensions of children's rights. Missing from our current frameworks for protection of children are robust protections of children's dignity, privacy, empowerment, and equality rights.

We also seem to elevate principles of retribution against evildoers above principles of protection of innocents. The judicial system's reaction when children have the courage to tell the scariest secrets may be more harmful than therapeutic. Although much progress has been made in avoiding retraumatizing child victims during investigation and trial, too often, children who report sexual abuse are still subjected to repeated examinations and interviews, removed from their homes instead of seeing their abuser removed, and subjected to intrusive court procedures and cross examinations that make it difficult for them to heal.[2] The stories that follow explore some of the most difficult issues in child protection. Telling them from a child-centered perspective places children, not perpetrators, at the center and allows us to understand their needs and capacities and examine our policies through a developmentally sensitive lens.

The little girl whom I shall call Jeannie was about five years old when she was given a secret to keep. The year was 1950. She had no name for what happened but she was told it was a secret and that she was not supposed to tell anyone. Somehow, she understood that this secret had the power to break apart the web of relationships she relied upon for security and love.

Before the secret, her world had seemed secure. It was a small family circle she inhabited, embedded in several larger circles. At the center were Jeannie, her parents Amy and Bill, and her older brother. Her parents made their living as musicians. "Hippies" before such a word had been invented, they had left Greenwich Village to raise their family in a house they had built with their own hands in the middle of the woods not far from New York. Their two acres of woods on the side of Salt Hill boasted a main house, a cottage, a studio, and a pump house. An outside observer would have seen these structures as little more than a collection of back woods shacks scattered among the trees. They had no running water or electricity, but the walls of the houses were lined with shelves and shelves of books.

Jeannie and her brother spent their days in the woods, playing in favorite places to which they had given names like "The Mossy Trail," "The Picnic Place," and "The Observatory." At night, their parents read aloud to them by the light of kerosene lamps from the *Wizard of Oz*, Sherlock Holmes, Robert Louis Stevenson, and H. G. Wells. When Jeannie was about three or four, her father had built her a playhouse—a teepee constructed of wood timbers covered with roofing shingles. She helped him build it, but when it was done, she decided something was missing. She asked him to make a sign and dictated the text. "This Teepee Belongs to Jeannie." Still not satisfied, she asked him to add more words. Now it read: "This Teepee Belongs to Jeannie—Amy and Bill's little girl." Should any strangers have stumbled upon the cluster of buildings and rusting cars hidden in the woods, she wanted the visitors to know that this was her teepee, and she wanted them to know exactly who she was and the names of the grown-ups to whom she belonged. This was how Jeannie understood her place in what family scholars call her "nuclear family of origin."

Fortunately, strangers rarely ventured up the rocky dirt road to Salt Hill. If they had, they might have decided that these children were neglected—their surroundings were messy and littered with what other people might call junk. Their clothes and their bodies were often dirty. They were covered with mosquito bites, scabs, and scrapes from falling out of trees and tumbling down cliffs. But only their closest neighbors, who were like family, and various aunts and uncles who lived near enough to come to share a meal or an overnight visit, ever came to Salt Hill. (There was also one astonished delivery driver from Macy's Department Store.) This second ring of intimate friends and "extended family" supported and encircled the "nuclear" core.

On the third ring were members of the extended family who lived so far away they could not come and go in one day, but who were bound to Jeannie and her nuclear family by strong ties of kinship that pulled across the miles. Sometimes they came to visit at Salt Hill, but mostly Jeannie and her family traveled to visit them. One of these relatives was Jeannie's Aunt Meg, who lived in New Jersey. Aunt Meg, her mother's older half sister, had married very young, wanting to get her independence. She married a man who made his living as a farmer. Aunt Meg was a very pretty woman, with long smooth brown hair that she kept pinned up in a complicated knot. Her husband's name was Luke. He wore his short gray hair in a brush cut and drove a red tractor. As Jeannie would later decide, struggling to describe him accurately, he looked a lot like the actor George C. Scott. His face was red and leathery from the sun and the skin next to his blue eyes was deeply creased with lines from squinting at the horizon. He grew some vegetables and raised some cows, chickens, and pigs on his farm, but his cash crop was flowers and flower bulbs—gladiolas. In summer, the farm was a glorious blaze of color, and Uncle Luke could name each of the hundreds of varieties of "glads" that he kept sorted in separate bins in the barn.

Jeannie and her family visited the farm twice every year for about a week—usually at Easter and again in the summer. One summer, Jeannie's mother went on a long trip to visit a sister. Her father took care of Jeannie while her mother was gone. He was an experienced caregiver. Being a musician, he worked at night so he was usually at home during the day. He was easygoing and funny, very comfortable and reassuring to be around. Jeannie liked being with her father, but she was unhappy when he left her to stay with Aunt Meg and Uncle Luke for a week during that summer her mother was gone. He had a regular summer band date that lasted about a week, playing his bass fiddle in a dance band on the Boardwalk in Atlantic City. So he arranged to drop Jeannie off at the farm and pick her up on the way home. She felt lonely and could not wait for Daddy to come and take her home. Although she loved and trusted her father, she was unable to tell him or anyone else the secret.

She could not tell because, if she did, Uncle Luke would cut her throat with his razor. Luke's razor was not like a modern safety razor. It was a long sharp knife made of steel and had a long sharp straight-edged blade that folded back on a hinge into its dull metal case. Whenever she went into the bathroom at the farm (and there was only one bathroom so it could not be avoided) she would see it in its usual place on a shelf under the mirror. Next to the razor hung a leather strop. She had seen Uncle Luke sharpen the razor by drawing it back and forth along the strop. She knew the razor was very sharp. She knew this because, one day, she had used the razor to cut off her own hair. She had chopped her bangs into a strange spiky fringe that looked like a badly mown hedge. When Aunt Meg asked her why she had done that, she could not say. Later, she told her mother a lie—she said she had burned her hair on a birthday candle and had to cut off the burned ends. Perhaps it was her way of telling the secret without actually telling it. It marked an end of something.

From the time she cut her hair, she did everything she could to stay away from Luke. When the family visited at the farm, she stayed away from the living room where he sat on the couch listening to the radio, or, later, watching TV. She knew that if she peeked around the door, he would motion to her and tell her to come over and sit in his lap. Direct orders from grown-ups were to be obeyed—but they could not tell you what to do if they could not see you. So she stayed out of sight. She could tell he was angry and afraid at the change in her. One hot summer day when Uncle Luke was headed to the market with his flowers, he patted the seat next to him. "Come on, Jeannie, want to go to the market?" She used to love going to the roadside market, where she could see all the flowers and vegetables lined up for display and get an ice cream cone on the way home. Her parents pushed her toward the passenger seat, which was very high up, and they were starting to lift her up and put her in the cab of the truck. She could see Uncle Luke smiling at her and reaching out his arms. She struggled free, and ran. She could hear them saying, "Sorry, Luke—don't know what's gotten into her." But *he* knew.

So when she fell on the front hall stairs and tumbled to the bottom, she knew why. As she fell, the steps came up and hit her in the face, smashing her teeth into her cheek and cutting a deep gash in the corner of her mouth. Her parents pressed a towel on the bleeding wound and took her to the local doctor. He had only one arm. The grown-ups whispered that he had lost his other arm in the War (meaning the Second World War). He did not sew up her mouth with a needle and thread, as the grown-ups had expected and she had feared. Instead, he wrapped a bandage around her entire head and under her chin, to keep her mouth shut. The doctor instructed her not to speak or open her mouth until it healed. She could drink soup and chocolate milk through a straw. When she got back to the farm, she heard her Aunt Meg say the doctor must have been afraid to try stitching her mouth closed with only one hand.

Jeannie knew, mysteriously but with absolute certainty, that the fall on the stairs was a warning. No matter what, she had to keep her mouth shut—and she did. When she got back to her home town, her mother took her to a plastic surgeon with two arms who stitched up her mouth. The repair was successful and left her with a crooked smile that her family considered charming—a little lopsided but certainly not disfiguring, as they had feared. There would be no permanent scars.

The summer before third grade, she found among the books in the attic at the farm a multivolume set of stories, poems, and biographies written for young readers. It was an old-fashioned set dating to the 1920s, but she loved those stories and poems and she read them avidly. She also found a box of paperbacks that belonged to Uncle Luke. They were what we would call "porn." She read these with a mixture of fear and curiosity, sitting on the attic stairs, looking for clues to the strange things she had seen and experienced but had never understood.

Her fears did not stay cooped up at the farm—they traveled with her wherever she went. She began biting her fingernails to the quick. She had trouble sleeping and had recurrent nightmares. But these were the Eisenhower years and nobody was attuned to these signals of a child in trouble. Her teacher was worried at the changes in her and called a conference to ask her parents if something was wrong. No one asked her, or if they did, she probably would not have been able to explain. And, of course, she continued to visit the farm at Easter and in the summer although she now dreaded these trips. Family is family.

The last time she visited the farm, she was nine. It was a Sunday, so her mother and Aunt Meg were cooking dinner at midday. Aunt Meg was standing in the kitchen, preparing vegetables, when she gave a loud moan and clutched at her forehead. She said her head hurt so much it felt like it was splitting open. Jeannie thought of a ripe watermelon she had seen split open in the field. Then Meg collapsed, and Jeannie watched as Uncle Luke and the other men carried her to the couch in the living room—the place Jeannie most feared to go. She continued to watch, scared and fascinated, from the hallway door as Meg vomited into a pail. Someone had taken the pins out of her long brown hair and it fell around her face and in her eyes. Jeannie and her brother were chased away into the dining room. They were given a treat to keep them quiet and out from under foot. They ate slice after slice of bread covered with layers of butter and thick globs of honeycomb scooped from a big glass jar. They knew something was very wrong or the grown-ups would have stopped them from gorging themselves on honey before dinner. Then the ambulance came and took Aunt Meg to a hospital in Burlington—Uncle Luke rode with her and Jeannie and her family followed in their car. Aunt Meg was already dead before they arrived at the hospital. The next day, Jeannie's father took Jeannie and her brother home, while her mother stayed to help with the funeral arrangements. Jeannie never saw the farm again. She never saw Uncle Luke again.

It was a long time before she realized she was now free to tell the secret. Actually, most of the time she forgot it existed—like something that has been put away out of sight and out of mind. In the end, it turned out that her secret was not really a secret. "Everyone knew" that Uncle Luke had what, in those days, they discreetly called "a weakness for little girls." So Jeannie realized that her closely guarded secret was not really a "deep dark secret," just a shameful "family secret." When she first told her mother, it was several years after Aunt Meg had died and the family had stopped going to the farm. She was in the kitchen of the house in the woods so she must have been around eleven. She told her mother that Uncle Luke had done some funny stuff with her when she was little. Her mother laughed uneasily. "Well, that doesn't surprise me. He had a reputation." There was a basket of laundry sitting on the kitchen floor and, as Jeannie stared at the bright cotton dresses waiting to be folded, she could feel the waves of her mother's fear and discomfort flowing over her. It was clear to her that she had made a mistake. She had been right before—this was not something she was supposed to talk about. She put it back in the box and closed the lid.

Fifteen years later, when she was traveling through New Jersey with her young husband and baby daughter, she caught sight of a familiar landmark from those long past trips on the New Jersey Turnpike and suddenly thought of the farm and of Uncle Luke. There was a strange buzzing in her ears and she felt paralyzed, as if she had lost the power to move or speak. She told her husband how she was feeling, and she told him very briefly about what had happened so many years ago. And then she put it away again, back in its box.

By the time she spoke again to her mother about the secret, society had made great strides in recognizing the prevalence and effects of child abuse, and the topic of child sexual abuse was no longer taboo. This time, her mother shook her head sadly, and said, "Luke was always susceptible to little girls." Again, it was as if they had taken an object for which they had no use, a torn garment or a broken dish, out of a box in the attic. They had held it at arm's length and examined it for a moment, remarked on its sad history, and put it back in the box so they could get on with their lives. No more was said.

Eventually, Jeannie was able to talk her secret through with a therapist. With her newfound insight and confidence, and her youngest child in first grade, she decided to go back to school and train for a "career outside the home." She was lucky it had taken so long to find her equilibrium. In a leap of imagination that would have been impossible at age eighteen or twenty, she decided to become a lawyer. In 1980, some thirty years after the molestations, she began her studies at Columbia University School of Law. As a law student, she rarely thought about Uncle Luke. Until one day, as she was working in the library, developing topics for student articles for the *Columbia Law Review*, she happened to open a volume of the New York Reports and it happened to fall open to a case about a child. Like the landmark on the New Jersey Turnpike, the opinion stopped her in her tracks. She could not breathe or move. As the head note on the case explained, the judge had disqualified the child victim from testifying in a case alleging sexual molestation. The judge reasoned that the child's testimony should be excluded because it would be so detrimental to the defendant. So ugly and despicable was the nature of the crime the child would be alleging, the judge feared the jury would be led by its revulsion to convict based on a mere child's testimony. Only if the child's testimony were independently corroborated would it be admissible in a court of law. She felt a wave of anger rise in her. "Well, of course," she thought. "Isn't the victim's testimony always the most damning evidence in any crime? And how could it ever be corroborated? Would any person do what this man did in front of a witness?" She looked at the caption and saw that the case dated from the period of her own molestation—the early 1950s. In some ways, she found it comforting. Even if she had had the courage to speak out, this case told her that it would have been pointless. As she had known all along, no one in the world in which she grew up, including the judge, would have wanted to listen to such awful scary secrets. But Uncle Luke was long dead and she was a grown-up woman, with children of her own. Times had changed and she was no longer bound to silence. She took a deep breath, and, quaking like a rabbit, she forced herself to read the entire case. She wrote up a topic proposal about evidentiary issues in child sexual abuse cases, but she was not yet ready to tackle the topic herself. Instead, she encouraged a younger law review student (who had no idea of Jeannie's secret) in writing what became one of the earliest articles discussing the newly created statutory exceptions to the hearsay rule for child witnesses in sex abuse cases.

The last time she and her mother spoke of Uncle Luke she was a professor of law, specializing in family and children's law. This time, it was her mother who opened the box and took out the family secret. She was staying at Jeannie's home recuperating after a hospital stay when, one evening, she told her daughter there was something she wanted to talk about. She said that she knew more now about child sexual abuse—everyone did. Back then, it was just not talked about. Now, she couldn't help feeling guilty that she had not prevented the molestation. She should have known that Luke might be up to his old tricks. He had never "bothered" her, but he had "bothered" her younger sister when she was a little girl. Jeannie assured her mother she had done the best she could and that she should not blame herself.

Each of these conversations was very important to Jeannie. They confirmed what she remembered. They also confirmed why she had found it so hard to tell the secret. It was because she sensed, as children do, that this secret would be even harder for those who loved her to hear than it was for her to tell. Perhaps that is why she never did tell her father and, as far as she knew, neither did her mother.

By now, Jeannie had come to understand that there was no use trying to keep this secret locked away, even from herself. It was better to know and to own it—to be prepared and ready to put the fear in its place. She never knew when it might jump out and confront her without warning, but now she knew how to deal with it. Take, for example, that day in 2001 when she had been walking through the Jacksonville, Florida, airport terminal. She was pulling behind her one of those silly-looking suitcases on wheels, thinking of nothing more important than whether the Avis car she had reserved would be ready for pick up once she and her husband got to the counter. She stopped in her tracks, rooted to the spot. There, in front of her, stood half a dozen glass display cases scattered across the concourse. She had seen them before, on earlier trips, filled with exhibits of local or cultural interest. Today, they held a nostalgic exhibit of old-fashioned barbershop shaving gear. She stood transfixed, staring at the leather strop, shaving brush, and straight razor in the case in front of her. The razor gleamed. There were razors all around her, in all of the glass cases. She could not move. She could not breathe. She felt as if she were enveloped in a cloud, and a buzzing in her ears obscured the other ordinary sounds around her.

Her husband stopped and called back to her, "What's the matter?" She could not speak. He came back and touched her arm. "Are you all right?" She spoke from inside the cloud of fog, "Uncle Luke had a straight razor. I thought he would cut my throat." Over fifty years had passed since she had last laid eyes on Uncle Luke or his razor, and yet the shock of recollection was still so powerful it could take her breath away and rob her of the power of movement and speech. But only for an instant. She drew a deep breath and walked on.

Undoubtedly, you have guessed that the child in this story and the woman she became are me (Fig. 9). I was not a heroic child— just an ordinary child suffering an all too common experience, remaining silent out of fear and guilt, and eventually learning to conquer that fear and guilt. Although adults recoil at the data, statistics show that child sexual abuse is so common it qualifies as ordinary. Approximately 87,200 cases of sexual abuse of children were substantiated nationwide in 2004, a typical year.[3] The actual numbers of children subjected to sexual abuse is actually far larger. According to survey data, one out of five females and one out of ten males are victims of some form of sexual abuse during childhood.[4] Victims are far younger than is often supposed. Of the 87,200 confirmed cases of child sexual abuse, 5,000 involved children under three, 17,000 involved children age four to seven, and 18,000 involved children age five to eleven.[5] While the experience of molestation may be ordinary, the stigma attached to it is extraordinary. Child victims are isolated by the same shame and revulsion that historically surrounds perpetrators of sexual crimes against children, and victims often must suffer in silence. Perpetrators' threats to harm children or their families if they "tell" have especially damaging effects. A child who is forced to cooperate by keeping the abuse a secret carries a heavy burden of guilt for her

Fig. 9. Author, at about age four (photograph by Boyd F. C. Bennett, 1949, courtesy of the author).

complicity—a burden that makes the secret even harder to disclose.[6]

I have always relied on Maya Angelou's far braver and more eloquent voice to speak about child sexual abuse. I have included her work in readings for my classes on child abuse and I have cited it in footnotes to the articles I wrote about the importance of listening to the child's voice. Her work has given me, and I am sure countless others before and after me, the courage to speak about (and listen to) some of the scariest secrets a little person can share. I first read Maya Angelou's 1970 book *I Know Why the Caged Bird Sings* after I began teaching family law. Like Louisa Alcott who was too busy working to work for suffrage, I was too busy in the 1970s raising children and learning to represent them to read about them. A student in one of my classes recommended Angelou's book and I read it with awe. The book is an autobiography, a rich and wonderful story, told through a child's eyes, of growing up as part of a tightly knit and strongly loyal extended family. Nicknamed "Rittie" by her family, Marguerite (who later renamed herself Maya) devoured books like most children devour chocolate chip cookies. Something happened to Rittie when she was eight years old that affected her for many years. Her mother's boyfriend raped her. Although he threatened to kill her brother if she told, she was unable to keep the secret because her bloodstained panties told the story for her. The perpetrator was arrested and tried. She testified against him, in a scene that conveys all the confusion and guilt a child witness can feel when placed on the witness stand and asked questions beyond her ability to explain or to answer. Maya was asked if the perpetrator had ever touched her before. In her child's mind, she believed that, because she earlier had accepted his fondling as pleasant and evidence of his affection, she was somehow complicit in his crime. If she were to admit that he had "touched her" before the actual rape, she would surely be punished. So she told a lie and said he had never touched her before. He was convicted and released on bail, but the next day, he was found dead—kicked to death. Angelou recounts how the child, "Rittie," knew she was somehow to blame. She is overwhelmed at the thought that the words she uttered caused the man's death. "The only thing I could do was stop talking to people. . . . If I talked to anyone else, that person might die too. Just my breath, carrying my words out, might poison people and they'd curl up and die like the fat black slugs that only pretended. I had to stop talking." At first her family accepts her silence. But "then came the last visit from the visiting nurse, and the doctor said I was healed. That meant that I should be back on the sidewalks playing handball or enjoying the games I had been given when I was sick. When I refused to be the child they knew and accepted me to be, I was called impudent and my muteness sullenness. For a while I was punished for being so uppity that I wouldn't speak; and then came the thrashings by any relative who felt himself offended."[7] For Rittie, silence is a refuge. She remains silent, speaking only to her beloved brother, for over a year, buried in books and communicating only in writing. She is coaxed out of her silence by a wonderful woman named Miss Flowers whose melodic voice and sensitive treatment bring her back to life.

Angelou's story illustrates how a child's experience of trauma is shaped by, and in turn shapes, the child's development. While young children may lack the tools to understand maltreatment, fortunately, they have tools of imagination and instincts for survival that allow them to cope with things beyond their capacity to comprehend. Play can be a serious, even a life-saving business. Adults, and the laws and programs created by adults, often fail to honor or understand the child's perspective. In the adult world, there are perpetrators and victims. Grown-ups rush to punish the guilty and protect the innocent. Often, the issues that are most important to the child get lost in the shuffle. Certainly, confining a perpetrator may protect the child and other potential future victims from harm. But the process of catching, convicting, and punishing a perpetrator may have unforeseen consequences for the child he has abused. Maya Angelou's story shows how the harm she suffered was compounded when the adults who loved her sought revenge on her molester. The trial at which she testified to a courtroom full of angry faces and the vigilante killing that followed her testimony only added to her trauma. Maya's abuser was her mother's live-in boyfriend. In today's punitive climate, a mother whose paramour molests her child is often charged with "failure to protect." When parents are incarcerated they cannot work or take care of their children. Children already in crisis find themselves shuffled to a foster home at the time when they most need to be with the people they love.

Especially shocking is the huge disparity between the resources we spend on the criminal and the resources we spend on the child.

In my area, a child who has been sexually abused will routinely wait two to three month to see a therapist trained in treating sexual abuse victims, if she sees a therapist at all. Take the case of a child I will call Nicole—a fictitious name for a real child. Raped by her father when she was six, she was removed from her home and placed in foster care. The justice system went into overdrive, arresting, trying, and convicting the perpetrator. Nicole was placed on the witness stand and testified against her father, sending him to the prison where he will remain for many years to come, at a cost to the taxpayer of some $100,000 annually. What about Nicole? When I learned of her case, over a year had passed, and she had never had any therapy. The agency claimed there was no money for therapy in the budget. Besides, she was doing just fine.

What about another child I shall call Eric? At age three, Eric was severely physically and sexually abused. Placed in a foster home, he too "did fine" until age ten. Then he suddenly began acting out his fears and angers in increasingly aggressive ways. Alarmed at the change in him, his foster mother begged the state (a different state from the one where Nicole lives) to provide him with outpatient therapy. The agency stonewalled for a year, pleading insufficient funds. Finally, Eric's foster mother got the agency's attention by stating that she feared he would harm her or her other foster children if he did not get help. The agency removed Eric from his foster family and placed him in a locked institution.

These stories are anecdotal—and must remain that way to protect the privacy of the children—but the published and verified studies show that Nicole's and Eric's stories are far too common. Forty to 60 percent of cases in which maltreatment is substantiated get no further services.[8] In other words, each year about half a million abused children and their parents receive no treatment or assistance whatsoever, even after they have been identified and the abuse has been confirmed. When services are provided, the vast majority of services go to adults, rather than children. There are many hundreds of "parenting classes" aimed at abusive or neglectful adults for every group therapy program for abused or neglected children. Providing one-on-one therapy for foster children is especially difficult, and not only because therapy is costly. Successful therapy depends on far more stability and continuity than a child in foster care can expect. The risks are unusually high that therapy will be discontinued for lack of funds, or that the child will be moved to a different health system or geographic community.[9]

It is possible, however, to create effective and affordable therapeutic services for traumatized children. The Department of Health and Human Services has identified a number of model programs that have proven track records for success and can be implemented at reasonable cost.[10] One such method is called TF-CBT, or Trauma-Focused Cognitive-Behavioral Therapy. Studies comparing TF-CBT to other forms of therapy show its effectiveness. Children's symptoms of posttraumatic stress disorder, or PTSD, were reduced by 63 percent, depression by 41 percent, acting out by 23 percent, and these benefits were maintained over two years. How does TF-CBT work? As described by Doctors Cohen, Deblinger, and Mannarino in a recent article in *Psychiatric Times*,

> Core components of TF-CBT are psychoeducation about child sexual abuse and PTSD; affective modulation skills; individualized stress-management skills; an introduction to the cognitive triad (relationships between thoughts, feeling and behaviors); creating a trauma narrative (a gradual exposure intervention wherein children describe increasingly distressing details of their sexual abuse); cognitive processing; safety skills and education about healthy sexuality; and a parental treatment component. Parents are seen separately from their children for most of the treatment and receive interventions that parallel those provided to the child, along with parenting skills. Several joint parent-child sessions are also included to enhance family communication about sexual abuse and other issues.[11]

I saw this opaque description translated into practice at a conference at the Field Center in Philadelphia, where a pair of doctors, one a pediatrician and one a PhD in psychology, described how they used this model program. The presenters worked as a team with sexually abused children from their first contact at the physical examination.[12] They introduced themselves to children as the body doctor and the feelings doctor. Armed with knowledge of children's cognitive and emotional development as well as knowledge of the physical aspects of child sexual abuse, they were able to help the child understand and tell her story in a language appropriate to the child's age and stage of development. The feelings doctor continued to meet with the child in subsequent weeks, helping her to tell her story, first to the therapist and then to her family, so thoroughly and fully that it lost its power. Families also benefited from this therapy and were able to be more supportive of their children. The body doctor was always on call to help a child understand and lay to rest her fears about bodily harm. Reforms in the legal system have also reduced the trauma of gathering evidence from child victims. As we saw earlier, in the narrative of Frederick Douglass, historically, children were not permitted to testify at all, because they were deemed to lack legal capacity or were thought to be unreliable witnesses. Research into child development has replaced myths about children's propensity to fabricate with actual data about children's ability to recall and relay details of events they witness or experience. Children can now tell their stories in court and be believed, but the process may be as traumatic as the original crime.[13] Skilled interviewing techniques can maximize the reliability and validity of the child's testimony and minimize the trauma. Media technologies, such as closed circuit television and videotaped interviews, preserve the child's statements, minimize repetitive questioning, and allow the child to speak without being intimidated by the defendant or the courtroom setting.[14] New laws creating exceptions to the rule against hearsay allow an adult to repeat the child's statements in court, without requiring that the child herself be present. Recalling what we know of child development, reputational issues are very important to school-aged children, and it is important to protect their privacy.[15]

In Gainesville, Florida, we have a Child Advocacy Center and a Child Protective Team that provide specially equipped playrooms with closed circuit TVs and cameras. Here, children can tell their stories their own way in nonthreatening surroundings. They can be interviewed by a trained interviewer as they play while all those who need access to the information—prosecutors, child welfare staff, police, and doctors—can watch without being seen. Through a telephone, these observers can instruct the interviewer to ask follow-up questions, without intimidating or disturbing the child. In the past two decades, the U.S. Supreme Court has decided several cases holding that courts may make accommodations to avoid trauma to child witnesses without violating the rights of criminal defendants. Gradually, rules designed for adults are being reinterpreted through the eyes of children. For example, the confrontation clause was predicated on the idea that a witness will not lie when confronted by the person he or she is accusing. But research indicates children are far more likely to recant a truthful accusation when confronted by the perpetrator than to make a false accusation. Stress does not sharpen the child's attention; it decreases the child's ability to recall events and accurately report them. A child who testifies by closed circuit TV is more likely, not less likely, to be able to tell the truth, the whole truth, and nothing but the truth. Viewing the courtroom from a child-centered perspective, we are finding ways to make it possible for children to tell these scary secrets without being victimized in the process.

For most of our history, Americans have been in denial about child abuse, and especially about child sexual abuse. Denial is no longer possible—thanks in large part to the courage of boys and girls who survived and grew into men and women willing to speak out. As Maya Angelou's story shows us, words can kill but words can also heal. Sometimes children need to keep their secrets in order to feel safe. Sometimes they need to tell their secrets in order to feel free. It is at least as important how society responds to these children, when they do speak out, as how it responds to their abusers. Do we see the children only as witnesses for the prosecution or do we see them as small and vulnerable but courageous individuals with cognitive understandings and responses that reflect their developmental needs? Do we offer them our support after they tell their stories or do we spend our resources on their abusers while they go without necessary care? Do we honor their silence and address their fears, or do we force them to confront trauma for which they are unready? We are learning, from listening to these children, about children's spirit and resilience as well as their pain.

I cannot close this chapter without acknowledging a personal debt I owe to a seventeen-year-old girl I will call Emma. A woman who had been her mentor over many years referred Emma to the Center on Children and Families. Emma's start in life was not easy. Sexually molested as a child by her parents, she had been removed from their custody and placed in foster care. Later, she went to live with relatives, and now she was in her last year of high school. She told me, in quite a matter-of-fact way, about her background and then explained her current legal problem. She had moved to the university town where I was teaching in order to attend the local community college. The community college had a dual enrollment program that allowed high school seniors to do their first year of college and the last year of high school simultaneously, by taking college courses. Emma was supporting herself with a part-time job and had scholarships and subsidies to cover her schooling expenses. Emma had just one problem. She needed the signature of a parent or guardian to do so many routine things—apply for a driver's license, rent an apartment, open a bank account, go to the doctor. Emma was one of those children who had slipped through the bureaucratic cracks in the system and gotten "lost." She had had no contact with her parents for many years and was now on her own, a missing person in the foster care system. Legally, her parents or the system were her guardians, she did not know which. She did not want to get tangled up in the system again, having been there before. She asked, "How hard would it be to apply for emancipation?"

I told her it should be simple, as she was already self-supporting and showed such maturity and sense of purpose. She was exactly the sort of minor for whom emancipation statutes had been written. But as I walked her down to the clinic to introduce her to the student lawyers who would be able to help her with her paperwork, I felt humbled and ashamed. Why, I asked myself, did I not feel comfortable enough to tell her that I too had been molested as a child? Surely that would have been the friendly and helpful thing to do. Surely, seeing me in my office surrounded by my books and diplomas, would have given this young student's confidence a boost. It was that encounter with Emma, a straw among many other small straws, that convinced me I was old enough, at age fifty-nine, to stop keeping those scary old secrets once and for all. Thank you, Emma, wherever you are.

CHAPTER 13

AGE AND THE IDEA OF INNOCENCE

"Amal" and Lionel Tate

It would be extraordinary if our Constitution did not require [in juvenile justice cases] procedural regularity and the exercise of care implied in the phrase "due process." Under our Constitution, the condition of being a boy does not justify a kangaroo court.

—In re *Gault*, 387 U.S. 1 (1967)

The protection principle obligates adults to protect children—the small, the weak, and the vulnerable—from harm at the hands of adults. But what about children who are perpetrators of violence? The right to protection has another face quite different from the protection of crime victims. Children have a right to protection from the most severe consequences of their own immaturity. A hundred years ago, in an earlier movement for children's rights, juvenile courts were created in recognition that children's immaturity makes them less guilty when they commit a crime and more amenable to rehabilitation. But today, when children are the perpetrators of crimes, society's retributive instinct often seems to overpower the protective. The other side of the coin of the protection principle is the notion that children who make mistakes should not suffer life-shattering consequences.

Advocates for children joke that our systems try to pigeonhole children as "Mad, Bad, Sad, or Can't Add." Those who are "sad" we send to the child protection system. Those who are "mad" end up in the mental health system. Those who "can't add" are channeled into special education. The "bad" go into the justice system. Yet developmental theory would tell us many of these children are all of these things wrapped up in one evolving package. In this chapter I will explore stories of the "bad" children, kids who are accused of violent crimes. The protagonists in these narratives range from children who are actually innocent to those who are "less guilty by reason of adolescence."[1] From a children's rights perspective, all of them have distinct rights as young humans.

A twelve-year-old I shall call Amal was on trial for felony battery before the juvenile court in a small county in Florida. He could have pled guilty and received favorable treatment. But he insisted that he was innocent. I was in court to observe his lawyers—a clinical professor and two law students from our juvenile clinic. As I watched the familiar script of opening arguments, presentation of evidence, and cross examination of witnesses, it suddenly struck me that this trial was a passion play worthy of the 1960s movement era. As so often happens even where the population is largely black, the prosecutor, the judge, the police detective, and the state's medical expert were all white. The defendant, his family sitting in the front row, and all the witnesses in his defense were black. Amal was a very small boy who at the time of the incident for which he was charged weighed less than 68 pounds and stood only 4 feet 10 inches tall. He had grown in the year since the incident, but was still small for his age. He looked very vulnerable in a shiny green polyester suit with wide lapels that would have been more at home in a wedding party than a courtroom. Sitting beside him at the counsel table were not one or two but three lawyers. This was remarkable in itself. In the real world, "dream teams" are for rich people, and poor black children accused of a crime are lucky to get a single overworked public defender. If they are unlucky, they get a down-at-the-heels freelance lawyer who picks up the kid's case to earn a few bucks of pocket change. But this child lived in a university town, and his frantic mother had called the law school's juvenile clinic. Amal's dream team was all female and all black. Women and people of color were latecomers to the University of Florida but they have made up for lost time in their commitment to pro bono work on behalf of children. The first females graduated from the University of Florida's Levin College of Law in 1933, and in 1958, after resisting integration for decades, the College of Law admitted its first African American student. As of 2004, half the law students were female and 23 percent of the students were minority students—Black, Asian, Hispanic, and Native American. At the Center on Children and Families, which I codirect, we find that students of color and female students are drawn to advocacy for children in numbers far exceeding their percentages in the student body.

The intensity of Amal's two student lawyers, twin sisters who had just graduated cum laude, was palpable. The supervising instructor, a former public defender herself, projected an aura of calm and confidence, but I could see that she too was coiled as tight as a spring, ready to jump into action if needed. The repeat players in the courtroom—the regulars who had "seen it all before"—seemed to know their roles by heart and seemed far more relaxed than the three young women at the defense table. Unlike other courts I have known, the juvenile court in this county was clean and well run and staffed by dedicated people who care deeply about the goal of rehabilitation. They might have been excused for resenting the trial as a pointless and expensive distraction from the real work of getting help for a troubled child who would otherwise be headed for a life of crime.

The hitch was that Amal said he was innocent. Although many of the facts of the case were in dispute, here is a basic outline of the story that brought all these people to court. A woman with a history of drug abuse and child abuse had left her two-year-old and an infant with a relative, promising to return in a few hours. The woman did not return, and the next day, the relative, who had her own three children to support, had to go to work. She had left eleven-year-old Amal, his twelve-year-old brother, and his fourteen-year-old sister alone before. Nationwide, over 70 percent of married mothers of school-age children are in the workforce. Studies show that 5 percent of eight-year-olds, 13 percent of ten-year-olds, and 29 percent of thirteen-year-olds are in "self-care." Day care costs more than low-wage workers earn, and among poor families only 12 percent of those eligible to receive child-care subsidies are receiving them.[2] Obviously, leaving children without adult supervision raises a risk that someone will get hurt, but poor mothers often have few options.

The fourteen-year-old took charge of the infant, and the two-year-old girl went to play with Amal and his older brother. At some point, she either fell or was pushed from the top of a bunk bed. She fell approximately 5 to 6 feet to a concrete floor. The children called 911 and she was taken by ambulance to the hospital.

Because of the severity and type of her injury, the system for investigating child abuse swung into motion. A nurse who was an expert on child abuse examined the X-rays and said that a fall alone could not cause such severe injury. She diagnosed the injury as shaken baby syndrome. So the children were brought to the police station and interrogated by a police investigator. The investigator showed them photographs of the toddler as she had come out of surgery, with tubes in her nose and mouth and swathed in bandages. They were told she was horribly injured and were pressed over and over to say what *really* happened. There is no audio or videotape of the interview so we do not know what questions were asked or exactly how the children answered. But the detective confirmed on cross-examination that the children had tears running down their cheeks. According to notes made by the detective's partner, the twelve-year-old stated during the interrogation that Amal had been on the bunk bed playing with the two-year-old child. The state's theory, based on the shaken baby diagnosis, was that Amal had held the victim out at arm's length, had shaken her, and had thrown her from the bunk bed. Amal was brought back into the interrogation room, was read his Miranda rights, and was confronted with this version of events. He continued to maintain that he had put her in the top bunk of the bed to sleep (his Momma had told him girls and boys shouldn't sleep together and the bottom bunk was his) and was not there when she fell. But Amal was charged with the crime. Or, in the lingo of the juvenile courts, the prosecutor filed a petition seeking an adjudication that Amal was a delinquent child, based on Amal's having committed an act that, if committed by an adult, would be a crime. The criminal act was felony child abuse, later changed to felony battery.

Juvenile courts are an American invention. In the late nineteenth century, reformers became convinced that children who committed crimes should be segregated from adult criminals. Because they were young and easily influenced, they should be treated in a system that emphasized rehabilitation rather than punishment. A separate set of courts was created to handle cases involving youths.[3] Initially, procedures in these courts were very informal, but today defendants in juvenile courts have some but not all of the protections afforded adult criminal defendants. Juveniles do not have a constitutional right to a jury, so Amal's case would be tried before a judge. The judge would decide whether the state had proved its case and, if so, would have the authority to "adjudicate" Amal delinquent and to order him locked up in a juvenile facility. Like a criminal defendant, Amal had a constitutional right to a lawyer and to have the state prove beyond a reasonable doubt that he had committed the acts of which he was accused.[4]

No one will ever know exactly what happened in the one-story cinder-block house that morning. But the medical expert retained by the law school clinic had several reasons for believing Amal's story. He was ready to testify that a child can suffer injuries resembling shaken baby syndrome from an accidental fall, especially if a previous head trauma is reinjured. There were indications of prior abuse, probably by the toddler's mother, who was already under supervision by the Department of Children and Families. And the expert was ready to testify that Amal was not physically capable of holding out at arms length and shaking the two-year-old, as the prosecution alleged. At the time of the incident, the two-year-old weighed 25 pounds and Amal, at only about 60 pounds, did not have the ability to exert sufficient force to inflict a shaken baby brain injury.

The two student lawyers, Talibah and Nailah, also believed that Amal was innocent. But that was beside the point. As his attorneys, they advocated zealously on his behalf, exactly as they had been trained to do. The state's case had hit a brick wall when Amal's older brother refused to testify against him. Every time the state's attorney came near their key witness, he would start to sob. So the state was in no hurry to try the case. But Amal's lawyers feared the case would drag on indefinitely. So the defense filed a motion for a speedy trial—something that was common in the big city but apparently unheard of in this court where all the repeat players felt they were on the side of the angels. The student lawyers also filed a motion to suppress the statements from the interrogation of the children on the grounds that failure to tape record the interview had made it impossible to tell if the questions were leading or suggestive, and arguing that the tactics used were likely to confuse and frighten the children into making false statements. The motion was denied.

At the trial, the defense was on message from the opening statements. They stressed that the court could not convict Amal unless the prosecution showed beyond a reasonable doubt that he touched the child, causing her to fall, that he intended to touch her, and that the fall had caused her injuries. They cross-examined the pediatric nurse who had diagnosed shaken baby syndrome, calling to her attention journal articles and studies showing that a simple fall from a 5-foot height has resulted in life-threatening brain injury in other toddlers. How could she be sure the injury resulted from shaking by Amal and not a simple accidental fall? She remained adamant. She had seen X-rays of many cases of shaken baby and this looked just like them.

I watched as these young women, only a few years out of their teens, went through their ritual paces—rising to make objections, walking to the podium, seeking permission to approach the bench, marking and entering items in evidence. They had been carefully trained: "No matter how angry you feel, no matter how unfair the judge's ruling seems to you, you must never, never lose control. You must quietly but clearly register your objection—to preserve the issue for appeal—and then you must sit down. And no matter how the judge rules, you must always say 'Thank you, you Honor' or 'Yes, your honor.' Even when the ruling feels like a punch in the gut and you know in your heart and head that he is wrong."

As I watched them stand up and take these body blows (for this judge had been consistently ruling against them) I thought of Dr. Martin Luther King Jr. and his admonition to his young recruits: "He would tell you to come forward to fight for what was right. But you had to take an oath. You had to agree to be nonviolent. You had to agree that if anything would happen, you would turn the other cheek. He said, 'If you can't do it, don't come.' "[5] These young women had trained for three years at the premier law school in their state. They were not naive—they expected to be beaten, since the prosecution wins a vast majority of cases that go to trial. In addition, they had been unable to depose the prosecution's medical expert, because the prosecution had given them a long list of potential witnesses and had refused to narrow it further. As if this weren't enough, fate had delivered one last blow their client could ill afford. Their expert had suffered a heart attack and, barring a miracle, would be unable to testify. Without his presence in court, they would have to depend on his deposition. How likely was it that a written document could succeed in rebutting testimony from the state's two expert witnesses?

If Martin Luther King Jr. were here, I thought, he would cheer for these girls. They exemplified his dream—having overcome the racial divide, they had studied side by side with white peers, and been judged by their character and accomplishments and not their color. They were now equipped to fight nonviolently against injustice. But Dr. King would certainly weep for Amal and the thousands like him who are treated as criminals for behaving like foolhardy kids. Amal's case was not as dramatic as Emmett Till's. Fourteen-year-old Emmett paid with his life for supposedly flirting across the color line. Some white people, and even some black people, said at the time that it was Emmett's own poor judgment that got him killed. But Emmett did not know that a word or a look could get him killed. In Chicago, in 1955, even an angry white husband would have cut him some slack. But not in Mississippi. Eleven-year-old Amal also lacked mature judgment. He put a two-year-old in the top bunk of a rickety improvised bunk bed—not a wise thing to do. But even assuming, as the state believed, that he had played a role in her fall, why was it necessary to charge him with a felony?

We have seen a phenomenon in the last two decades that I can only call the "demonization" of children, and especially black children. We have a long history of stereotyping children from ethnic and racial minorities as lawbreakers and dangerous delinquents. The civil rights movement, it seems, provided only the briefest of intermissions in a pattern of presuming black boys guilty until proven innocent. From 1955 to 1965, we saw black children portrayed as heroes. Within a few years, that moment had passed. Nowadays, when a black child commits an act of defiance or even of foolishness, we often cut him no slack at all. This is not just an issue affecting black children. It affects all children and is eroding the rights of all children.

As civil rights lawyer Steven Bright has said, there is only one thing we promise our children. We don't promise them good schools, or food, or a roof over their heads. But we do promise them a jail cell. The criminal justice system is always open for business, whether the economy is strong or weak, whether we are at war or at peace. And during the 1990s it became a yawning pit swallowing large numbers of children. Of the children in the justice system, a disproportionate number are children of color. In 1999, there were 1,000 black children in detention for every 100,000 in the population, five times the rate of white children.[6] In the years since the Montgomery and Selma protests, we have gone from a society that treated the arrests of children as an outrage to a society that routinely tries children—especially children of color—for all kinds of things we used to assume were accidents or youthful lapses in judgment.

Although rates of juvenile crime are declining, more and more children are being tried in the adult rather than the juvenile system.

Contrary to popular perception, the children tried as adults are not hardened killers. For many, it is their first encounter with the justice system. Others are tried as adults because they have a prior conviction as a juvenile. They are being tried for crimes against property, possession of illegal substances, and other offenses that used to be handled in juvenile delinquency courts or informally, within the community.[7]

For many of the children and grandchildren of those who marched in Birmingham, like the young lawyers I was observing that day, the movement opened doors to a new world of opportunity. But for too many other children, the doors to opportunity slam shut, as they are channeled into jails and juvenile detention facilities where the color line is almost as stark as in the schools and buses their grandparents fought to integrate. Four decades ago the world reacted with revulsion to the arrest of children. Today it is business as usual.

On this particular day, the system was in for a surprise. When the court reconvened, all that was left before the prosecution rested its case was testimony from its medical expert. Nailah and Talibah knew that they had no rebuttal expert—only his deposition. But neither the judge nor the prosecution knew this—Nailah and Talibah were playing their cards close to their vests. Minutes before the trial was to recommence, the state's medical expert entered the courtroom. This was the defense lawyers' first opportunity to interview him, and they pounced. They asked if they could speak with him outside, and he agreed. They were back in the courtroom before the startled state's attorney realized what had happened.

On direct examination, the doctor stated his impeccable credentials. The chair of the university's department of pediatric neurosurgery, he was a nationally known expert, and it was he who had operated on the injured child and had saved her life. He described her injuries and testified to their severity. Now it was time for the defense to cross-examine him. Nailah asked simply, "Can an injury like this be caused by an accidental fall?" "Yes," he answered. "Can it be caused by falling from a 5 foot height onto a concrete floor?" "Yes." "Have you ever operated on children who had the injuries like this from an accidental fall?" "Yes, many times." Nailah thanked the witness and sat down.

The defense rested without calling any witnesses. There was no need. The prosecution's witness had provided the final crucial piece of evidence. The state had failed to establish Amal's guilt beyond a reasonable doubt. In fact, the state's expert had demolished the state's theory of the case. As Nailah and Talibah delivered their closing arguments, Amal and his family were still in suspense but I knew the case was over and that they had won. A few days later, the judge handed down his formal ruling. He dismissed the petition on the ground that the state had failed to prove its case.

What if Amal had not believed in himself enough to fight for his own innocence? What if his dream team had lost its courage and had cut a deal, as the state fully expected? Amal would be another statistic in the juvenile justice system with a strong likelihood of ending up in the criminal justice system. To me, the saddest aspect of this case was not what the child protection and juvenile justice systems did but what they failed to do. The systems we have created were so busy looking for a culprit in this tragic accident they forgot about protecting Amal and his siblings from harm that was not just speculative but absolutely certain. Imagine the impact of seeing a little child in convulsions and near death, and the shame and guilt of being older and supposedly "taking care" of the littler child when she was hurt. Imagine the trauma of being interrogated at the police station, of being shown the picture of the toddler swathed in bandages, and of being given a choice of confessing or accusing a sibling. At the time of trial, none of the children had been offered any therapy to deal with the trauma and guilt they must have experienced.

Amal is lucky—other children his age are being tried in adult criminal courts for similarly ambiguous crimes. When kids are playing unsupervised, bad things can happen. In 2001, the Florida case of Lionel Tate attracted national attention when Lionel became the youngest child in America ever sentenced to life in prison without parole (Fig. 10). For twelve-year-old Lionel, this was a first offense. As in the case of Amal, no one will ever know what actually happened. Whatever the circumstances, in Lionel Tate's case, there was no doubt the six-year-old victim had suffered fatal injuries and that Lionel had caused those injuries. Six-year-old Tiffany weighed about 45 pounds and was no match for Lionel's 170 pounds. Lionel's mother, a state trooper, was babysitting the six-year-old and left the two children playing while she slept on another floor of their townhouse. When the kids made too much noise she told them to be quiet or she would come down and "beat their butts." Later, Lionel claimed he did not mean to hurt Tiffany and had been imitating moves he had seen on World Wide Wrestling TV shows. He admitted to body slamming the little girl and jumping on her from a stairway. When he realized that she was badly hurt, he ran to his mother to tell her Tiffany had stopped breathing. The emergency medics were unable to revive the child.

Instead of treating this as an accident or blaming the tragedy on lack of parental supervision, the prosecutor decided to charge Lionel. In the drive to get tough on juvenile crime, much of the discretion about trying children as adults has been shifted from judges to prosecutors, who are perceived as tougher and more responsive to the voters. Florida law gave the prosecutor a range of choices and he elected to "direct file" this case in adult criminal court, charging Lionel with felony murder. As we saw with Amal's case, juvenile courts generally handle cases in which a minor is charged with conduct that would be criminal if the actor were an adult. But Florida law allows a district attorney to indict a person *of any age* in adult court if the crime he or she is accused of committing could be punishable by death or life in prison. Judges have no choice but to accept this unilateral decision by the prosecution. If an innocent person is killed in the course of a felony, the state can charge the defendant with "felony murder" even if he or she did not intend to kill the victim. Typical scenarios are an armed robbery where a gun goes off or a kidnapping where the victim is accidentally suffocated. What was the predicate felony for which Lionel was charged? Lionel was charged with aggravated child abuse, a class three felony. Aggravated child abuse occurs when a person willingly or knowingly abuses a child and the abuse results in great

Fig. 10. Lionel Tate, age fourteen, being tried as an adult for murder in 2002, in Florida (with permission of the Associated Press).

bodily harm. In order to convict Lionel of felony murder, the state did not need not show that Lionel intended to kill or even seriously harm Tiffany, only that he intended to perform the physical actions that caused her fatal injuries. The jury decided he had, based on evidence that Tiffany had suffered such severe injuries and Lionel's admission to having wrestled with and jumped on her. Some jurors expressed shock when the judge sentenced Lionel to life in prison without parole. They had assumed the sentence would be lenient given the defendant's young age. But the judge had no choice. Under Florida law the minimum sentence for felony murder is life without parole.

I became involved with this case when the Center on Children and Families at the University of Florida College of Law joined with the Children and Family Justice Center at Northwestern School of Law in researching and writing an amicus brief to the appeals court, asking it to overturn Lionel's conviction.[8] An amicus brief, also known as "friend of the court" brief, is a means for judges to hear from experts in a given area about the potential impact of a case on the larger legal landscape. Amicus briefs are intended as aids to the judges in understanding the case in broader context. We argued a number of complex issues of criminal law, but my part of the brief involved the history of child abuse laws. I argued that child abuse laws had never been intended to be used against children who injured other children in play. The whole history of child abuse laws showed their purpose was to protect children from adult caretakers, not to subject children themselves to criminal penalties when their caretakers failed to supervise them. The brief also argued that Lionel, at age twelve, was too immature to understand the real world consequences of his acts. Drawing on much of the same neurological and psychological research that in 2005 would persuade the Supreme Court to overturn the juvenile death penalty in *Roper v. Simmons*, we showed that the adolescent brain is far less developed than the brain in adulthood, and adolescents are far less capable of understanding the seriousness of their acts.

For me, one of the most troubling aspects of Lionel's case was the role his mother may have played in his defense strategy. Trying a child as an adult produces a strange Catch 22. Parents often continue to make decisions for children, even when the child is tried as an adult, so the person making the decision is not the one who must pay the price. Before the trial began the prosecutor offered a generous plea bargain—three years in a juvenile facility where Lionel would get expert mental health services, followed by ten years probation. At Lionel's mother's insistence, the bargain was rejected. It is hard enough for a preteen to understand the risks of drinking and driving, let alone of standing trial for murder. Circumstances suggest Lionel had very little idea about what was at stake. When the jury found Lionel guilty, he turned to his lawyer and asked, "Does that mean I can go home now?" Lionel's mother could go home, but he could not. He was sent to an adult prison, where he was kept in isolation so he would not be with the adult prisoners, and then to a juvenile facility. Neither setting provided the kind of intensive mental health interventions he needed.

However, Lionel was given a second chance. The appeals court decided the trial court had erred in failing to consider evidence of Lionel's lack of capacity to participate in his own representation. This time, rather than go through a new trial, he agreed to plead guilty in exchange for time served and ten years probation. Some observers may have been confident Lionel would turn out fine. I was not one of them. Now fifteen, he had spent three years in the criminal justice system, he had not received any of the mental health interventions he needed, and he was going home as a much larger and more aggressive teen, to a parent who had failed to provide adequate supervision when he was twelve. Any infraction of his parole conditions, even a small infraction, could send him back to jail. He was going back to a neighborhood and peer group where violence and lawbreaking were a fact of life.[9]

What kind of odds would an expert have given on a boy like Lionel Tate? Would he become a career criminal or a solid citizen? As James Garbarino would say, "It depends." Garbarino is the country's foremost expert on violence in children. He is a scientist and not a lawyer. In addition to reporting his scholarly research in academic journals, he has written a number of books aimed at the general reading public.[10] He wrote about boys who kill in *Lost Boys*, and recently published a new book on the increase in violence among girls, *See Jane Hit*. Garbarino has spent thousands of hours with young people, listening to their experiences and studying the various factors that come into play in determining how they will turn out as adults. He utilizes Urie Bronfenbrenner's ecological framework on child development as well as drawing upon the ego development theories of Erik Erikson to understand how children interact with their environments. He is against sentimentalizing children as "innocents" or demonizing them as predators, and insists on rejecting stereotypes and looking at the evidence. He is firmly committed to solutions based in sound theory and evaluated for effectiveness.

The Center on Children and Families recently invited Dr. Garbarino to speak to an audience of children's lawyers on the topic "What Lawyers for Children Should Know about Social Science." A small, intense man with an impish grin and a wicked sense of humor, he is a spellbinding speaker. Here, in a nutshell, is what he told us:

> Context matters. Rarely does the process of cause and effect work universally. Rather, it operates in the context established by culture, gender, ethnicity, prior experience, and historical circumstances. This is the fundamental lesson we learn from scientific research on human development. When we look at development of children and ask, "Does X cause Y?" the best scientific answer is always "It depends."[11]

For example, studies show that 30 percent of children who show a chronic pattern of aggression at age nine develop into seriously violent delinquents. In some neighborhoods, however, the figure is 15 percent and in others it is 60 percent. These differences reflect the disparity of developmental assets and risk factors from one environment to another. Rarely, if ever, does a single influence determine the course of a child's life. According to Garbarino, "it is the accumulation of risk factors and the accumulation of developmental assets that describe the level of social toxicity and social robustness, which, when coupled with the forces of human biology, tell the story of a child's development."[12]

Let's look first at developmental assets. Looking at assets that enhance positive behavior, experts at the Search Institute identified forty such assets in categories such as Family, School, Neighborhood, Peers, Expectations, and the child's own mode of thinking. For example, "Family has clear rules and consequences, and monitors the young person's whereabouts." "Young person's best friends model responsible behavior." "School provides clear rules and consequences." "Neighbors take responsibility for monitoring young people's behavior."[13] The more assets a child had, the less likely he or she was to engage in problem behavior, including aggression (defined as engaging in three or more acts of fighting, hitting, injuring a person, carrying a weapon, or threatening physical harm in the past twelve months). With zero to ten assets, 61 percent of kids were in the violent category. With eleven to twenty assets the figure fell to 35 percent. With thirty-one to forty assets, it fell to 6 percent. Add to this the fact that adolescence is an especially vulnerable time. The average number of assets for children *declines* as they move through adolescence, from 21.5 in sixth grade to 17.2 in twelfth grade.[14]

What about risk factors? Obviously, the converse of an asset is usually a risk. An absent parent, a lack of quality schooling, and a toxic peer environment all contribute negatively to the child's development. Let's look at one risk factor in particular—a history of abuse. The data are clear that having been abused as a child is a risk factor for a child's developing "conduct disorder"—a psychological diagnosis based on a chronic pattern of aggression, bad behavior, acting out, and violating the rights of others. Most abused children, however, do not develop conduct disorder. Recent research has uncovered some fascinating connections between biology, genetics, and child development. Psychologists have long believed that children are born with basic personality traits that affect how they interact with their worlds. A child who is outgoing and optimistic by nature may respond differently than a timid or fearful child to the very same caregiver. The optimistic infant may sail through situations that leave the sensitive infant deeply affected. In chapter 1, we looked at theories of attachment and saw that developmental theorists believe a secure attachment to the caregiver provides the very young child with ego strengths of hope and trust. What about children who do not develop this sense of trust? They may develop a habit of thinking about their world and their own place within it— Garbarino calls it a "social map"—that is negative rather than positive. Negative thinking is a risk factor for conduct disorder.

Psychologist Kenneth Dodge discovered that the odds of a child developing conduct disorder increase if the child thinks in the following four ways: (1) is hypersensitive to negative social cues, (2) is oblivious to positive social cues, (3) has a narrow repertoire of responses when aroused or agitated, and (4) has concluded from experience that aggression is a successful social strategy.

The first two modes of thinking, hypersensitivity and pessimism, are easy to imagine and affect many adults as well as children. We know that a child who lacks a secure attachment is more likely to develop the lack of trust and negative thinking that characterize the first two modes of thinking. What do we mean by a "narrow repertoire of responses?" Garbarino, in his lecture, described a teenager with whom he had worked who had only one response to every hypothetical. "What would you do if someone took your pen?" "Hit him." "What would you do if another kid said something bad about your mother?" "Punch him." "What would you do if you met some kids from a gang on the street?" "Beat 'em up."

As Garbarino points out, aggression is a child's normal response to frustration. Studies show aggression at its height in one-year-olds and beginning to decline in the second year of life, a decline that continues throughout the life course.[15] Tiny children can be seen hitting, punching, and biting in any toddler playgroup in order to express their emotions or get their way. But most children are eventually socialized to more acceptable approaches. In other words, they are taught by interactions with adults and other children that physical aggression does not produce good results or win you many true friends. Yet many children in today's social environment can rationally draw the conclusion that aggression is the safest strategy in dangerous neighborhoods where authority figures are powerless to protect kids from violent peers. As one boy put it, speaking bluntly to Dr. Garbarino, "If I join a gang, I am 50 percent safe; if I don't, I am zero percent safe."[16]

We see how the biology of a child's temperament can interact with the early experiences of nurturing (including the caregiver's temperament) and be compounded or mitigated in later developmental stages, depending on the surrounding social, familial, and peer environments. In addition to these many complex factors, scientists have discovered a specific gene, the monoamine oxidase A, or the *MAOA* gene, that affects how chemicals are processed in the brain. These chemicals affect the brain's response to threat or stress. A child who has the *MAOA* gene turned off is less able to deal with stressful situations and more apt to react aggressively. Researchers wondered if this gene might have something to tell us about why some abused children develop conduct disorder and others do not. In one study, the rate of conduct disorder in children who had the *MAOA* gene turned off and had been abused was 85 percent. In children who had been abused and had the *MAOA* gene turned on, the rate was 40 percent. Children who had not been abused were 20 percent likely to develop conduct disorder, regardless of whether they had the *MAOA* gene turned on or off.

I almost hesitate to report this study out of fear that some readers may stop right here and say, "Ah, hah! Some kids are just destined to be bad. We should take all the abused kids, test them for a defective *MAOA* gene, and then lock them up and throw away the key." But the study did not stop with childhood conduct disorder. In examining the likelihood that these children (the ones with the double whammy of the bad gene and a history of abuse) would develop into antisocial adults, the researchers found that many other factors came into play, including whether there was therapeutic intervention, what school he attended, who were his friends, and even the person whom the individual married. In other words, "It depends."

Looking at Lionel Tate, what we know of his childhood indicates many risk factors at work, both biological and social. His family situation was unstable. His parents separated when he was under a year old and he did not see his father for seven years. His paternal grandmother cared for him for several years while his mother was overseas in Desert Storm, as well as when his mother played basketball for the U.S. Army. Later on, his teachers described him as a big kid, often ostracized by his peers, who lacked social skills and reacted with emotional outbursts when frustrated. He interpreted every interaction with peers in a negative manner.

While not physically aggressive with other children, he had difficulty expressing his emotions and frustrations. His fourth grade teacher in Mississippi reported that he was written up for "disrupting the class, making noises, disruptive behavior in the hallway, disruptive behavior in the bathroom," the teacher Smyth said. "And when I say disruptive, I don't mean violent-type disruptive. I mean anything he could think of doing to start something—even if in the cafeteria flicking the corn kernel at someone." Another teacher described him as "very loud, very boisterous . . . like a bull in a china shop . . . he was almost out of control." This teacher liked her students to work in groups, and she would persuade Lionel to join a group, but "it wouldn't be 15 minutes and he'd be dragging his desk away, slamming his books. . . . Honestly, the other students were relieved that he had left the group." She said that Lionel, then about ten years old, was once punished for physically "hoisting" a tiny girl in his class without her permission, but he never got violent or physical with other children when he was angry. "He would usually hit the walls, stomp his feet and then totally withdraw into himself," the teacher said. "It was a pouty type of anger."[17]

These traits frayed the nerves of teachers and family alike. His mother had sent him to live with his father in Mississippi when he was about ten, so she could train to become a Florida state trooper, but after a year in Mississippi he was back in Florida. He was back again in Mississippi the next year, after having trouble in his Florida school. The teachers in Broward County, Florida, had recommended he be placed in a special school for children with behavioral problems, but there was no room in the program.

His teachers back in Mississippi saw a deterioration in his behavior. "He seemed to have less control over the impulses than he had before," said one, "And there was more a tendency to be a little bullying. I'm not saying he was a bully, but I would say that he had discovered he was bigger and he could get what he wanted sometimes with that. . . . Toward the end of the year, there did seem to be more vulgarity and hostility toward authority."[18]

When the school year was over, he was sent back to Florida. A month later, in July of 1999, he was left to play late into the night, unsupervised, with a very small child. In these pages, we have met some twelve-year-olds whom we could trust with the care of a younger child. Lionel Tate was not one of them. But the years between twelve and eighteen were critical developmental years for Lionel, as for any child. Who can say how he would have responded to the skilled interventions and rehabilitative approaches that he never received?

Studies have shown that adult sanctions do more harm than good. The catch phrase that kids should do "adult time for adult crime" makes a snappy slogan but, if measured in terms of reduction of crime, it appears the "get tough" policy has been a failure. Legal academics use the terms "general deterrent" and "specific deterrent" to describe law's effects. General deterrence occurs when a law has the effect of discouraging people from committing crimes because they are afraid of the consequences. Specific deterrence comes into play when an individual who has committed a crime is deterred by the punishment he receives from committing more crimes. The problem with general deterrence, when it comes to teenagers, is that adolescents, because of their stage of development and the changes taking place in their brains, are notoriously bad at assessing risks and matching their acts to the likely consequences. They are impulsive and have limited ability to see into or weigh the future. I always think of the exchange my father, a music teacher, had with one of his adolescent students. The boy was making a pretty good sound on the trumpet but the position of his lips on the mouthpiece was all wrong. "You can play like that now," warned my father, "but your lip will be shot before you're forty." The kid rolled his eyes. "Forty-schmorty! Who wants to be forty!" To many an adolescent, the idea of ten years, let alone a lifetime, behind bars is simply incomprehensible.

The studies to date on recidivism make clear that applying adult penalties to juveniles does not act as a specific deterrent either. In several controlled studies that followed groups of juveniles sent to adult court and those tried in juvenile courts, all of whom committed similar acts and have similar demographic backgrounds, the ones who were transferred to criminal courts had higher rates of rearrest (30 percent versus 19 percent) and reoffended sooner (135 days versus 227 days). What accounts for this difference? Many factors have been suggested, and it is likely more than one is implicated in any given case. As early reformers knew, throwing kids in with adults exposes them to brutalization (they are ten times more likely to be raped, for example) and immerses them in a culture of crime where they can learn from the real pros. Adult prisons are less likely to offer access to rehabilitative programs, mental health interventions, or even access to education. Studies suggest that juveniles tried in adult courts have higher recidivism rates even when they serve their sentences in juvenile facilities. It seems that the criminal court *process* has negative effects—interviews of kids show they feel they are being judged not only for what they have done but as personifications of their bad behavior. In juvenile courts, they were offered hope and made to feel as if they retained some "fundamental worth." In Florida, despite the surge in punitive rhetoric about juvenile justice, studies showed that the kids in the juvenile facilities felt like the adults around them cared about them as people and taught them appropriate behaviors. Compared to juveniles in adult prisons, they felt far more ready to reintegrate in their communities and far more confident they would not reoffend.[19] While the public may get instant gratification when a child who commits a serious crime is charged as an adult, it is now clear that the public's long-term interests are better served by keeping kids in juvenile courts.

The sequel to Lionel's story is still unfolding. In May 2005, Lionel allegedly went to a neighbor's apartment and borrowed the phone to order four pizzas. Apparently, he did not plan to pay for them. When the deliveryman came to the door, he saw a masked kid with a gun, dropped the pizzas, and ran. He later identified the kid as Lionel. Where did Lionel get the gun? Recall that his mother was a state trooper; she had left her service revolver in a place where Lionel could find it, and he did. Reportedly, Lionel's fingerprints were on the pizza box. He also allegedly ate the pizza. This story would be funny if it were not so sad. Based on Lionel's possession of a gun, strictly forbidden under his probation agreement, the judge revoked his probation and sentenced him to thirty years in prison. He admitted to taking the gun but claims the evidence will show another boy used it to rob the pizza man. Lionel is awaiting trial and faces a life sentence if he is convicted of the armed robbery charge.

This time, instead of portraying Lionel as a chubby kid with a tear-streaked face, the media portrayed him as a tall lean young man with a smirk. These portrayals may well be accurate, but what if we had been able to shift the balance of assets and risks when he was six or eight or ten or twelve, and not yet involved in the criminal justice system? Could it have made the difference? As James Garbarino would say, "It depends."

At what age do we begin attributing full-blown criminal intent to children? The lines we draw in juvenile justice are often arbitrary and reflect fears and biases rather than sound research about either culpability or rehabilitation. Even my law students have trouble deciphering Florida law, which allows a child of any age to be charged with murder and treats fourteen-, fifteen-, and sixteen-year-olds differently not only depending on their age but also depending on slight variations among their crimes.[20] Lines must be drawn, but should legislators be free simply to pick them out of a hat? Should prosecutors and elected judges be given such wide discretion to throw children into the deep end of the system, influenced as they are by the public mood and their own reelection prospects?

I believe the Supreme Court got it right in *Roper v. Simmons* when it decided that the age of eighteen, an age that marks the passage to adulthood in the vast bulk of our laws, should mark a bright line boundary. I believe that draconian penalties, not only death but also life in prison without parole, violate the human rights of children. Such punishments may sometimes be justified for the most heinous and depraved of criminals—mass murderers like Adolph Hitler come to mind. But, regardless of one's position on the death penalty, this is one area in which children should and must be treated differently because they *are* different. The developmental line between childhood and maturity is fuzzy, suggesting the brain continues to develop into the middle twenties.[21] But the cultural line is relatively clear. As our amicus brief to the Supreme Court in the *Roper* case demonstrated, eighteen is the benchmark American law has set for juveniles to be given full responsibility for decision-making, from getting a tattoo or body piercing to enlisting in the army. It is also the age set in international human rights documents. Young children should be given help, not handcuffed, and teenagers, whatever the crime, should be given a chance to show that they can be rehabilitated.[22]

This is not to suggest that juveniles should receive a free pass when they commit antisocial acts. But any effective system for addressing juvenile crime must be focused on prevention and grounded in solid research and theory. Several of my colleagues have proposed an approach that is based in an ecological theory of child development.[23] Its purpose would be to prevent the juvenile from developing into a criminal by changing the balance of risk factors and assets. Rather than focusing on the child's mental state at the time of the crime, as we do in assessing adults' culpability, treat the issue as one of risk management. Each juvenile offender would have an Individualized Risk Management Plan (IRMP) managed by a multidisciplinary team including school, police, mental health, and vocational counseling to work with the child and his family and community on addressing the dynamic (i.e., changeable) risk factors and assets in the child's life. Such an approach would serve values of fairness, efficiency, and personal responsibility while protecting society from juvenile crime and preventing as many children as possible from graduating into the adult criminal justice system.

Innocence has many faces. Our first story, that of Amal, was a story of "actual innocence" about a child who narrowly escaped being locked up for a crime he did not commit. His story reminds us that due process is important even in special courts whose objective is benign and therapeutic. Our second story, that of Lionel Tate, was the story of a confused child in a dangerously adult body—less guilty by reason of adolescence. We know he committed the physical acts that led to Tiffany's death and may well have intended to hurt her, but did he have a real understanding of the consequences?

Three competing approaches exist, and overlap, for dealing with cases involving children who commit criminal acts. In the first approach, we treat them as cases where adults, not children, are at fault. Often, a child's acting out is a symptom of abuse or neglect. Looking at the situation through the broad lens of child protection, we discover that the real culprit is not the child but lack of supervision, parental abuse, or just a toxic environment in which children witness and are taught to enact violence. Rather than blaming the child, we work on improving his environment, adding protective factors, and addressing risk factors.

In the second approach, we hold the perpetrator accountable, but in a different way. Juveniles are tried for acts that would be criminal if committed by an adult but are considered less guilty and more amenable to rehabilitation on account of their young age. We act on the belief that it is morally wrong to hold a child accountable to the same extent as an adult because children lack the full capacity to comprehend their acts. This is the basic premise behind the *Roper* decision, holding that the Constitution's prohibition against "cruel or unusual punishment" is infringed when minors are executed. Applying an established doctrine of proportionality, the Court ruled that minors, because they are underage, are not sufficiently culpable to merit the ultimate penalty.

The third approach is to decide that immaturity has no bearing on innocence. A crime is a crime. This was the position taken by the police arresting a nine-year-old Florida child. She was handcuffed and taken away in a squad car, suspected of having taken $10 and a bunny rabbit from her neighbor's home. "Somebody entered a residence without permission and stole money and a pet rabbit. That's burglary," a police spokesman told the press. "I don't know what other explanation you need. Nine years old is enough to know right from wrong."[24]

Looking at human rights through the lens of child development, we know this approach is far too simplistic. Knowing right and doing right are among the most daunting developmental challenges of childhood. Children are not on a level playing field with adults, including the adults they will one day become, when it comes to understanding and doing right. The concepts of needs-based and capacity-based rights, and the principles of human dignity, equality, agency, privacy, and protection explored throughout this book all come together to explain why, in the area of criminal justice, children *are* different and need systems designed to protect their due process rights as well as recognize their rights to rehabilitation.

CONCLUSION

The Future of Rights

We want a world fit for children, because a world fit for children
is a world fit for everyone.
> —Children of the U.N. Special Session on Children, May 8, 2002

In May of 2002, over three hundred child delegates from around the world traveled to the United States for a Children's Forum, the first of its kind to be held in connection with a U.N. Special Session. They produced a document titled "A World Fit for Us" and presented it as a message to the Special Session of the General Assembly on May 8, 2002.[1] Quickly dubbed the "U-18s" (for delegates under age eighteen), they participated on an equal basis in the Special Session programs, appearing as panelists, offering comments, and asking questions from the floor. Their participation transformed the usually stuffy halls of the United Nations. The underground passages were packed with exhibits about children, young people of every nation mingled and exchanged information, queues of kids formed at a bank of computer terminals, young reporters covered the proceedings, and young people were everywhere, contributing their honesty, vitality, color, and energy. Their participation was a direct consequence of the adoption of the Children's Rights Convention (CRC), and its commitment in Articles

12 and 13 to include children and youth in proceedings that affect their lives.

At the World Summit on Children in 1990, young people had played a largely ceremonial role, "handing the pens to the adult delegates so they could sign the documents."[2] In the intervening decade, responding to the CRC's mandate, governments had sponsored numerous children's summits and a new generation of U-18s had come of age. The young delegates were polite and respectful but brutally and sometimes dangerously honest. In one electrifying moment, an adult delegate from an African country who had boasted of overcoming the problem of child soldiers found his story contradicted by the youngest member of the panel. Saying that he himself had been kidnapped and made to fight, the boy told us that many children in his country were still held by the militia from which he had escaped.

Worldwide, the CRC has unlocked the honesty, energy, and creativity of children. Children have brought us fresh insights and fresh perspectives on old problems. In 2004, I was invited to Belfast by Cornell, Ulster, and Queen's Universities to study children's responses to living in a violent environment and to see how children in Northern Ireland were participating in defining their own rights as envisioned by the CRC. The 1998 Good Friday Agreement that brought some measure of peace to Northern Ireland included groundwork for a Bill of Rights. A new post of Commissioner of Children and Young People had been created and the commissioner, together with Queen's University, Belfast, embarked on a project to get input from children about their rights.[3] In a pilot project to develop methods, a team of Queen's University graduate students in law and political science had fanned out over the city schools, bringing with them huge sheets of paper and magic markers. They asked the children to draw their neighborhoods and the things that made them feel good and bad and what they thought about words like "crime" and "police." They did not ask about "the troubles" that were still simmering in Belfast—they did not have to. In one hour viewing the children's posters I learned more about the troubles than I had in a day of scholarly presentations.[4] The children talked freely about the violence, and their magic marker maps were brimming with symbols of the sectarian divide—curb painting, wall murals, warring flags, swathes of orange and green, and the fortresslike wall that literally divides Protestant from Catholic Belfast. Children were especially sensitive to these symbols, and many said they felt afraid when they saw curbs painted orange or green or flags of either camp displayed, because they knew it meant there would be fighting. Most Belfast children attend sectarian schools. They said they hated having to wear uniforms because it made them targets when passing through the other side's territory to get to school. They had fresh ideas for resolving the divisions. Here's one suggestion from an eight-year-old to stop the fighting over flag displays: "Let's make a new flag for everybody that has the design of the Orangeman's flag but is green like the Irish flag." A sensible solution worthy of eight-year-old Sheyann Webb.

A book cannot replicate a gathering of flesh-and-blood children, but in this book, I have introduced the reader to many different children who have worked hard and risked much to perfect our rights and have earned their place as delegates. Each is a unique individual and at the same time a symbol of children's rights. In this final chapter, let me gather them here in an imaginary hall for a Children's Forum on the future of rights. In my book, I have assigned them special roles, as standard-bearers for various human rights principles. I am sure, knowing the agency and voice of my invitees, that many will bridle at their assigned roles and will have a lot to say about how I misinterpreted or misunderstood their lives. But let's assume those issues have been thrashed out and we are ready to get down to work.

Fred Bailey, who became Frederick Douglass, and Dred Scott's daughters, Eliza and Lizzie, are in the room under the banner of *privacy*. They have been joined by foster children John G., fighting for the house his father left him, and Tony, who took charge of his own destiny and found himself an adoptive mother. I assigned them the privacy principle because their stories illustrate the importance of belonging and of the right to family relationships and the difference between being raised by strangers and being raised by family.

Ben Franklin is in the room, under the banner of *agency*. He stands for children's role in defending free expression and freedom of the press. He has been joined by the Tinker children who won for American schoolchildren the right to peaceful protest and to due process. Also present is Zachary, the kindergartner whose picture of Jesus was taken out of the hallway display, and he is joined by a throng of twenty-first-century children now using the Internet as a meeting place and platform for expression.

We cannot fit the thousands of young marchers of the civil rights movement into the room, but two of them, John Lewis and Sheyann Webb are here together, as they were on Edmund Pettus Bridge when they were assaulted and tear-gassed by troopers. They have a lot to teach us about how children experience discrimination as they pass through developmental stages, and they have also taught us what children gain, as well as risk, when they are empowered to fight injustice.

Louy Alcott and William Cather are in the room, and they have been joined by Nikki and Kelli, wearing their tuxedoes, and by Sandra, in her jeans and cowboy boots. Each in her own way and her own time stands for the *equality* principle, and the right to define oneself and not to be confined by gender stereotypes. Also present is Helen Keller, who used her precious "sense of think" to break the prison of darkness and silence. She has been joined by Mara, the Russian child who wanted to play her own music, and by Naomi, the child who finally learned to walk. They stand for another aspect of equality—a fair opportunity for each child to reach his or her potential.

The world-renowned journalist of the Holocaust, Anne Frank, is in the room, under the banner of individual *dignity*. Liu, the refugee from the Chinese one-child policy, is also there. They are joined by representatives of the undocumented alien children graduating from high school who are waiting for action on the DREAM Act. These children stand for the right to be treated as individuals and not persecuted, exiled, or stigmatized because of one's parentage, ethnicity, or religion. Already waiting to greet them under the banner of dignity was the newsboy, an icon of the early children's rights movement. He and other working children have been joined by Evelyn, the nine-year-old entrepreneurial window washer. They symbolize another aspect of dignity—that children's work and play be valued and respected.

Finally, we come to Maya Angelou, a sexually abused child who lost her voice but found it again in *I Know Why the Caged Bird Sings* and grew up to become a beloved storyteller. She stands for a child-centered approach to *protection* that takes into account the whole child and protects the full panoply of her rights, rather than retraumatizing her in the process of gaining revenge against her abuser. Joining her are Lionel Tate who crushed his playmate, and Amal, the child who put the baby in the top bunk. Both of these children were caught up in the juvenile justice system when they were accused of committing crimes. They are here to remind us that there are many forms of innocence and vulnerability calling for our protection, from actual innocence to the vulnerability of adolescence. They show us that adolescents are still, developmentally and legally, children and need protection from their own immaturity. These are our U-18s, and in thinking about the future of rights I ask you to imagine them present and to listen to their voices.

In preparation for this Children's Forum summit, I have laid out a scheme of rights grounded in basic human rights values—privacy, agency, equality, individual dignity, and protection—and informed by the science of human development that emphasizes needs as well as capacities, dependency as well as autonomy. I have shown how these values take on more complex and nuanced meanings when viewed through the lens of child development and its stages and critical tasks. And I have sketched out a model of childhood that places children in an ecological context. The ecological model pushes us to think about the environment in which children grow: the microsystems (i.e., family, school, community) in which children are embedded, the exosystems (i.e., parents' workplace, health care systems, the economy) that indirectly affect children, and the macrosystem that provides a cultural context and moral framework for our conduct toward children. I have presented all those attending with narratives about real children to show rather than merely tell how these human rights and developmental principles play out in children's lives. By linking modern children's stories with stories drawn from American history, I have shown that these values are not a recent invention but are deeply rooted in American history and tradition. Children's rights are new in the same way that women's rights and African Americans' rights, and rights for the differently abled were once new. They are a new extension of existing rights principles to a class of persons who have suffered unjust discrimination and who have been marginalized in the past.

In my Introduction, I proposed that thinking seriously about justice for children would have a maturing effect on our capacity to understand the fundamental meaning of human rights. Here is my opportunity to test my hypothesis. The purpose of our gathering is to address the future of rights for all humans, not just for children. Rather than taking as our template the scheme of rights designed by adults to meet the needs of adults and tailoring it to meet children's needs, I would explore whether making children's rights the template provides a better pattern for thinking about human rights in general.

Suppose one were to think about all human activity within the ecological and developmental framework we have applied to children's rights? Illusions of autonomy, so dear to adult-centric schemes of rights, would dissolve, making room for the reality of dependency and interdependency. We would see each person's struggle for trust, will, hope, competence, and generativity described by Erik Erikson as part of a human journey and get away from thinking of rights as a form of special treatment for "minorities," including children.[5] We would have to look at all persons, parents and workers as well as children, more realistically and in ecological context. Our obsession with the individual as the fundamental unit of rights would expand to include family, community, and relational interests. We could shift our focus from punishing individuals for stumbling and falling to creating an environment that catches and strengthens them before they hit the ground. Taking a cue from the environmental and medical sciences, we would gauge our success by how well we protected the most fragile, not by how strong we made the strongest. We would start worrying when the physical, cultural, and economic environment became toxic to the young and not measure it by whether adults could survive a heavy daily dose of stress and pain. I have called this paradigm shift "Ecogenerism" to emphasize the core value of generativity—commitment to the next generation. Ecogenerism's goal is a world that is fit for children, now and in the future.

The philosophy I propose would require a major transformation in the American macrosystem. As we saw in chapter 1, the macrosystem is the patterning by history, power, and ideas of the broader society in which the child lives. Law is the system that carries these norms throughout the various systems, as blood flows through veins and arteries in the human body and water through streams and rivers in the natural world. Currently, the American macrosystem is characterized by a number of mutually reinforcing values and ideologies that strike me as toxic to children, including a blind belief in individual responsibility; the myth of individual autonomy; a belief in free market efficiency as the measure of good and consumption as the engine of the free market; deep-seated prejudices dividing people along lines of race, class, gender, and religion; and a success ethic that rejects as unworthy those who falter in climbing the ladder of success.[6] I will use the term "privatization" as shorthand for this complex of ideologies and values. As Martha Albertson Fineman has commented, "[Americans] have an historic and highly romanticized affair with the ideals of the private and the individual, as opposed to the public and the collective, as the appropriate units of focus in determining social good."[7] Social critic Orlando Patterson talks about a "privatization of freedom" that has dramatically shifted the way Americans perceive the meaning of this basic value. "Freedom in this conception means doing what one wants and getting one's way. It is measured in terms of one's independence and autonomy, on the one hand, and one's influence and power, on the other."[8]

If these are accurate descriptions of the American macrosystem, we should not be surprised at the increase in child poverty in America or be baffled by our nation's underinvestment in children as a group. Accumulation of private wealth for one's own children displaces a shared commitment to all children as a paramount goal. In politics, individual success within the "ownership society" displaces the New Deal emphasis on collective insurance against the shared risks of personal or climate disaster and systems failure. Each individual looks after himself and his own and government should step out of the way as he climbs the ladder to prosperity and power. Meanwhile, our public infrastructure declines and children become isolated from one another in affluent gated communities and ghettos. It seems inevitable, given this paradigm of freedom, that the conceptual divide between "our children" and "other people's children" has widened to the detriment of all American children.

The autonomy myth and the focus on individual responsibility are profoundly unjust to children. Very young children are not autonomous nor can they be charged with responsibility for their "condition" in life. Children make no choices about when or where or to whom they will be born or the caretaking assets available to them. Whatever chances they have at reaching mature autonomy are dependent on the emotional and material resources invested in them during childhood. Market efficiency is also a poor match for children's needs. Children are not a profit center and get left behind when profit is the only motivation, as we are learning to our dismay in states that have privatized the child protection system. The emphasis on consumption has led to a society where children's primary role is as consumers—of junk foods, of junk media, and junk education generated for profit. Parents working double shifts in order to give their children "everything" are victims of this toxic message from the American macrosystem. The autonomy myth, market efficiency, and the high value of consumption color every aspect of children's lives. These ideals influence how we define the quality of childhood, attitudes toward family, and how we define the good parent. These flawed ideals are responsible for the toxic environment in which Americans are raising their children. We can see these toxic effects in the increase in child poverty, the obesity epidemic, and the culture of violence that makes America the most dangerous developed country in the world.

Nevertheless, different versions of "the good" continue to compete with this version and have deeper roots in American history and tradition. Property rights are only one among many values embodied in the Constitution and, as Frederick Douglass reminded us, we betray that "Glorious Liberty Document" when we place property above all else. American values recognize that the pursuit of life, liberty, and happiness are unalienable rights. Looking at rights through a developmental lens forces us to dig deeper in understanding what these values mean. An understanding of human development in ecological context belies the myth that autonomy is the foundation of life, liberty, and happiness, even when applied to adults. It also puts consumption of material goods into perspective, elevating the role of personal interaction and emotional engagement above profit in defining the "good life."

A change in our macrosystem would not be easy and would not happen overnight. But such paradigm shifts have occurred before and continue to occur. One can point to the abolition of slavery and gender equality as examples. Our national response to the excesses of the robber barons and the Depression created many social programs, some of which have survived the era of privatization. In recent years, America's commitment to international law has eroded, but I see a backlash developing against unilateralism and rejection of human rights.

The example of paradigm shift that is most closely related to Eco-generism is the environmental movement. Rachel Carson published her book *Silent Spring* in 1962, and within a short period of time our views and policies toward the environment shifted radically. We were able to respond to the environmental crisis by designing new laws and adopting evidence-based practices to preserve, protect, and prevent the degradation of our natural world. Environmentalists have waged an uphill battle because they are asking that we make significant sacrifices for a future good. But Americans do care about their natural world. At this writing, it is fair to say that the debate over whether global warming exists has ended and we are moving toward implementing preventive measure to address this real problem. I believe we can do the same with our social world, using similar approaches, in order to create an environment fit for children. Recall that Berry Brazelton identified a seventh "irreducible need" of children. He called it "Protection of the Future" from threats such as ecological crises, social inequality, and war. As he pointed out, "all needs pale before the need to survive and give birth to succeeding generations."[9]

What is the role of children's *rights* in my utopian scheme? Children's rights, as conceived in the CRC and in this book, include needs-based rights as well as capacity-based rights. They create a moral environment for thinking about what we owe to our children. Recall that human rights are a kind of ozone layer of the law. Like a healthy ozone layer, they cast a protective shield over the humans below. With the universal adoption of the CRC, children's rights are now firmly entrenched as an element of international law. The CRC has not instantly transformed the Earth into a child-friendly planet, but it has begun to shift the international macrosystem of power and ideologies to make a place for children as priorities and as participants. Because I see children's rights as rooted in American values as well as international human rights, I view it as inevitable that children's rights will be made increasingly explicit in American constitutional decisions and statutory law. This will happen regardless of whether the United States ever ratifies the CRC, although our progress is likely to be more halting and less informed if we isolate ourselves from the rest of the world.

If we were to take the bold step of committing ourselves to children's rights, integrating the central human rights values I have outlined for children into our national macrosystem, and *acting* upon them, I imagine we would find that the children at the U.N. Special Session for Children got it right. A world fit for children *is* a world fit for everyone.

NOTES

Introduction. Ain't I a Person?

1. Arthur M. Schlesinger Jr. "Folly's Antidote," www.nytimes.com/2007/01/01/opinion/01schlesinger.html, accessed January 1, 2007.

2. The only other nation that has not ratified the CRC is Somalia, which lacks a functioning government.

3. Haley and Malcolm X, *Malcolm X*, 21.

4. Truth, "Ain't I a Woman."

5. Ross, "A Place at the Table," 1335–36.

6. Compare the concerns of liberals who critique children's rights, such as Martin Guggenheim, in *What's Wrong with Children's Rights* and "How Children's Lawyers Serve the State," with those of conservatives, such as Bruce Hafen and Jonathan Hafen, in "Abandoning Children to Their Autonomy." Guggenheim's concern is that child rights will be misused as a weapon against the poorest and most vulnerable families, while the Hafens' concern is that rights for children will imperil authority structures within the traditional family.

Chapter 1. How to Think about Childhood

1. Coles, *Their Eyes Meeting the World*, 1.

2. Mintz, *Huck's Raft*, 1–5.

3. Pufall and Unsworth, "The Imperative and the Process for Rethinking Childhood," 2.

4. Woodhouse, "Youthful Indiscretions," 763.

5. Konner, *Childhood*, 13, 87, 141; Singer, "Developmental Variations," Table P.1, xxxi.

6. Mintz, *Huck's Raft*, 1–5.

7. Brazelton and Greenspan, *Irreducible Needs*, x.

27. Fagan and Zimring, *Changing Borders of Juvenile Justice*, 13–19.

28. United Nations General Assembly, CRC, Art. 5.

29. Ibid., Art. 1.

30. *Moore v. City of East Cleveland*, 431 U.S. 494 (1977). "Our decisions teach that the Constitution protects the sanctity of the family precisely because the institution of the family is deeply rooted in this Nation's history and tradition."

Chapter 3. Boys in Slavery and Servitude: Frederick Douglass

1. My retelling of Frederick Douglass's childhood is drawn primarily from his first book, *Narrative of the Life of Frederick Douglass an American Slave by Himself*, written in 1845 when he was twenty-seven years old. To the extent this differs from his later autobiographical writings, I have chosen to focus on this first and more contemporaneous recollection. Some of the material in this chapter appeared earlier in Woodhouse, "Dred Scott's Daughters," *Buffalo Law Review*, 669–79. I also draw upon Preston, *Young Frederick Douglass*, and McFeely, *Frederick Douglass*, and on various visual images and facsimiles of documents from his lifetime, available on the Internet. See Frederick Douglass National Historic Site, at http://www.nps.gov/frdo/; Indiana University–Purdue University at Indianapolis's The Frederick Douglass Papers, at http://www.iupui.edu/~douglass; The Frederick Douglass Papers at the Library of Congress, http://memory.loc.gov/ammem/doughtml/doughome.html, all accessed June 30, 2006.

2. Berlin, *Slaves without Masters*, 54–55; McFeely, *Frederick Douglass*, 26.

3. Douglass, *Narrative*, 31–32; McFeely, *Frederick Douglass*, 34.

4. Douglass, *Narrative*, 34.

5. Ibid., 35 (emphasis in original).

6. Ibid., 34.

7. Ibid., 36–37.

8. Blassingame, Introduction, xv, xl.

9. Preston, *Young Frederick Douglass*, 104.

10. Douglass, *Narrative*, 45; McFeely, *Frederick Douglass*, 44.

11. Douglass, *Narrative*, 70.

12. Ibid., 72.

13. Douglass and Murray raised a family together and were married from shortly after his escape until her death in 1882. McFeely, *Frederick Douglass*, 312.

14. Douglass, *Narrative*, 74.

15. Johnson, *Soul by Soul*, 21.

16. These themes are developed in greater detail in Woodhouse, "Who Owns the Child?" 1041–50.

17. Aristotle, *Nicomachean Ethics*, 1161b.

18. Woodhouse, "Who Owns the Child?" 1041–50.

19. Mason, *From Father's Property*, 104; Mintz, *Huck's Raft*, 32–33.

20. Woodhouse, "Who Owns the Child?" 1046.

21. Mason, *From Father's Property*, 2, 31; Mintz, *Huck's Raft*, 32–33.

22. *Prigg v. Pennsylvania*, 41 U.S. 536 (1842) (Margaret Mason and her four children, one of whom was born in Pennsylvania, were taken by force back to Maryland by bounty hunter Prigg under authority of Fugitive Slave Acts and U.S. Const. art. IV, § 2, cl. 3).

23. Higginbotham, *Shades of Freedom*, 28–37.

24. Grossberg, *Governing the Hearth*, 197; Mason, *From Father's Property*, 24–27, 96.

25. Stampp, "Chattels Personal," 203; Higginbotham, *Shades of Freedom*, 34–36.

26. Preston, *Young Frederick Douglass*, 113.

27. Mason, *From Father's Property*, 24–31; Higginbotham and Kopytoff, "Racial Purity," 1971, 2006.

28. Berlin, *Slaves without Masters*, 222–23.

29. Ibid., 222–28; Mason, *From Father's Property*, 31–39.

30. Douglass, *Narrative*, 32.

31. Grossberg, *Governing the Hearth*, 211; Mintz, *Huck's Raft*, 154–60.

32. Bremner, *Children and Youth*, 691, quoting Elijah Devoe, *The Refuge System, or, Prison Discipline Applied to Juvenile Delinquents* (New York: J. B. M'-Gown, 1848), 27–28; Mintz, *Huck's Raft*, 160, quoting Elijah Devoe.

33. Berlin, *Many Thousands Gone*, 279.

34. Mintz, *Huck's Raft*, 94.

35. Holt, *Orphan Trains*, 100, quoting from an editorial in the *Belleville Weekly Democrat*, April 17, 1858.

36. Davis, *Neglected Stories*, 116.

37. Weld, *American Slavery*, 123.

38. Cong. Globe, 39th Cong., 1st Sess. 504 (1866).

39. Foner, *Reconstruction*, 80.

40. Davis, *Neglected Stories*, 147; Mintz, *Huck's Raft*, 115.

41. Johnson, *Soul by Soul*, 21.

42. Zainaldin, *Antebellum Society*, 68–69.

Chapter 4. Girls at the Intersection of Age, Race, and Gender: Dred Scott's Daughters

1. Woodhouse, "Dred Scott's Daughters," 684–85. For facsimiles of legal documents in the case, visit the Washington University Virtual Library Digital Collection, The Dred Scott Case, http://library.wustl.edu/vlib/dredscott/, last accessed June 29, 2006.

2. National Park Service, Jefferson National Expansion Memorial, African

American Community, http://www.nps.gov/jeff/planyourvisit/african-american community.htm.

3. Berlin, *Slaves without Masters*, 33. For petitions from Dred Scott's era, see http://library.wustl.edu/vlib/dredscott/.

4. Wilson, *The Dred Scott Decision*, 21–22.

5. VanderVelde and Subramanian, "Mrs. Dred Scott."

6. By contrast, a free black man could marry a female slave without losing his freedom. In an 1857 case from Kentucky, a manumitted slave married a slave woman whom he then purchased from her master in order to ensure that they could not be separated. Unfortunately, he went bankrupt and his debtors attached and sold his wife as an article of his property and used the proceeds to satisfy his debts. *Kyler & Wife v. Dunlap*, 18 B. Mon. 561 (Ky. 1857) discussed in Woodhouse, "Who Owns the Child?" at 1043, note 222.

7. The speech of Abraham Lincoln, delivered in Springfield, Illinois, on June 26, 1857, is available from the Teaching American History Project of Ashland University, at http://teachingamericanhistory.org/library/index.asp?document=52, accessed June 30, 2006.

8. Catterall, *Judicial Cases*, 121.

9. See *Dred Scott v. Sandford*, 60 U.S. (19 How.) 393, 398 (1857).

10. As with many of the facts in the *Dred Scott* case, inconsistencies exist between the historical record and reports or recitations in the court records. For example, Sanford's name was misspelled by the Supreme Court reporter, acquiring an extra *d*. The trial judge in the federal case, tried in 1854, apparently instructed the jury that Eliza was about fourteen but she may have been as old as sixteen. Compare *The Case of Dred Scot in the United States Supreme Court*, 3–4 with VanderVelde and Subramanian, at note 27 (reporting Eliza's most probable year of birth as 1838, and noting that one historian estimated Eliza was nineteen and Lizzie eighteen). I will assume here that Eliza's birth year was 1838 and Lizzie's was 1846, making Eliza eight and Lizzie a newborn at the time of the first case. Swain, *Dred and Harriet Scott*, 91–92.

11. Hopkins, *Dred Scott's Case*, 23.

12. Mintz, *Huck's Raft*, 95, 110.

13. White, "Female Slaves," 106–7.

14. Mintz, *Huck's Raft*, 110; VanderVelde and Subramanian, "Mrs. Dred Scott," 1064–65, estimating the value of the Scott family members based on statistics compiled in 1914 by Harrison Anthony Trexler, *Slavery in Missouri 1804–1865* (Baltimore: Johns Hopkins Press, 1914), 38–39.

15. Mintz, *Huck's Raft*, 95.

16. Woodhouse, "Who Owns the Child," 1064–65.

17. Catterall, *Judicial Cases*, 428–29, reprinting *Meekin v. Thomas*, 17 B. Mon. 710 (Ky. 1857).

18. Catterall, *Judicial Cases*, 334, reprinting Catherine Bodine's Will, 4 Dana

476 (Ky. 1836); Catterall, *Judicial Cases*, 183, reprinting *Kitty v. Commonwealth*, 18 B. Mon. 522 (Ky. 1857).

19. Jean Fagan Yellin, in her book *Harriet Jacobs: A Life*, has provided a wonderfully detailed examination of the life of this remarkable woman, and the story she wrote under the pseudonym of Linda Brent is borne out by Yellin's exhaustive research.

20. Brent, *Incidents*, 374.

21. Fox-Genovese, *Within the Plantation Household*, 290–92; Austin, "Sapphire Unbound!" 539; Harris, "Finding Sojourner's Truth," 384; Tarpley, "Black Women, Sexual Myth," 1343.

22. VanderVelde and Subramanian, "Mrs. Dred Scott," 1074 and note 179, quoting from "Dred Scott Free at Last: Himself and His Family Emancipated," *St. Louis Daily Evening News*, May 26, 1857, at 2.

23. Mintz, *Huck's Raft*, 104.

24. Brent, *Incidents*, 374.

25. The text of Frederick Douglass's speech delivered in May of 1857, is available from the Teaching American History Project of Ashland University, at http:// teachingamericanhistory.org/library/index.asp?document=772, accessed June 30, 2006.

26. The speech of Abraham Lincoln, delivered in Springfield, Illinois, on June 26, 1857, is available from the Teaching American History Project of Ashland University, at http://teachingamericanhistory.org/library/index.asp?document=52, accessed June 30, 2006.

27. VanderVelde and Subramanian, "Mrs. Dred Scott," 1074 and note 179, quoting from "Dred Scott Free at Last: Himself and His Family Emancipated," *St. Louis Daily Evening News*, May 26, 1857, at 2.

28. "Visit to Dred Scott." *Frank Leslie's Illustrated Newspaper*, June 27, 1857, 49–50.

29. Swain, *Dred and Harriet Scott*, 84.

30. Gates, Introduction, xvii.

31. Roberts, "Racism and Patriarchy," 3.

32. Johnson, *Soul by Soul*, 21.

33. Mintz, *Huck's Raft*, 101–3.

34. Swain, *Dred and Harriet Scott*, 4.

Chapter 5. Growing Up in State Custody: "Tony" and "John G."

1. Hilliard-Nunn, *Youth Speak!*

2. Children's Aid Society, "Aging Out of Foster Care," at http://www .childrensaidsociety.org/about/whatwethink/agingoutoffostercare, accessed June 8, 2007.

3. Fellmuth, *Child Rights and Remedies*, 23.

4. Statistics in this paragraph are taken from the Child Welfare League of America's National Data Analysis System, located at http://ndas.cwla.org/data_stats/, accessed June 8, 2006.

5. Waldfogel, *Future of Child Protection*, 60–64.

6. Russell-Brown, *Underground Codes*, 5–18.

7. Child Welfare League of America's National Data Analysis System, located at http://ndas.cwla.org/data_stats/, accessed June 8, 2006. Data is also available from Centers for Disease Control and Prevention, located at http://www.cdc.gov/ncipc/factsheets/svfacts.htm, accessed June 8, 2007.

8. Data from Centers for Disease Control and Prevention, located at http://www.cdc.gov/ncipc/factsheets/svfacts.htm, accessed June 8, 2007.

9. In *The Book of David*, Richard Gelles paints a stark picture of what can happen to children when the system fails to intervene in high-risk cases, while Dorothy Roberts paints a stark picture of the social effects of excessive intervention in poor families in *Shattered Bonds*. Studies suggest that foster care can be beneficial to many children we now label "neglected," if only because they are better housed, fed, and cared for than in their own homes, but moving children who are not truly at risk of harm from poor or dysfunctional homes into better homes is contrary to American law and family values.

10. Statistics from the Administration for Children and Families, Department of Health and Human Services, Child Maltreatment 2004, at http://www.acf.hhs.gov/programs/cb/pubs/cm04/table3_21.htm, accessed April 10, 2007.

11. Roberts, "Community Dimensions," 23–35.

12. Sally Kestin, "Lost Children Easily Found: Sun-Sentinel Turns Up Nine of DCF's Missing Children," (August 11, 2002), at http://www.sun-sentinel.com/news/local/southflorida/sfl-amissing11aug11,0,1816955.story?page=3, accessed June 20, 2006.

13. Department of Children and Families, http://www.dcf.state.fl.us/missingkids/, accessed June 11, 2006.

14. The data are taken from the October 2002 National Incidence Studies of Missing Abducted Runaway and Thrownaway Children, or NISMART, Bulletin: Runaway/Thrownaway Children: National Estimates and Characteristics, authored by Heather Hammer, David Finkelhor, and Andrea J. Sedlak, located at http://www.ncjrs.org/html/ojjdp/nismart/04/ns1.html, accessed June 11, 2006.

15. Brazelton and Greenspan, *Irreducible Needs*, x.

16. Sheryl Dicker, Elysa Gordon, and Jane Knitzer, "Improving the Odds for the Healthy Development of Young Children in Foster Care," National Center for Children in Poverty (January 2002), located at National Center on Children in Poverty, http://www.nccp.org/pub_pew02b.html, accessed Jan. 22, 2007.

17. Rob Geen, Anna Sommers, Mindy Cohen, "Medicaid Spending on Foster Children," The Urban Institute (2005), located at Urban Institute, www.urban.org/publications/311221.html, accessed Jan. 23, 2007.

18. Hardin, "Safety and Stability for Foster Children," 31–48; American Academy of Pediatrics, "Developmental Issues for Young Children in Foster Care."

19. Administration for Children and Families, Department of Human Services, AFCARS Report, at http://www.acf.hhs.gov/programs/cb/stats_research/afcars/tar/report13.htm, indicates over 50,000 children exited foster care to adoptive placements in 2005, compared with 38,000 in 1998, an increase of 3 percent. But adoption is not the best answer for every child and every family. Coupet, "Swimming Upstream," 430–35.

20. Eric Frazier, "N.C. Taking Foster Kids' Social Security Money," *Charlotte Observer*, June 16, 2006; Hatcher, "Foster Children," 1798.

21. Delgado et al., *Expanding Transitional Services*, 23–24.

22. Courtney and Dworsky, *Midwest Evaluation*, 1. This report is a longitudinal study of the transition to adulthood for a sample of foster youth who came of age after the passage of the Foster Care Independence Act of 1999. The 282 youths who were still in care were compared with the 321 who had already been discharged. Comparison groups were taken from the age nineteen cohort of the National Longitudinal Study of Adolescent Health, generally referred to as "Add Health," a federally funded study that examines how social contexts affect health related behaviors of adolescents. University of North Carolina Population Center, Add Health, at http://www.cpc.unc.edu/projects/addhealth/, accessed July 7, 2006.

23. Courtney and Dworsky, *Midwest Evaluation*, citing Add Health 2002.

24. Ibid., 7–8.

25. Ibid., 7.

26. Ibid.

27. Foster Care Independence Act of 1999. See Pub. L. No. 106–169, 113 Stat. 1822 (codified as amended in scattered sections of 42 U.S.C.).

28. Courtney and Dworsky, *Midwest Evaluation*, 1–2.

29. Ibid., 5, 8, 9.

30. Ibid., 14.

31. Ibid., 5.

32. NBC6, Tape Released Showing Teen Beaten at Boot Camp, February 17, 2006, at http://www.nbc6.net/news/7158282/detail.html, accessed June 8, 2006.

33. Richard Mendel, *Less Hype, More Help: Reducing Juvenile Crime, What Works—and What Doesn't* (Washington, DC: American Youth Policy Forum, 2003), cited in Office of Juvenile Justice and Delinquency Prevention Model Programs Guide, at http://www.dsgonline.com/mpg2.5/correctional_facility.htm, accessed June 10, 2006.

34. Alex Leary, "Law Puts End to Boot Camps: The Martin Lee Anderson Act Replaces the Camps with Programs That Focus More on Education," *St. Petersburg Times*, at http://www.sptimes.com/2006/06/01/State/Law_puts_end_to_boot_.shtml; Jason Garcia, "New Law Revamps State Boot Camps," *Orlando Sentinel*,

June 1, 2006, at http://www.orlandosentinel.com/news/local/state/orl-bootcamp
0106jun01,0,4754462.story?coll=orl-news-headlines-state, accessed June 10,
2006. The Martin Lee Anderson Act, 2006 FL H.B. 5019, is codified in various sections of Chapters 39 and 985 of the Florida Statutes Annotated.

35. While there are genuine challenges in representing children, see Buss,
"Confronting Developmental Barriers," 918, they are not insurmountable obstacles. As Jane Spinak argues, pointing to the collective work of decades of scholars
and attorneys, it is time to stand firm on the issue of whether children deserve and
can benefit from legal counsel to give them voices in the legal system. The majority position among experts in the field is now clearly in favor of children in state
custody, as our most vulnerable citizens, being assigned lawyers trained to represent this class of clients and meet those challenges. Spinak, "Simon Says," 1385;
Woodhouse, "Talking about Children's Rights," 130.

Chapter 6. The Printer's Apprentice: Ben Franklin and Youth Speech

1. Brands, *First American*, 29.

2. Franklin, *Autobiography*, 70. My citations of Franklin's autobiography are
from the University of Virginia's E-book version, a use of electricity that would
surely have delighted him.

3. Brands, *First American*, title page.

4. Franklin, *Autobiography*, 18.

5. Ibid., 13.

6. Ibid., 14.

7. Ibid., 17–18.

8. Mintz, *Huck's Raft*.

9. *Tinker v. Des Moines Independent Community School District*, 393 U.S.
503 at 737 (1969).

10. *Hazelwood School District v. Kuhlmeier*, 484 U.S. 260 at 266 (1988),
quoting *Tinker*, 393 U.S. 503 at 506.

11. *Hazelwood*, quoting *Bethel School Dist. No. 403 v. Fraser*, 478 U.S. 675
(1986) and *Tinker*.

12. Mintz, *Huck's Raft*, 54–55, 118–21, 311–13.

13. *Meyer v. Nebraska*, 262 U.S. 390 (1923).

14. *West Virginia v. Barnette*, 319 U.S. 624 (1943).

15. For more information on these televised hearings, which took place
between April and June of 1954, see Museum of Broadcasting, "The Army-
McCarthy Hearings," at http://www.museum.tv/archives/etv/A/htmlA/army-
mccarthy/army-mccarthy.htm, accessed July 1, 2006

16. The Rosenbergs were executed on the evening of June 19, 1953. For a
photograph of their sons, Michael and Robbie, see "Heir to an Execution," located at http://www.films42.com/columns/rosenberg.asp, accessed April 15, 2007.

17. The words "under God" were added on June 14, 1954, as a result of advocacy by the Knights of Columbus. See Ben's Guide to U.S. Government for Kids, at http://bensguide.gpo.gov/3-5/symbols/pledgeallegiance.html, accessed April 15, 2007, and Knights of Columbus, "How the Words Under God Came to Be Added to the Pledge of Allegiance," at http://www.kofc.org/rc/en/about/activities/community/pledgeAllegiance, accessed July 2, 2006.

18. *Tinker*, 393 U.S. 503, 508.

19. Ibid. at 511.

20. Black, dissenting, ibid. at 516.

21. C. H. as Guardian ad Litem for *Z. H. v. Oliva*, 226 F.3d 198 (3rd Cir. 2000) (en banc). A similar case is *Peck v. Baldwinsville School District*, 426 F.3d 617 (2d Cir. 2005), in which students were asked to draw pictures of "ways to save our environment."

22. *Z. H. v. Oliva*, 226 F.3d, 213–14.

23. *Peck,* 426 F.3d 617 (2d Cir. 2005).

24. *Demers v. Leominster School Department*, 263 F. Supp. 2d 195 (D. Mass. 2003) (eighth grader suspended because of drawings depicting violence at school); *Porter v. Ascension Parish School Board*, 2004 U.S. Dist. Lexis 1175 (M.d. La. 2004) (fourteen-year-old suspended for drawing depicting torching of school).

25. *Gules v. Marineau*, 349 F. Supp. 2d 871 (D. Vt. 2004) (T-shirt critical of George Bush); "Teen high school paper seized," CNN.Com, November 28, 2005, at http://www.cnn.com/2005/education/11/28/studentnewspaper.seize.ap/index.html.

26. Woodhouse, "Speaking Truth to Power," 481.

27. Cox Media Network, "Study Reveals 14% of Teens Have Had Face-to-Face Meetings with People They've Met on the Internet," May 11, 2006, at http://www.netsmartz.org/pdf/cox_teensurvey_may2006.pdf, accessed July 2, 2006.

28. For coverage of this topic aimed at parents, see "MySpace Invader," on MSNBC, at http://www.msnbc.com/id/12192496/, accessed June 16, 2006.

29. The Child Online Protection Act (COPA) is codified at 47 U.S.C. section 231(c)(1).

30. *U.S. v. American Library Association*, 539 U.S. 194 (2003).

31. See "MySpace Safety Tips," at http://www1.myspace.com/misc/safetyTips .html, accessed April 15, 2007; www.netsmartz.org, accessed June 16, 2006.

32. Mintz, *Huck's Raft*, 25–27, 215.

33. Woodhouse, "Ecogenerism"; Woodhouse, "Reframing the Debate"; Woodhouse, "Cleaning Up Toxic Violence."

34. Kunkel and Zwarun, "How Real Is the Problem of TV Violence?" 203; Gentile and Anderson, "Violent Video Games," 225.

Chapter 7. Youth in the Civil Right's Movement:
John Lewis and Sheyann Webb

1. Lewis, *Walking with the Wind*, 318.

2. Webb and West Nelson, *Selma, Lord, Selma*, 11.

3. Williams, *Eyes on the Prize*, 39–43.

4. Ibid., 44.

5. Williams, *Eyes on the Prize*, 56–57; Lewis, *Walking with the Wind*, 46–47.

6. PBS, *American Experience*, "The Murder of Emmett Till," at http://www
.pbs.org/wgbh/amex/till/sfeature/sf_remember.html, accessed April 17, 2007.

7. King, *Call to Conscience*, 95.

8. Southern Poverty Law Center, "Center Information: The Civil Rights Martyrs," at http://www.splcenter.org/centerinfo/lci-12.html, accessed September 16, 2003.

9. Lewis, *Walking with the Wind*, 318.

10. Halberstam, *Children*, 30–31.

11. Ibid., 31.

12. Lewis, *Walking with the Wind*, 107.

13. Ibid., 31; Halberstam, *Children*, 239.

14. Lewis, *Walking with the Wind*, 31.

15. Ibid., 43–44.

16. Ibid., 47.

17. Ibid., 66–67.

18. Ibid., 69–70.

19. Ibid., 115.

20. Halberstam, *Children*, 391.

21. Ibid., 438–39.

22. *Brown v. Board of Education*, 347 U.S. 483 (1954).

23. Levine, *Freedom's Children*, 130–33.

24. King, *I Have a Dream*, 88.

25. Halberstam, *Children*, 439–43.

26. Williams, *Eyes on the Prize*, 189.

27. Ibid., 190 (959 children arrested on the first day); Halberstam, *Children*, 441 (over six hundred children arrested on the first day).

28. Williams, *Eyes on the Prize*, 190.

29. Halberstam, *Children*, 441; Levine, *Freedom's Children*, 81.

30. Levine, *Freedom's Children*, ix–xi. The author explains that she was unable to include material from all the children with whom she spoke. Following is a list of the names and approximate ages or grades in school at the time they became involved in some form of protest: Delores Boyd (eight), Arlam Carr (five), Myrna Carter (HS), Ben Chaney (eleven), Claudette Colvin (fifteen), Roy DeBerry (HS), Thelma Eubanks (fifteen), Frances Foster (fifteen), Mary Gadson (HS), Ernest

Green (HS Jr.), Audrey Faye Hendricks (nine), Towanner Hinkle (sixteen), Barbara Howard (six), Princella Howard (sixteen), Jawana Jackson (four and a half), Joseph Lacey (thirteen), Larry Martin (eleven), Gwendolyn Patton (nine), Bernita Roberson (fourteen), James Roberson (ca. thirteen), Larry Russell (sixteen), Fred Shuttlesworth Jr. (ten), Patricia Shuttlesworth (eleven), Ricky Shuttlesworth (thirteen), Euvester Simpson (seventeen), John Steele (ten), Judy Tarver (seventeen), Fred Taylor (thirteen), Sheyann Webb (eight), Gladis Williams (thirteen).

31. Levine, *Freedom's Children*, 78.

32. Ibid., 79.

33. Ibid., 84.

34. Halberstam, *Children*, 440.

35. Ibid., 395.

36. Levine, *Freedom's Children*, 86.

37. Ibid., 29.

38. Webb and West Nelson, *Selma, Lord, Selma*, 31–33.

39. Levine, *Freedom's Children*, 126.

40. Webb and West Nelson, *Selma, Lord, Selma*, 11.

41. Levine, *Freedom's Children*, 129.

42. Ibid., 129.

43. Webb and West Nelson, *Selma, Lord, Selma*, 91–116.

44. Levine, *Freedom's Children*, 136.

45. Ibid., 155.

46. Ibid., 153.

47. Beals, *Warriors Don't Cry*, xx–xxi.

48. Jackson *Sun*, "Civil Rights 40th Anniversary Edition, at http://www .jacksonsun.com/civilrights/sec3_arrestlist.html, accessed June 11, 2003.

49. Canada, *Fist Stick Knife Gun*.

50. The conference became the springboard for a volume edited by my codirector Nancy Dowd, with Dorothy Singer and Robin Wilson, titled *Handbook on Children, Culture, and Violence*.

Chapter 8. Old Maids and Little Women: Louisa Alcott and William Cather

1. Aldrich, *My Child and I*, 323.

2. Buechler, *Women's Movements*, 13.

3. Alcott, *Her Girlhood Diary*, 1.

4. Alcott, *Little Women*, 6.

5. Blackstone, *Commentaries*, 430.

6. For an insightful discussion of the Victorian concept of separate spheres and attendant legal and social limitations on women's lives, see Wright, "Well-Behaved Women," 226–43.

7. Siegel, "Home as Work," 1090. Reva Siegel explores the early feminist

attempts to obtain rights to the fruits of their own labors, both in the household and in the wage economy.

8. Aldrich, *My Child and I*, 323.

9. Woodhouse, "Who Owns the Child?" citing to Elizabeth Hampsten, "A German-Russian Family in North Dakota," *Heritage Great Plains* 20 (1987): 8, quoting from the recollections of a woman raised on a farm in the plains states.

10. Alcott, *Her Girlhood Diary*, 34.

11. Letter of October 1, 1873, from Louisa May Alcott to Lucy Stone, reprinted in Stern, *Signature of Reform*, 211.

12. Stern, *Signature of Reform*, 123–24, letter of March 1869. Alcott's fans would have been shocked to learn she was publishing lurid Gothic tales under the pseudonym A. M. Barnard. Read her 1863 story, "Pauline's Passion and Punishment," at Project Guttenberg, http://www.gutenberg.org/etext/8384, accessed Sept. 19, 2007.

13. Cather's best-known novels are *O Pioneers!* published in 1913, *The Song of the Lark*, published in 1915, and *My Ántonia*, published in 1918.

14. Robinson, *Willa*, 123.

15. Ibid., 23.

16. O'Brien, *Willa Cather*, 86.

17. Ibid., 83–84.

18. Ibid., 78.

19. Ibid., 99.

20. O'Connor and Day, *Lazy B.*; O'Connor, *Chico*.

21. *United States v. Virginia*, 518 U.S. 515 (1996).

22. Pierpoint, "Postscript," 53.

23. Nemours Foundation, TeensHealth, "Eating Disorders: Anorexia and Bulimia," at http://www.kidshealth.org/teen/your_mind/mental_health/eat_disorder.html (suggesting images in media contribute to such disorders), accessed January 23, 2007.

24. *Romer v. Evans*, 517 U.S. 620 (1996).

25. *Lawrence v. Texas*, 539 U.S. 558 (2003).

26. Associated Press, "Florida Student Sues after Being Left Out of Yearbook," June 23, 2002.

27. National Center for Lesbian and Gay Rights, "NCLR and Equality Florida Applaud Clay County School Board's Decision to Settle Claim by High School Senior," at http://www.nclrights.org/releases/pr-claycountyschool10902105_print.htm? Press release, September 21, 2005, accessed May 29, 2006.

28. *Time*, October 10, 2005, The Battle Over Gay Teens, at http://www.time.com/time/magazine/article/0,9171,1112856,00.html, accessed April 20, 2007.

29. Statement of Brittany Bjurstrom, Point Foundation, at http://www.pointfoundation.org/scholars.html, accessed July 3, 2006.

Chapter 9. Breaking the Prison of Disability: Helen Keller and the
Children of "Greenhaven"

1. Keller, *My Life*, 27. While hundreds of editions of Keller's 1903 autobiography have been published in many languages, I used the restored classic edition, edited by Roger Shattuck with Dorothy Hermann and published by W. W. Norton, which contains the complete version of Helen's story and the accounts of Annie Sullivan and John Macy that were part of the original edition.

2. Ibid., 25.

3. Ibid., 21.

4. Ibid., 22.

5. Ibid., 17–18.

6. Ibid., 23–24.

7. Ibid., 22.

8. Ibid., 27–28.

9. Ibid., 149–50 (letter of Annie Sullivan dated April 5, 1887).

10. Ibid., 285ff., reprinting juvenile letters.

11. Ibid., 288.

12. Ibid., 318 (reprinting Oliver Wendell Holmes's letter to Keller of August 1, 1890).

13. Ibid., 324.

14. Ibid., 31–32.

15. Ibid., 32.

16. As Mintz points out in *Huck's Raft*, 188–91, the systematic study of child development was just beginning in America in the 1880s.

17. Keller, *My Life*, 154 (Annie Sullivan, letter of May 8, 1887).

18. Ibid., 164.

19. Ibid., 77–81.

20. Fleischer and Zames, *Disability Rights Movement*, 19, 31–32.

21. 20 U.S.C. § 1412(1) (1994).

22. *Rowley v. Hendrick Hudson Central School District*, 458 U.S. 176, 203–4 (1982).

23. *Rowley*, 458 U.S., 215.

24. Fleischer and Zames, *Disability Rights Movement*, 184–99.

25. Steven Erlanger, "Vienna Buries Child Victims of the Nazis," *New York Times*, April 29, 2002.

26. *Buck v. Bell*, 274 U.S. 200, 207 (1927).

27. While the Court has never explicitly overruled *Buck v. Bell*, the Court's 1943 decision in *Skinner v. Oklahoma*, 316 U.S. 535 (1942), striking down a eugenics law providing for forced sterilization of felons, sounded its death knell.

28. Waldfogel, *Future of Child Protection*, 84, 120.

29. *No Child Left Behind Act of 2001*, Pub. L. No. 107–110, 115 Stat. 1425 (2002) (codified at 20 U.S.C. §§ 6301–777 (2000)).

30. Raymond Simon, Assistant U.S. Secretary for Elementary and Secondary Education, "Letter to Chief State School Officers Regarding Inclusion of Students with Disabilities in State Accountability Systems," March 2, 2004, at http://www.ed.gov/admins/lead/account/csso030204.html, accessed April 15, 2007.

31. Title 34, Code of Federal Regulations, part 200.

32. U.S. Department of Education, "Flexibility for States Raising Achievement for Students with Disabilities," May 10, 2005, at http://www.ed.gov/policy/elsec/guid/raising/disab-factsheet.html, accessed April 15, 2007.

33. Crain, *Theories of Development*, 384–91.

34. Martha Minow, in her book *Making All the Difference: Inclusion, Exclusion, and American Law*, explores how we might reconsider fundamental values of equality through recognition of the reality and richness of difference.

35. Keller, *My Life*, 154–55 (emphasis in original).

Chapter 10. Hide and Survive: Anne Frank and "Liu"

1. Marks, *Hidden Children*, 35 (recollection of Renee Roth-Hano).

2. Frank, *Diary*, 651. Version A is Anne's first version, Version B is her edited version from March 1944, and Version C is from Otto Frank's compilation published as *Anne Frank: Diary of a Young Girl*. This quotation is from Version A, May 3, 1944.

3. Ibid., 591 (March 25, 1944).

4. Ibid., 669 (April 11, 1944).

5. Ibid., 623 (April 9, 1944).

6. Müller, *Anne Frank*, 264–65.

7. Frank, *Diary*, 610 (April 4, 1944).

8. Müller, *Anne Frank*, 246.

9. Ibid., 107, 124.

10. Ibid., 142.

11. Rol and Verhoeven, *Photographic Remembrance*, 100.

12. Hidden Child Foundation's Web page, hosted by the Anti-Defamation League, at http://www.adl.org/hidden/history.asp, accessed July 6, 2006.

13. Marks, *Hidden Children*, 4.

14. Ibid., 44.

15. Ibid., 54.

16. HIAS and Council Migration Service of Philadelphia, About HIAS and Council Migration Service of Philadelphia, at http://www.hiaspa.org, accessed June 6, 2007.

17. Affidavit, on file with author.

18. Affidavit, on file with author.

19. For a description of the one-child policy see Center for Reproductive

Rights, "China Turns One-Child Policy into Law," June 13, 2006, at http://www
.crlp.org/ww_asia_1child.html, accessed April 16, 2007.

20. Refugees, The United States and the Holocaust, Holocaust Encyclopedia,
United States Holocaust Memorial Museum, Washington, DC, at http://www
.ushmm.org/wlc/en/, accessed July 6, 2006.

21. Martin, *United States Refugee Admission Program*, Introduction.

22. Carolyn J. Marr, *Assimilation through Education: Indian Boarding
Schools in the Pacific Northwest*, American Indians of the Pacific Northwest, University of Washington Digital Collections, 2003, at http://content.lib.washington
.edu/aipnw/marr.html#movement, accessed May 25, 2006. For additional sources
visit Bibliography of Indian Boarding Schools: Approximately 1875 to 1940,
Labriola National American Indian Data Center, University Libraries, Arizona
State University, compiled by Vickey Kalambakal (Fall 2001), at http://www.asu
.edu/lib/archives/boardingschools.htm, accessed May 25, 2006.

23. For example, the Indian Child Welfare Act of 1978 (ICWA), 25 U.S.C. §§
1901 et. seq., reads: "The Congress hereby declares that it is the policy of this Nation to protect the best interests of Indian children and to promote the stability
and security of Indian tribes and families by the establishment of minimum Federal standards for the removal of Indian children from their families and the placement of such children in foster or adoptive homes which will reflect the unique
values of Indian culture, and by providing for assistance to Indian tribes in the operation of child and family service programs."

24. Ortiz, "Growing Up Native American," 646–68.

25. The Senate, in the 109th Congress, passed the DREAM Act on May 25,
2006, as sections 621–32 of Senate Bill S.2611, The Comprehensive Immigration
Reform Act of 2006, but opposition in the House defeated the bill. Senate Bill
S.1348, the Secure Borders and Economic Opportunity and Reform Act of 2007,
introduced May 9, 2007, also includes a version of the DREAM Act, but at this
writing, it remains unclear whether the 110th Congress will succeed in passing
any immigration bills.

26. One blogger, Brad Warbiany, on May 1, 2006, on a site titled The Liberty
Papers, while conceding the weight of many anti-immigration arguments, captured the dilemma thus: "But do we want to hang a big 'No Vacancy' sign on the
land of opportunity?! No. That stands in the way of everything [we] purport to
stand for. That stands in the way of freedom and of individual rights. I hesitate
to throw out words like this, but that is **blatantly anti-American**." At http://-
www.thelibertypapers.org/2006/05/01/immigration-the-american-dream/ (emphasis in original).

27. Several Web sites have continued to update the status of immigration reform on an almost daily basis, including Federation for American Immigration
Reform, at http://www.fairus.org/, and the National Immigration Law Center, at
http://nilc.org/, accessed June 6, 2007.

28. Rich Lowry, "Let Them Eat Diversity," National Review Online, September 2, 2003, at http://www.nationalreview.com/lowry/lowry090203.asp, accessed May 25, 2006; Unknown blogger, The Truth about the DREAM Act Immigration Reform: Monitoring the Propaganda from Supporters of Massive Immigration, at http://immref.com/spin/dream-act-truth/, accessed June 5, 2007.

29. *Plyler v. Doe*, 457 U.S. 202 (1982).

30. Immigration Law & Policy: Immigrant Student Adjustment/DREAM Act, National Immigration Law Center, April 2006, at http://www.nilc.org/immlawpolicy/DREAM/index.htm, accessed May 25, 2006.

31. Victor's and Pamela's stories both come from the Web page of the Movimiento Estudiantil Chicano de Aztlán, at http://www.nationalmecha.com/mechablog/2005/12/the_dream_act_o.html, accessed May 25, 2006. For stories about student activism in support of the DREAM Act, visit the Coalition of Student Advocates (CoSA), at http://www.cosaonline.org/001detail.html, accessed May 25, 2006; and Carrie Kilman, Deferred Dreams: Undocumented Students Fight for Rights, Tolerance.org, A Project of the Southern Poverty Law Center, at http://www.tolerance.org/news/article_tol.jsp?id=1067, accessed May 25, 2006.

32. Kilman, Deferred Dreams.

33. These are the closing words of "A World Fit for Children," the statement authored by over three hundred child delegates to the U.N. Special Session on Children held in New York in May of 2002, the text of which is available at http://www.unicef.org/specialsession/documentation/childrens-statement.htm.

34. Patricia Cohen, In Old Files, Fading Hopes of Anne Frank's Family," *New York Times*, February 15, 2007, front page.

35. Barbara Slavin, "Few Iraqi Refugees Allowed into U.S.," at http://www.usatoday.com/news/world/iraq/2007-04-29-iraqi-refugees_N.htm, accessed June 15, 2007 (only sixty-eight refugees were admitted during six months through March 2007).

Chapter 11. Children at Work: Newsboys, Entrepreneurs, and "Evelyn"

1. Holt, *Orphan Trains*, 46, quoting Charles Loring Brace, Founder of the New York Children's Aid Society.

2. Bartoletti, *Kids on Strike*, 58.

3. Brazelton and Greenspan, *Irreducible Needs*, 4.

4. Bartoletti, *Kids on Strike*, 54.

5. Schorsch, *Images of Childhood*, 148.

6. Hoyt, *Horatio's Boys*, 64–97, 237.

7. Riis, *How the Other Half Lives*, 196–97.

8. Holt, *Orphan Trains*, 137–38.

9. Riis, *How the Other Half Lives*, 203.

10. Hoyt, *Horatio's Boys*, 111.

11. Hawes, *Children's Rights Movement*, 19.

12. Fass and Mason, *Childhood in America*, 237–68; Mintz, *Huck's Raft*, 139–46.

13. Holt, *Orphan Trains*, 92–93.

14. Ibid., 74.

15. Ibid., 62–63, 99–101.

16. Freedman, *Kids at Work*, 2.

17. Grubb and Lazerson, *Broken Promises*, 43–66.

18. Mintz, *Huck's Raft*, 139.

19. Holt, *Orphan Trains*, 184–85. Linda Gordon tells a fascinating story about the orphan trains movement, and its racist elements, in *The Great Arizona Orphan Abduction*.

20. Hawes, *Children's Rights Movement*, 28.

21. Woodhouse, "Out of Children's Needs, Children's Rights," 321.

22. Holt, *Orphan Trains*, 47; Mintz, *Huck's Raft*, 164–67; Gordon, *Pitied but Not Entitled*, 23.

23. PBS, *American Experience*, Orphan Trains Transcript, at http://www.pbs .org/wgbh/amex/orphan/orphants.html, accessed July 6, 2006.

24. Holt, *Orphan Trains*, 185.

25. Todres, "Importance of Realizing 'Other Rights,' " 906.

Chapter 12. Telling the Scariest Secrets: Maya Angelou and "Jeannie"

1. Angelou, *I Know Why the Caged Bird Sings*, 80, 87.

2. McGough, *Child Witnesses*, 1–7.

3. Department of Health and Human Services, Administration for Children and Families, *Child Maltreatment 2004* (Washington, DC: U.S. Government Printing Office, 2006), at http://www.acf.hhs.gov/programs/cb/pubs/cm04/ chapterthree.htm#types, accessed April 19, 2007.

4. About 20 percent of adult women and 5–10 percent of adult men report being sexually abused as children. Finkelhor, "Current Information," 31.

5. Department of Health and Human Services, Administration for Children and Families, *Child Maltreatment 2004*, Table 3-1.

6. American Academy of Child and Adolescent Psychiatry, Child Sexual Abuse, Bulletin No. 9, updated July 2004, at http://www.aacap.org/publications/ factsfam/sexabuse.htm, accessed July 7, 2006.

7. Angelou, *I Know Why the Caged Bird Sings*, 87–88.

8. English, "Extent and Consequences of Child Maltreatment," 49.

9. Steinhauser, *Least Detrimental Alternative*, 250–57.

10. Department of Health and Human Services, Substance Abuse and Mental Health Services Administration, at http://modelprograms.samhsa.gov/model.htm, accessed April 17, 2007.

11. Cohen et al., Trauma-Focused Cognitive-Behavioral Therapy for Sexually Abused Children, Psychiatric Times, vol. 21, no. 10 (September 2004), at http://www.psychiatrictimes.com/article/showArticle.jhtml?articleId=175802444, accessed April 17, 2007.

12. Presentation of Esther Deblinger, PhD and Martin Finkel, DO, at Field Center on Children's Policy Practice and Research, University of Pennsylvania, "One Child, Many Hands: A Multidisciplinary Conference on Child Welfare," June 3, 2005.

13. Goodman et al., "Testifying in Criminal Court."

14. *Maryland v. Craig*, 497 U.S. 836 (1990).

15. Putnam and Finkelhor, "Mitigating the Impact," 115.

Chapter 13. Age and the Idea of Innocence: Amal and Lionel Tate

1. Steinberg and Scott, "Less Guilty by Reason of Adolescence," 1009.

2. Larner et al., "Caring for Infants and Toddlers," 4; Waldfogel, *What Children Need*, 140.

3. Fondacaro and Fasig, "Judging Juvenile Responsibility," 355; Mintz, *Huck's Raft*, 176–78.

4. In re *Gault*, 387 U.S. 1 (1967); *McKeiver v. Pennsylvania*, 403 U.S. 528 (1971).

5. Levine, *Freedom's Children*, 86 (Myrna Carter recalling Dr. King's words).

6. In 1999, 1,004 black juveniles out of every 100,000 were in detention while the rate for white juveniles was 212. Rates for Hispanics were twice those of whites. "Nationally, Custody Rates Were Highest for Blacks," at http://www.ncjrs.gov/html/ojjdp/202885/page10.html, accessed April 18, 2007. This and the following statistics are taken from data from 1999 to 2003 provided by the federal Office of Juvenile Justice and Delinquency Prevention, at http://ojjdp.ncjrs.gov/ojstabb/, accessed April 18, 2007. The proportion of the national population of youths aged 10 to 17 is 61 percent white, 16 percent black, and 19 percent Hispanic. Blacks and nonwhite Hispanics were three times as likely to live in poverty. While 60 percent of children in juvenile detention are white, 37 percent are black. The rates of those arrested who are referred to court are 18 percent for whites compared to 25 percent for blacks. Cases involving black teens were less likely (46 percent for whites and 36 percent for blacks) to be handled informally.

7. Bortner et al., "Race and Transfer."

8. The text of our brief in *State of Florida v. Tate* is posted on the Center on Children and Families Web site, at http://www.law.ufl.edu/centers/childlaw/library.shtml#legalbriefs, accessed April 18, 2007.

9. Guerra, "Intervening to Prevent Childhood Aggression," 277.

10. Garbarino, *See Jane Hit*; Garbarino, *Lost Boys*.

11. Garbarino, *See Jane Hit*, 62.

12. Ibid.

13. Ibid., 198–99, citing Search Institute (1997), "The Assets Approach: Giving Kids What They Need to Succeed," at www.search-institute.org, accessed April 18, 2007.

14. Garbarino, *See Jane Hit*, 201, citing Search Institute.

15. Ibid., 36, citing studies of Richard Tremblay.

16. Ibid., 225.

17. Carolyn J. Keough, "Teen Killer Described as Lonely, Pouty, Disruptive," *Miami Herald*, Monday, February 5, 2001, front section, final edition, page 1A.

18. All quotes are from Keough, "Teen Killer."

19. Bishop and Frazier, "Consequences of Transfer," 227–76; Redding, "Adult Punishment for Juvenile Offenders," 375–94.

20. *Brief of Juvenile Law Center, Children and Family Justice Center, Center on Children and Families, Child Welfare League of America, Children's Defense Fund, Children's Law Center of Los Angeles, National Association of Counsel for Children and 45 Other Organizations as Amici Curiae in Support of Respondent*, in *Roper v. Simmons*, available on the Center on Children and Families Web site at http://www.law.ufl.edu/centers/childlaw/library.shtml, accessed July 10 2006.

21. Singer, "Developmental Variations," xlv.

22. Options like blended sentences allow a juvenile to be sentenced as a juvenile and released when he turns twenty-two, but only if he can show he has been rehabilitated and no longer poses a danger. Redding and Howell, "Blended Sentencing," 146–47.

23. Fondacaro and Fasig, "Judging Juvenile Responsibility," 366–68; Slobogin et al., "Prevention Model of Juvenile Justice," 186–226; Slobogin and Fondacaro, "Rethinking Deprivations of Liberty," 499–516.

24. "Girl, 9, Cuffed for Rabbit Heist: Cops Take Her Away after Missing Bunny Found in Her Home," CBS News, New Port Richey, FL, April 9, 2004, at www.cbsnews.com/stories/2004/04/09/national/main611108.shtml, accessed April 18, 2007.

Conclusion. The Future of Rights

1. Documents from the Children's Forum are available at UNICEF's Web site, United Nations Special Session on Children, at http://www.unicef.org/specialsession/child_participation/childrens_forum.html, accessed April 18, 2007.

2. Woodhouse, "Enhancing Children's Participation," 753.

3. A copy of the report, Commissioner of Children and Youth and Queens University, Belfast, "An Analysis of Research Conducted with School Children into Children's Rights in Northern Ireland," is available at http://www.niccy.org, accessed April 18, 2007.

4. I am grateful to Professor Laura Lundy and her colleagues at Queen's University, Belfast, for sharing the artwork done by the children and to University of Ulster, Queen's University, and Professor Martha Fineman's Feminism and Legal Theory Project for supporting my Belfast research fellowship.

5. Yoshino, *Covering: The Hidden Assault on our Civil Rights.*

6. Woodhouse, "Cleaning Up Toxic Violence," 422, citing Guinier and Torres, *Miner's Canary*; Pew Research Center, "Religion and Public Life"; Etzioni, *The Limits of Privacy*; McCord, "Placing American Urban Violence in Context"; and Fineman, *The Autonomy Myth.*

7. Fineman, *The Autonomy Myth*, xiv.

8. Orlando Patterson, "The Speech Misheard Round the World," *New York Times*, January 22, 3005, A2.

9. Brazelton and Greenspan, *Irreducible Needs*, 178.

BIBLIOGRAPHY

Alcott, Louisa May. *Little Women*. New York: Little, Brown, 1994.

———. *Louisa May Alcott: Her Girlhood Diary*. Edited by Cary Ryan. Mahwah, NJ: Bridgewater Books, 1993.

———. *The Selected Letters of Louisa May Alcott*. Edited by Madeleine B. Stern. Athens: University of Georgia Press, 1995.

Aldrich, F.L.S. *My Child and I, in Sickness and Health, from Pre-Natal Life until Sixteen*. Philadelphia: P. W. Ziegler, 1903.

Amar, Akhil R., and Daniel Widawsky. "Commentary: Child Abuse as Slavery: A Thirteenth Amendment Response to *DeShaney*." *Harvard Law Review* 105 (1992): 1359–83.

American Academy of Pediatrics Committee on Adoption, Early Childhood, and Dependent Care. "Developmental Issues for Young Children in Foster Care." *Pediatrics* 106, no. 5 (2000): 1145–50.

Angelou, Maya. *I Know Why the Caged Bird Sings*. New York: Bantam, 1993.

Aristotle. *Nicomachean Ethics*. Translated by Christopher Rowe. Oxford: Oxford University Press, 2002.

Austin, Regina. "Sapphire Bound!" *Wisconsin Law Review* 3 (May/June 1989): 539–78.

Bartholet, Elizabeth. *Nobody's Children: Abuse and Neglect, Foster Drift, and the Adoption Alternative*. Boston: Beacon Press, 1999.

Bartoletti, Susan Campbell. *Kids on Strike*. Boston: Houghton Mifflin, 1999.

Bass, Sandra, Margie K. Shields, and Richard Behrman. "Children, Families, and Foster Care: Analysis and Recommendations." In Packard Foundation, "Children, Families, and Foster Care," 5–29.

Beals, Melba Pattillo. *Warriors Don't Cry: A Searing Memoir of the Battle to Integrate Little Rock's Central High*. New York: Washington Square Press, 1994.

Berlin, Ira. *Many Thousands Gone: The First Two Centuries of Slavery in North America*. Cambridge, MA: Harvard University Press, 1998.

———. *Slaves without Masters: The Free Negro in the Antebellum South*. New York: Pantheon Books, 1974.

Bishop, D. M., and Charles E. Frazier. "Consequences of Transfer." In Fagan and Zimring, *The Changing Borders of Juvenile Justice*, 227–76.

Blackstone, William. *Commentaries on the Laws of England: Book the First*. Birmingham, AL: Legal Classics Library, 1983.

Blassingame, John W. Introduction. In Blassingame et al., *Narrative of the Life of Frederick Douglass*, ix–xl.

———, John R. McGiven, Peter P. Hinks, and Gerald Fulkerson, eds. *Narrative of the Life of Frederick Douglass, an American Slave Written by Himself*. New Haven, CT: Yale University Press, 2001.

Bortner, M. A., Marjorie S. Zatz, and Darnell F. Hawkins. "Race and Transfer: Empirical Research and Social Context." In Fagan and Zimring, *The Changing Borders of Juvenile Justice*, 277–320.

Brands, H. W. *The First American: The Life and Times of Benjamin Franklin*. New York: Doubleday, 2000.

Brazelton, T. Berry, and Stanley I. Greenspan. *The Irreducible Needs of Children: What Every Child Must Have to Grow, Learn, and Flourish*. Cambridge, MA: Perseus, 2000.

Bremner, Robert H., John Barnard, Tamara Hareven, and Robert Mennel, eds. *Children and Youth in America: A Documentary History*. 3 vols. Cambridge, MA: Harvard University Press, 1970–74.

Brent, Linda. *Incidents in the Life of a Slave Girl, Written by Herself* (Maria Child, ed., 1861). In Gates, *The Classic Slave Narratives*.

Bronfenbrenner, Urie. *The Ecology of Human Development*. Cambridge, MA: Harvard University Press, 1993.

Buechler, Steven M. *Women's Movements in the United States: Woman Suffrage, Equal Rights, and Beyond*. New Brunswick, NJ: Rutgers University Press, 1990.

Buss, Emily. "Confronting Developmental Barriers to the Empowerment of Child Clients." *Cornell Law Review* 84 (1999): 895–966.

Campbell, Edward D. C., and Kym S. Rice, eds. *Before Freedom Came: African-American Life in the Antebellum South*. Charlottesville: University of Virginia Press, 1991.

Canada, Geoffrey. *Fist Stick Knife Gun*. New York: Beacon Press, 1996.

The Case of Dred Scott in the United States Supreme Court: The Full Opinions of Chief Justice Taney and Justice Curtis and Abstracts of the Other Opinions of the Other Judges. New York: Greeley and McElrath, 1857.

Cather, Willa. *My Ántonia*. Boston and New York: Houghton Mifflin, 1918.

———. *O Pioneers!* Boston and New York: Houghton Mifflin, 1913.

———. *The Song of the Lark*. Boston and New York: Houghton Mifflin, 1915.

Catterall, Helen Tunnicliff. *Judicial Cases concerning American Slavery and the Negro*. Vol. 5. New York: Negro University Press, 1968.

Cherminsky, Erwin. *Constitutional Law Principles and Policies*. New York: Aspen Law and Business, 1997.

Clark, Elizabeth B. "Religion, Rights, and Difference in the Early Women's Rights Movement." *Wisconsin Women's Law Journal* 3 (1987): 29–45.

Cobbs, Elizabeth H., with Petric J. Smith. *Long Time Coming: An Insider's Story of the Birmingham Church Bombing That Rocked the World*. Birmingham, AL: Crane Hill Publishers, 1994.

Coles, Robert. *Children of Crisis: Studies of Courage and Fear*. Boston: Little, Brown, 1967.

———. *The Moral Life of Children*. Boston: Atlantic Monthly, 1986.

———. *The Spiritual Life of Children*. Boston: Houghton Mifflin, 1990.

———. *Their Eyes Meeting the World: The Drawings and Paintings of Children*. Edited by Margaret Sartor. Boston: Houghton Mifflin, 1992.

Coupet, Sacha. "Swimming Upstream against the Great Adoption Tide: Making the Case for Impermanence." *Capital University Law Review* 34 (Winter 2005): 405–58.

Courtney, Mark E., and Amy Dworsky. *Midwest Evaluation of the Adult Functioning of Former Foster Youth: Outcomes at Age 19*. Chicago: Chapin Hall Center for Children, 2005.

Crain, William. *Theories of Development: Concepts and Applications*. 5th ed. Upper Saddle River, NJ: Pearson/Prentice Hall, 2005.

Crenshaw, Kimberle. "Mapping the Margins: Intersectionality, Identity Politics, and Violence against Women of Color." *Stanford Law Review* 43 (1991): 1241–99.

Davis, Peggy Cooper. *Neglected Stories: The Constitution and Family Values*. New York: Hill and Wang, 1997.

Delgado, Melanie, Robert Fellmeth, Thomas R. Packard, Karen Prosek, and Elisa Weichel. *Expanding Transitional Services for Emancipated Youth: An Investment in California's Tomorrow*. San Diego: Children's Advocacy Institute, 2007.

Detrick, Sharon. *A Commentary on the United Nations Convention on the Rights of the Child*. The Hague, the Netherlands: Martinus Nijhoff, 1999.

Douglass, Frederick. *Narrative of the Life of Frederick Douglass, an American Slave, Written by Himself*. Boston: Antislavery Office, 1845. Reprinted in Blassingame et al., *Narrative of the Life of Frederick Douglass*.

Dowd, Nancy E., Dorothy G, Singer, and Robin Fretwell Wilson, eds. *Handbook of Children, Culture, and Violence*. Thousand Oaks, CA: Sage, 2006.

Duquette, Donald N. *Advocating for the Child in Protection Proceedings: A Handbook for Lawyers and Court Appointed Special Advocates*. Lexington, MA: Lexington Books, 1990.

Elder, Glen H., Jr. "Human Lives in Changing Societies: Life Course Developmental Insights." In *Developmental Science*, edited by Robert B. Cairns, Glen H. Elder Jr., and E. Jane Costello, 31–62. New York: Cambridge University Press, 1996.

English, Diana J. "The Extent and Consequences of Child Maltreatment." In Packard Foundation, "Protecting Children from Abuse and Neglect," 39–53.

Erikson, Erik H. *Insight and Responsibility*. New York: W.W. Norton, 1964.

———. *The Life Cycle Completed*. New York: W.W. Norton, 1982.

Etzioni, Amitai. *The Limits of Privacy*. New York: Basic Books, 1999.

Fagan, Jeffrey, and Franklin E. Zimring. *The Changing Borders of Juvenile Justice: Transfer of Adolescents to the Criminal Court*. Chicago: University of Chicago Press, 2000.

Fass, Paula S., and Mary Ann Mason. *Childhood in America*. New York: New York University Press, 2000.

Fehrenbacher, Don E. *Slavery, Law, and Politics: The Dred Scott Case in Historical Perspective*. New York: Oxford University Press, 1981.

Fellmuth, Robert C. *Child Rights and Remedies*. Atlanta: Clarity Press, 2002.

Fineman, Martha. *The Autonomy Myth: A Theory of Dependency*. New York: New Press, 2004.

Finkelhor, David. "Current Information on the Scope and Nature of Child Sexual Abuse." In Packard Foundation, "Sexual Abuse of Children," 33–55.

Fleischer, Doris Zames, and Frieda Zames, *The Disability Rights Movement: From Charity to Confrontation*. Philadelphia: Temple University Press, 2001.

Fondacaro, Mark R., and Lauren G. Fasig. "Judging Juvenile Responsibility: A Social Ecological Perspective." In Dowd et al., *Handbook of Children, Culture, and Violence*, 355–73.

Foner, Eric. *Reconstruction: America's Unfinished Revolution, 1863–1877*. New York: Harper and Row, 1988.

Fox-Genovese, Elizabeth. *Within the Plantation Household: Black and White Women of the Old South*. Chapel Hill: University of North Carolina Press, 1988.

Frank, Anne. *The Diary of Anne Frank: The Revised Critical Edition*. Prepared by the Netherlands Institute for War Documentation, edited by David Barnouw and Gerrold van der Stroom, translated by Arnold J. Pomeranz and B. M. Mooyraart-Doubleday and Susan Massotty. New York: Doubleday, 2003.

Franklin, Benjamin. *The Autobiography of Benjamin Franklin*. Charlottesville: University of Virginia Library, 1995; Boulder, CO: NetLibrary: E-book ISBN 9780585233574, 1995.

Freedman, Russell. *Kids at Work: Lewis Hine and the Crusade against Child Labor*. New York: Clarion Books, 1994.

Freeman, Michael. *The Moral Status of Children: Essays on the Rights of the Child*. The Hague, the Netherlands: Kluwer Law International, 1997.

Garbarino, James. *Lost Boys: Why Our Sons Turn Violent and How We Can Save Them*. New York: Free Press, 1999.

———. *See Jane Hit: Why Girls Are Growing More Violent and What Can Be Done about It*. New York: Penguin, 2006.

Garbarino, James, F. M. Stott, and Faculty of Erikson Institute. *What Children Can Tell Us: Eliciting, Interpreting, and Evaluating Information from Children.* San Francisco: Jossey-Bass, 1992.

Gates, Henry Louis, Jr. Introduction. In Gates, *The Classic Slave Narratives*, i–xviii.

———, ed. *The Classic Slave Narratives.* New York: New American Library, 1987.

Gelles, Richard. *The Book of David: How Preserving Families Can Cost Lives.* New York: Basic Books, 1996.

Gelles, Richard, and Murray A. Strauss. *Intimate Violence: The Causes and Consequences of Abuse in the American Family.* New York: Touchstone, 1988.

Gentile, Douglas A., and Craig A. Anderson. "Violent Video Games: Effects on Youth and Public Policy Implications." In Dowd et al., *Handbook of Children, Culture, and Violence*, 225–46.

Goodman, G. S., E. P. Taub, D. P. Jones, P. England, L. K. Port, and L. Rudy. "Testifying in Criminal Court: Emotional Effects on Child Sexual Assault Victims." *Monographs of the Society for Research in Child Development* 57, no. 5 (1992): 1–142.

Gordon, Linda. *The Great Arizona Orphan Abduction.* Cambridge, MA: Harvard University Press, 1999.

———. *Pitied but Not Entitled: Single Mothers and the History of Welfare.* New York: Free Press, 1994.

Grossberg, Michael. *Governing the Hearth: Law and the Family in Nineteenth-Century America.* Chapel Hill: University of North Carolina Press, 1985.

———. "How to Give the Present a Past? Family Law in the United States, 1950–2000." In Katz et al., *Cross Currents*, 1–30.

Groves, Betsy McAlister. *Children Who See Too Much: Lessons from the Child Witness to Violence Project.* Boston: Beacon, 2002.

Grubb, W. Norton, and Marvin Lazerson. *Broken Promises: How Americans Fail Their Children.* Chicago: University of Chicago Press, 1988.

Guerra, Nancy G. "Intervening to Prevent Childhood Aggression in the Inner City." In McCord, *Violence and Childhood in the Inner City*, 256–312.

Guggenheim, Martin. "Child Welfare Policy and Practice in the United States, 1950–2000." In Katz et al., *Cross Currents*, 547–64.

———. "How Children's Lawyers Serve State Interests." *Nevada Law Journal* 6 (2006): 805–35.

———. *What's Wrong with Children's Rights?* Cambridge, MA: Harvard University Press, 2005.

Guinier, Lani, and Gerald Torres. *Miner's Canary: Enlisting Race, Resisting Power, Transforming Democracy.* Cambridge, MA: Harvard University Press, 2002.

Hafen, Bruce, and Jonathan Hafen. "Abandoning Children to Their Autonomy: The United Nations Convention on the Rights of the Child." *Harvard International Law Journal* 37 (1996): 449–91.

Halberstam, David. *The Children.* New York: Fawcett Books, 1999.

Haley, Alex, and Malcolm X. *The Autobiography of Malcolm X.* New York: Grove Press, 1964.

Haralambie, Ann M. *The Child's Attorney: A Guide to Representing Children in Custody, Adoption, and Protection Cases.* Chicago: American Bar Association, 1993.

Hardin, Brenda Jones. "Safety and Stability for Foster Children." In Packard Foundation, "Children, Families, and Foster Care," 31–48.

Harris, Cheryl I. "Finding Sojourner's Truth: Race, Gender, and the Institution of Property." *Cardozo Law Review* 18 (1996): 309–401.

Hatcher, Daniel L. "Foster Children Paying for Foster Care." *Cardozo Law Review* 27 (2006): 1797–852.

Hawes, Joseph M. *The Children's Rights Movement: A History of Advocacy and Protection.* Boston: Twayne Publishers, 1991.

Higginbotham, A. Leon, Jr. *Shades of Freedom: Racial Politics and Presumptions of the American Legal System.* New York: Oxford University Press, 1996.

Higginbotham, A. Leon, Jr, and Barbara K. Kopytoff. "Racial Purity and Interracial Sex in the Law of Colonial and Antebellum Virginia." *Georgetown Law Journal* 77 (1989): 1967–2028.

Hilliard-Nunn, Patricia, director, with Claudia Wright and Karen Keroak. *Youth Speak! Opinions about the Juvenile System.* CD produced in Gainesville, Levin College of Law, University of Florida, 2005.

Holt, Marilyn Irving. *The Orphan Trains: Placing Out in America.* Lincoln: University of Nebraska Press, 1992.

Hopkins, Vincent C. *Dred Scott's Case.* New York: Fordham University Press, 1967.

Hoyt, Edwin P. *Horatio's Boys: The Life and Works of Horatio Alger, Jr.* Radnor, PA: Chilton Book Co., 1974.

James, Allison. "Understanding Childhood from an Interdisciplinary Perspective: Problems and Potentials." In Pufall and Unsworth, *Rethinking Childhood*, 25–37.

Johnson, Walter. *Soul by Soul: Life Inside the Antebellum Slave Market.* Cambridge, MA: Harvard University Press, 1999.

Katz, Sanford N., John Eekelaar, and Mavis Maclean, eds. *Cross Currents: Family Law and Policy in the United States and England.* Oxford: Oxford University Press, 2000.

Keller, Helen. *The Story of My Life, with Supplementary Accounts by Anne Sullivan, Her Teacher, and John Albert Macy.* Edited by Roger Shattuck with Dorothy Herrmann. New York: W. W. Norton, 2003.

King, Martin Luther, Jr. *A Call to Conscience: The Landmark Speeches of Dr. Martin Luther King, Jr.* Edited by Clayborne Caron and Kris Shepard. New York: Warner Books, 2001.

———. *I Have a Dream: Writings and Speeches That Changed the World*. Edited by James M. Washington. San Francisco: Harper, 1992.

Kolchin, Peter. *American Slavery*. New York: Hill and Wang, 1993.

Konner, Melvin. *Childhood*. Boston: Little, Brown, 1991.

Kunkel, Dale, and Lara Zwarun. "How Real Is the Problem of TV Violence?" In Dowd et al., *Handbook of Children, Culture, and Violence*, 203–24.

Larner, Mary B., Richard E. Behrman, Marie Young, and Kathleen Reich. "Caring for Infants and Toddlers: Analysis and Recommendation." In Packard Foundation, "Caring for Infants and Toddlers," 7–20.

Lee, Hermione. *Willa Cather: Double Lives*. New York: Pantheon, 1989.

———. *Willa Cather: A Life Saved Up*. London: Virago, 1997.

Lerner, Gerda. *The Female Experience: An American Documentary*. Indianapolis: Bobbs-Merrill, 1977.

Levine, Ellen. *Freedom's Children: Young Civil Rights Activists Tell Their Own Stories*. New York: Putnam, 2000.

Lewis, Edith. *Willa Cather Living: A Personal Record*. New York: Knopf, 1953.

Lewis, John, with Michael D'Orso. *Walking with the Wind: A Memoir of the Movement*. New York: Simon and Schuster, 1998.

Macedo, Stephan, and Iris Marion Young, eds. *Child, Family, and State*. New York: New York University Press, 2003.

Malone, Linda. "The Effect of U.S. Ratification as a 'Self-Executing' or as a 'Non-Self-Executing' Treaty." In Todres et al., *The U.N. Convention on the Rights of the Child*, 33–36.

Marks, Jane. *The Hidden Children: The Secret Survivors of the Holocaust*. London: Bantam Books, 1995.

Martin, David. *The United States Refugee Admission Program: Reforms for a New Era of Refugee Resettlement*. Washington, DC: Migration Policy Institute, 2005.

Mason, Mary Ann. *From Father's Property to Children's Rights: The History of the Child in the United States*. New York: Columbia University Press, 1994.

McCord, Joan. "Placing American Urban Violence in Context." In McCord, *Violence and Childhood in the Inner City*, 78–115.

———, ed. *Violence and Childhood in the Inner City*. Cambridge: Cambridge University Press, 1997.

McFeely, William S. *Frederick Douglass*. New York: W. W. Norton, 1991.

McGough, Lucy S. *Child Witnesses: Fragile Voices in the American Legal System*. New Haven, CT: Yale University Press, 1994.

McWhorter, Diane. *Carry Me Home: Birmingham, Alabama: The Climactic Battle of the Civil Rights Revolution*. New York: Simon and Schuster, 2001.

Minow, Martha. *Making All the Difference: Inclusion, Exclusion, and American Law*. Ithaca, NY: Cornell University Press, 1990.

———. "Rights for the Next Generation: A Feminist Approach to Children's Rights." *Harvard Women's Law Journal* 9 (1986): 1–24.

Mintz, Steven. *Huck's Raft: A History of American Childhood.* Cambridge, MA: Belknap Press of Harvard University Press, 2004.

Müller, Melissa. *Anne Frank: The Biography.* New York: Henry Holt, 1998.

Nelson, Cathy L. "U.S. Ratification of the U.N. Convention on the Rights of the Child: Federalism Issues." In Todres et al., *The U.N. Convention on the Rights of the Child,* 87–95.

O'Brien, Sharon. *Willa Cather: The Emerging Voice.* New York: Oxford University Press, 1987.

O'Connor, Sandra Day, with illustrations by Dan Andreasen. *Chico: A True Story from the Childhood of the First Woman Supreme Court Justice.* New York: Dutton Children's Books, 2005.

O'Connor, Sandra Day, and H. Alan Day. *Lazy B: Growing Up on a Cattle Ranch in the American Southwest.* New York: Random House, 2002.

Ortiz, Simon. "Growing Up Native American: The Language We Know." In *Childhood in America,* edited by Paula S. Fass and Mary Ann Mason, 646–48. New York: New York University Press, 2000.

Packard Foundation. "Caring for Infants and Toddlers." *Future of Children* 11, no. 1 (2001).

———. "Children, Families, and Foster Care." *Future of Children* 14, no. 1 (2004).

———. "Protecting Children from Abuse and Neglect." *Future of Children* 8, no. 1 (1998).

———. "Sexual Abuse of Children." *Future of Children* 4, no. 2 (1994).

Pew Research Center. "Religion in Public Life: A Faith-Based Partisan Divide." In *Trends 2005,* edited by H. Morton. Washington, DC: Pew Forum on Religion and Public Life, 2005.

Pierpoint, Claudia Roth. "Postscript: Born for the Part, Roles that Katherine Hepburn Played." *New Yorker Magazine* 53 (July 14 and 21, 2003): 53–59.

Preston, Dickson J. *Young Frederick Douglass: The Maryland Years.* Baltimore: Johns Hopkins University Press, 1980.

Pufall, Peter B., and Richard P. Unsworth. "The Imperative and the Process for Rethinking Childhood." In Pufall and Unsworth, *Rethinking Childhood,* 1–21.

———. *Rethinking Childhood.* New Brunswick, NJ: Rutgers University Press, 2004.

Putnam, Charles, and David Finkelhor. "Mitigating the Impact of Publicity on Child Crime Victims and Witnesses." In Dowd et al., *Handbook of Children, Culture, and Violence,* 113–31.

Redding, Richard E. "Adult Punishment for Juvenile Offenders: Does It Reduce Crime?" In Dowd et al., *Handbook of Children, Culture, and Violence,* 375–94.

Redding, Richard E, and James C. Howell. "Blended Sentencing in American Juvenile Courts." In Fagan and Zimring, *The Changing Borders of Juvenile Justice*, 145–79.

Riis, Jacob A. *How the Other Half Lives: Studies among the Tenements of New York*. New York: Charles Scribner's Sons, 1890.

Roberts, Dorothy E. "The Child Welfare System's Racial Harm." In Macedo and Young, *Child, Parent, and State*, 98–133.

———. "Community Dimensions of State Child Protection," *Hofstra Law Review* 34 (2005): 23–35.

———. "Racism and Patriarchy in the Meaning of Motherhood." *American University Journal of Gender and Law* 1 (1993): 1–37.

———. *Shattered Bonds: The Color of Child Welfare*. New York: Basic Books, 2002.

Robinson, Phyllis C. *Willa: The Life of Willa Cather*. New York: Doubleday, 1983.

Rol, Ruud van der, and Rian Verhoeven. *Anne Frank, Beyond the Diary: A Photographic Remembrance*. New York: Viking, 1993.

Ross, Catherine J. "A Place at the Table: Creating Presence and Voice for Teenagers in Dependency Proceedings." *Nevada Law Journal* 6 (2006): 1362–72.

Rush, Sharon. *Huck Finn's Hidden Lessons: Teaching and Learning across the Color Line*. Lanham, MD: Rowman and Littlefield, 2006.

Russ, George H. "Through the Eyes of a Child, 'Gregory K.': A Child's Right to Be Heard." *Family Law Quarterly* 27 (1993): 365–93.

Russell-Brown, Katheryn. *Underground Codes: Race, Crime, and Related Fires*. New York: New York University Press, 2004.

Santrock, John W. *Adolescence*. 8th ed. New York: McGraw-Hill, 2001.

Schwartz, Ira M., and Gideon Fishman. *Kids Raised by the Government*. Westport, CT: Praeger, 1999.

Schorsch, Anita. *Images of Childhood: An Illustrated Social History*. New York: Mayflower Books, 1979.

Scott, Elizabeth S. "The Legal Construction of Adolescence." *Hofstra Law Review* 29 (2000): 547–98.

Scott, Elizabeth S, N. Dickon Reppucci, and Jennifer L. Woolard. "Evaluating Adolescent Decision-Making in Legal Contexts." *Law and Human Behavior* 19 (1995): 221–44.

Shachar, Ayelet. "Children of a Lesser God: Sustaining Global Inequality through Citizenship Laws." In Macedo and Young, *Child, Parent, and State*, 345–97.

Siegel, Reva. "Home as Work: The First Women's Rights Claims concerning Wives' Household Labor, 1850–1880." *Yale Law Journal* 103 (1994): 1073–216.

Singer, Dorothy G. "Developmental Variations among Children and Adolescents—An Overview of the Research and Policy Implications." In Dowd et al., *Handbook of Children, Culture, and Violence*, xxvii–xlvii.

Slobogin, Christopher, and Mark Fondacaro. "Rethinking Deprivations of Liberty: Possible Contributions from Therapeutic and Ecological Jurisprudence." *Behavioral Science and the Law* 18 (2000): 499–516.

———, Mark Fondacaro, and Jennifer Woolard. "A Prevention Model of Juvenile Justice: The Promise of *Kansas v. Hendricks* for Children." *Wisconsin Law Review* (1999): 185–226.

Spinak, Jane M. "Simon Says Take Three Steps Backwards: The National Conference of Commissioners on Uniform State Laws Recommendations on Child Representation." *Nevada Law Journal* 6, no. 3 (2006): 1385–95.

Stampp, Kenneth M. "Chattels Personal." In *American Law and the Constitutional Order*, edited by Harry N. Schreiber and Lawrence M. Friedman. Cambridge, MA: Harvard University Press, 1988.

Stanton, Elizabeth C., Susan B. Anthony, and Matilda J. Gage, eds. *The History of Woman Suffrage*, Vol. 1. New York: Fowler and Wells, 1881. Reprint edition, 1985.

Steinberg, Laurence, and Elizabeth S. Scott. "Less Guilty by Reason of Adolescence: Developmental Immaturity, Diminished Responsibility, and the Juvenile Death Penalty." *American Psychologist* 58 (2000): 1009–36.

Steinhauser, Paul D. *The Least Detrimental Alternative: A Systematic Guide to Case Planning and Decision-Making for Children in Care.* Toronto: University of Toronto Press, 1991.

Stern, Madeleine B., ed. *L. M. Alcott: Signature of Reform.* Boston: Northeastern University Press, 2002.

Swain, Gwyneth. *Dred and Harriet Scott: A Family's Struggle for Freedom.* St. Paul, MN: Borealis Books, 2004.

Tarpley, Joan R. "Black Women, Sexual Myth, and Jurisprudence." *Temple Law Review* 69 (1996): 1343–88.

Thomas, R. Murray. *Recent Theories of Child Development.* Thousand Oaks, CA: Sage, 2001.

Todres, Jonathan. "Analyzing the Opposition to U.S. Ratification of the U.N. Convention on the Rights of the Child." In Todres et al., *The U.N. Convention on the Rights of the Child*, 19–31.

———. "The Importance of Realizing 'Other Rights' to Prevent Sex Trafficking." *Cardozo Journal of Law and Gender* 12 (2006): 885–907.

Todres, Jonathan, Mark E. Wojcik, and Cris R. Revaz, eds. *The U.N. Convention on the Rights of the Child: An Analysis of Treaty Provisions and Implications for U.S. Ratification.* Ardsley, NY: Transnational Publishers, 2006.

Truth, Sojourner. "Ain't I a Woman?" In *The History of Woman Suffrage*, Vol. 1, 1848–1861, edited by Elizabeth C. Stanton, Susan B. Anthony, and Matilda J. Gage. New York: Fowler and Wells, 1881.

United Nations General Assembly. Convention on the Rights of the Child (CRC). 1989. UN General Assembly Document A/RES/44/25.

U.S. Congress. Adoption and Safe Families Act (ASFA). Public Law 105–89, U.S. Stat. 111 (1997): 2115, codified in scattered sections of U.S. Code 42.

U.S. Department of Health and Human Services (DHHS). The AFCARS Report: Preliminary FY 2003 Estimates as of April 2005 (10), 2005.

U.S. Department of Health and Human Services, Administration on Children, Youth, and Families. *Child Maltreatment 2004*. Washington, DC: Government Printing Office, 2006.

Van Beuren, Geraldine. *The International Law on the Rights of the Child*. Dordrecht, the Netherlands: Martinus Nijhoff, 1995.

———, ed. *International Documents on Children*. The Hague, the Netherlands: Martinus Nijhoff, 1998.

VanderVelde, Lea, and Sandhya Subramanian. "Mrs. Dred Scott." *Yale Law Journal* 106 (1997): 1033–121.

Veerman, Philip E. *The Rights of the Child and the Changing Image of Childhood*. The Hague, the Netherlands: Martinus Nijhoff, 1992.

Waldfogel, Jane. *The Future of Child Protection: How to Break the Cycle of Abuse and Neglect*. Cambridge, MA: Harvard University Press, 1998.

———. *What Children Need*. Cambridge, MA: Harvard University Press, 2006.

Webb, Sheyann, and Rachel West Nelson, as told to Frank Sikora. *Selma, Lord, Selma*. Tuscaloosa: University of Alabama Press, 1997.

Weithorne, Lois A. "Envisioning Second-Order Change in America's Response to Troubled and Troublesome Youth." *Hofstra Law Review* 44 (Summer 2005): 1307–506.

Weld, Theodore D. *American Slavery as It Is: Testimony of a Thousand Witnesses*. New York: Arno Press, 1968.

Welter, Barbara. "The Cult of True Womanhood." *American Quarterly* 18 (1966): 151–52.

White, Deborah Gray. "Female Slaves in the Plantation South." In *Before Freedom Came: African-American Life in the Antebellum South*, edited by Edward D. C. Campbell Jr. and Kym S. Rice, 101–21. Charlottesville: University of Virginia Press, 1991.

White, Susan O., ed. *Handbook for Youth and Justice*, New York: Kluwer/Plenum, 2000.

Williams, Juan. *Eyes on the Prize: America's Civil Rights Years, 1954–1965*. New York: Penguin, 1988.

Wilson, Charles Morrow. *The Dred Scott Decision*. Philadelphia: Auerbach Publishers, 1973.

Woodhouse, Barbara Bennett. "Children's Rights." In White, *Handbook for Youth and Justice*, 377–410.

———. "Children's Rights in Gay and Lesbian Families: A Child-Centered Perspective." In Macedo and Young. *Child, Parent, and State*, 273–305.

———. "Cleaning Up Toxic Violence: An EcoGenerist Paradigm." In Dowd et al., *Handbook of Children, Culture, and Violence*, 415–36.

———. "The Constitutionalization of Children's Rights: Incorporating Emerging Rights into the Constitutional Framework." *University of Pennsylvania Journal of Constitutional Law* 2 (1999): 1–52.

———. "Dred Scott's Daughters: Nineteenth-Century Urban Girls at the Intersection of Race and Patriarchy." *Buffalo Law Review* 48 (2000): 669–701.

———. "Ecogenerism: An Environmentalist Approach to Protecting Endangered Children." *Virginia Journal of Social Policy and Law* 12 (2005): 409–47.

———. "The Family Supportive Nature of the U.N. Convention on the Rights of the Child." In Todres et al., *The U.N. Convention on the Rights of the Child*, 37–46.

———. "Hatching the Egg: A Child-Centered Perspective on Parents' Rights." *Cardozo Law Review* 14 (1993): 1747–865.

———. "Out of Children's Needs, Children's Rights." *Brigham Young University Journal of Public Law* 8 (1993): 321–41.

———. "Reframing the Debate about the Socialization of Children: An Environmentalist Paradigm." *University of Chicago Legal Forum* (2004): 85–165.

———. "Re-Visioning Rights for Children." In Pufall and Unsworth, *Rethinking Childhood*, 229–43.

———. "Speaking Truth to Power: Challenging the Power of Parents to Control the Education of Their Own." *Cornell Law Journal* 11 (2002): 481–500.

———. "The Status of Children: A Story of Emerging Rights." In Katz et al., *Cross Currents*, 423–49.

———. "Talking about Children's Rights in Judicial Custody and Visitation Decision-Making." *Family Law Quarterly* 36 (Spring 2002): 105–33.

———. " 'Who Owns the Child?': *Meyer* and *Pierce* and the Child as Property." *William and Mary Law Review* 33 (1992): 1041–50.

———. "Youthful Indiscretions: Culture, Class Status, and the Passage to Adulthood." *DePaul Law Review* 51 (Spring 2002): 743–68.

Wright, Danaya C. " 'Well-Behaved Women Don't Make History': Rethinking English Family, Law, and History." *Wisconsin Women's Law Journal* 19 (Fall 2004): 211–318.

Wringe, Colin A. *Children's Rights: A Philosophical Study*. London: Routledge, 1981.

Yellin, Jean Fagan. *Harriet Jacobs: A Life*. New York: Basic Civitas Books, 2004.

Yoshino, Kenji. *Covering: The Hidden Assault on Our Civil Rights*. New York: Random House, 2006.

Zainaldin, Jamil. *Law in Antebellum Society: Legal Change and Economic Expansion*. New York: Alfred A. Knopf, 1983.

INDEX

The Public Square Book Series/Princeton University Press

Uncouth Nation: Why Europe Dislikes America by Andrei Markovits
The Politics of the Veil by Joan Wallach Scott

With Thanks to the Donors of the Public Square

President William P. Kelly, the CUNY Graduate Center